T&T Clark Studies in Systematic Theology

Edited by

John Webster
Ian A. McFarland
Ivor Davidson

Volume 17

TRINITY AND ORGANISM

Towards a New Reading of Herman Bavinck's Organic Motif

James Eglinton

B L O O M S B U R Y
LONDON · NEW DELHI · NEW YORK · SYDNEY

Bloomsbury T&T Clark
An imprint of Bloomsbury Publishing Plc

50 Bedford Square   1385 Broadway
London   New York
WC1B 3DP   NY 10018
UK   USA

www.bloomsbury.com

Bloomsbury is a registered trade mark of Bloomsbury Publishing Plc

First published 2012
Paperback edition first published 2013

British Library Cataloguing-in-Publication Data
A catalogue record for this book is available from the British Library.

ISBN: HB: 978-0-567-12478-4
PB: 978-0-567-41748-0

Library of Congress Cataloging-in-Publication Data
A catalogue record for this book is available from the Library of Congress

Typeset by Deanta Global Publishing Services, Chennai, India

Pourquoi croyez-vous que je date tout ce que je fais? C'est qu'il ne suffit pas de connaître les œuvres d'un artiste. Il faut aussi savoir quand il les faisait, pourquoi, comment, dans quelles circonstances.[1]

Picasso to Brassaï

---

[1] Picasso to Brassaï, *Conversations avec Picasso* (Paris: Gallimard, 1964). 'Why do you think I date everything I do? Because it is not enough to simply know the works of an artist. One must also know when he did them, why, how, in which circumstances.'

Contents

Abstract

This book provides a new reading of the organic motif as found in the works of the Dutch neo-Calvinist theologian, Herman Bavinck (1854–1921). Noting the recent collapse of the previously dominant 'two Bavincks' hypothesis, it explores the impact of this now defunct hermeneutic on the normative reading of Bavinck's organic motif in the work of Jan Veenhof. In probing Veenhof's general reliance on the failed 'two Bavincks' model and view of the motif through this lens, it becomes evident that a new general reading of Bavinck (which will be used to interpret specific portions of his theology) is required. One must 'reunite' the 'two Bavincks' by tracing the basis for conceptual unity in his thought.

This basis for unity is located in Bavinck's doctrine of God. In handling the divine paradigm of unity-in-diversity *via* both triadic and non-triadic emphases, one argues that Bavinck attempts to understand all of nature and history as a broad sweep of Trinitarian divine self-revelation. The redemption and modification of the Augustinian notion of the *vestigia trinitatis* enables Bavinck to see the Trinity revealed in all of life. He thus commandeers the common organic language of nineteenth-century Europe and, in so doing, loads it with Trinitarian meaning. The working hypothesis developed is that, for Bavinck, a theology of Trinity *ad intra* leads to a cosmology of organism *ad extra*.

Such a hypothesis is probed in chapters on Bavinck's doctrines of God, general revelation, Scripture and ecclesiology. In all of these, one finds that Bavinck invokes the organic motif to explain the sense in which the archetypal unity of the Godhead acts as the foundation for all consequent ectypal unity in the creation. As such, the *organisch* is understood to be Bavinck's motif of choice when accounting for the triniformity which abounds in all created reality.

In this exploration, it becomes apparent that as Bavinck uses the organic motif, he draws on the heritage of both Patristic and Reformation theology. However, he does not merely repristinate this tradition. Rather, his use of the motif is a highly creative development in the intellectual context of the late nineteenth-century.

Acknowledgements

This book is the product of three years of doctoral research at New College, University of Edinburgh. It is not a work produced in isolation. Rather, its content came together thanks to the input and stimulation of many people. In this respect, the primary place of honour must go to my doctoral supervisor, Professor David Fergusson. Over those three years, his scholarly excellence and gracious character taught me a great deal. Thanks are also due to Dr Paul Nimmo, my secondary supervisor, for regular and ongoing encouragement in my engagement with the Reformed tradition.

Gratitude is also due to two men whose profound influence upon my teenage years marks me to this day. Without a personal challenge to think theologically from Rev Robert Smith, my secondary school Religious Education teacher, this book would not exist. Indeed, I cannot imagine I would now be working as a theologian were it not for his input at a crucial time. To Rev David Meredith, from whom I inherited a love for 'contemporary Calvinism', I offer similar appreciation.

I first discovered the writings of Herman Bavinck in the Systematic Theology classroom of Professor Donald Macleod. I regard it a great privilege to have studied under this master dogmatician and hope that this book encourages him in his own theological endeavours.

Various individuals have kindly loaned me their ears in acting as a theological soundboard over the past few years: Drs Thomas Forster and William Schweitzer, Professor Carl Trueman and Revs David Strain and Michael Bräutigam have been loyal friends and faithful theological confidants. In his own way, each has contributed something to this book.

In 2007, I began my doctoral studies with only the dimmest realisation that I was stepping into a rapidly developing Bavinck movement. The recently completed English translation of *Reformed Dogmatics* has meant that current interest in Bavinck's work is considerable. This, in turn, has given me numerous opportunities to attend stimulating conferences and engage with outstanding scholars while preparing this work. Within this sphere, my

Kampen colleague, Professor George Harinck, has been a continual source of encouragement and assistance, as has Professor John Bolt. Without the generosity of Dr Rimmer de Vries, this book would be far poorer than it is. In April 2009, I spent three weeks conducting research as the resident Puchinger Scholar at Princeton Theological Seminary's Kuyper Research Centre. The Centre's warm welcome and constant assistance also greatly enriched my work.

On my first research trip to the Netherlands, Dr Wim Balke showed exceptional kindness in introducing me to various scholars who have, in turn, become important research colleagues and friends.

I must also offer thanks to the congregation and Kirk Session of St Columba Free Church and Rev Derek Lamont, among whom I served as Ministerial Assistant during the PhD years. Their willingness to accommodate a trainee preacher and teacher has ingrained in me what I hope to be the lifelong conviction that theology must always place itself in service of the church.

In terms of practical support, I am pleased to have written this book as a recipient of both the John Hope Scholarship and a New College Divinity Scholarship. To both the Hope Trust and New College, I express gratitude.

Gu mo bhean, an Dotair Eilidh Sìne NicDhòmhaill Eglinton; bidh mi taingeil gu bràth airson do ghaoil agus do chuideachaidh. Às d'aonais, bhithinn air chall. Tapadh leat airson a h-uile càil; tha fhios agam gun deach thu gu saothair mhòr air mo shon-sa, agus air sgàth an leabhar seo. Bidh mi fada nad chomain. Je serai toujours à toi.

Finally, I should thank those who have made the greatest, lifelong investment in my theological education: my parents James Perman and Ishbel Eglinton. This book is dedicated to you both, as you taught me all of the most important lessons in theology.

I acknowledge all mistakes and shortcomings as my own.

James Eglinton,
Kampen, September 2011
S.D.G.

List of Abbreviations

Chapter 1

Where Was Herman Bavinck?

In his own immediate geographical, ecclesiastical, academic and linguistic context, Herman Bavinck's unique contribution to theology was widely recognized. Indeed, even outwith the Dutch-speaking world, one finds hints in early twentieth-century anglophone theological literature that Bavinck was a theologian of some repute. In his Hastie Lectures,[1] a survey of nineteenth-century Dutch theology delivered between 1909 and 1911 at Glasgow University, James Hutton Mackay remarks: 'I had intended to notice the work of Professor Bavinck – Dr Kuyper's loyal and learned theological henchman – before concluding my final lecture. I may give as an excuse for omitting the name of the ablest living writer of Dogmatics in Holland, that Dr Bavinck is still a comparatively young man, and that his place, therefore, belongs to the present rather than to the past century.'[2]

As the pool of early twentieth-century anglophone theologians with an interest in Dutch theology, or furthermore the ability to read Dutch, was relatively small, such references to Bavinck were fleeting.[3] Interestingly, during his own lifetime, Bavinck was known in the English-speaking world primarily for his work on theoretical pedagogy. (It should be noted that the anglophones interested in Dutch Reformed pedagogy were also few in number). However, one century later, Bavinck has gained posthumous fame in the realm of anglophone systematic theology. In 2007, the completed

---

[1] Professor Hastie taught at Glasgow University in the late nineteenth century. He was well acquainted with German and Dutch theology.

[2] James Hutton Mackay, *Religious Thought in Holland during the Nineteenth Century* (London: Hodder & Stoughton, 1911), preface, xi.

[3] Mackay's knowledge of Dutch theology was gained during a decade spent in the Netherlands, six years of which were spent pastoring in Middelburg and Flushing. He acknowledges that prior to his arrival in the country he lacked a nuanced appreciation of its theological spectrum. 'When I went to reside in Holland, on my return from India ten years ago, I confess I knew very little about the subject I have undertaken to give some account of. The translated works of Kuenen and Tiele, men of world-wide reputation, I had read with interest. Scholten, when I took him up in Holland, seemed somewhat to be not unfamiliar, but Dr Kuyper was little more than a name, and I had never even heard of the *Doleantie*.' Mackay, *Religious Thought in Holland*, 13.

English translation of his *Gereformeerde Dogmatiek* was celebrated by a major conference at Calvin Theological Seminary. The centenary of his 1909 Stone Lectures was, in turn, marked by another Bavinck conference at Princeton Theological Seminary. In September 2010, the Edinburgh Bavinck Conference highlighted the growth of British (and broader European) interest in his writings.[1] As such, Bavinck has become a source of much interest beyond the borders of his original *Nederlands*-speaking context. It would not be fair to ascribe the new interest in Bavinck to a nostalgic, anti-modernist reaction; neither would it suffice to say that the lack of non-Dutch interest in Bavinck throughout the twentieth-century was a sign that he was merely an 'in house' theologian deemed unsuitable for export in his own day. Rather, the obvious barrier to earlier interest in his work was linguistic. Those in the anglophone world whose linguistic skills allowed them to penetrate this barrier recognized his significance and, to a certain extent, were responsible for mediating his theology to the English-speaking world. The likes of Geerhardus Vos, Louis Berkhof and Cornelius Van Til stand out in this regard.

The human being neither develops nor operates in a vacuum; thus the study of any prominent intellectual figure requires more than the reading of primary texts. Each life must be located within a particular context. In Bavinck's case, this context is primarily that of a fascinating life encompassing a childhood in a separatist manse, a daring decision to study theology at the modernist[5] school in Leiden, a brief ministry in Franeker, distinguished academic service in Kampen and Amsterdam and prolific theological and political output. In his own immediate context, Bavinck had two biographers, R.H. Bremmer[6] and Valentijn Hepp,[7] neither of whose works has been translated into English. As such, the previous century has been marked by a general poverty of English language biographical information within which to locate Bavinck.

However, recent years have seen a change in this respect. This shift has been such that the provision of a detailed Bavinck biography is perhaps

---

[1] The papers from the Edinburgh Bavinck Conference were published in the *Scottish Bulletin of Evangelical Theology* 29.1 (Spring 2011).

[5] The term 'modernist,' in a Dutch theological context, dates from 1858, when it first appeared in D.T. Huet's *Wenken opzigtelijk de Moderne theologie* ('s-Gravenhage: J. M. van 't Haaff, 1858), which applied the epithet to the movement begun by Johannes Scholten's *De leer der Hervormde Kerk* (Leiden: P. Engels, 1848–50) and Cornelis Opzoomer's *De weg der wetenschap* (Amsterdam: J. H. Gebhard 1849). This book's use of the term is thus with this specific meaning in order to describe the nineteenth-century Dutch theological movement preceding the rise of neo-Calvinism.

[6] R. H. Bremmer, *Herman Bavinck en zijn Tijdgenoten* (Kampen: Kok, 1966).

[7] Valentijn Hepp, *Dr. Herman Bavinck* (Amsterdam: W. Ten Have 1921).

unnecessary at the outset of this book. In the light of Bolt's useful sketch of Bavinck in the Editor's Introduction to each volume of Reformed Dogmatics,[8] Bristley's biography in his Guide to the Writings of Herman Bavinck[9] and Gleason's recently published biography,[10] it appears that the anglophone world is now considerably better informed of Bavinck's *Sitz im Leben*. Thus, this work concerns itself only briefly with the question 'who was Herman Bavinck?' Rather, it primarily attempts to frame a study of Bavinck's use of the 'organic' via the question 'where was Herman Bavinck?'

Various works were written during Bavinck's lifetime to set this scene. However, those published in English were few in number and, because they have been out of print for almost a century, are particularly difficult to access. As such, it seems appropriate to begin a book on Bavinck by recreating his backdrop.[11]

Viewed in terms of theology-in-history, Bavinck has an intriguing location. He appears at the close of a period which moves from the *Réveil* and its influence on rural Calvinism to the Groninger School of van Heusde and the Leiden school of his nephew, Johannes Scholten. Bavinck then emerges as a student in Leiden who (with Abraham Kuyper) leads an alternative theological movement: the neo-Calvinist renaissance. Within the exciting, rapid development of Calvin scholarship in the nineteenth-century, Bavinck emerged in Abraham Kuyper's slipstream as the neo-Calvinists' dogmatician *par excellence*.

To understand Bavinck generally, one must begin with some analysis of the eighteenth- and nineteenth-century circumstances which birthed Dutch neo-Calvinism at the turn of the twentieth-century. In analysing a highly specific area of his thought, namely the organic motif used throughout Bavinck's writings, one must begin the discussion with a historical overview.

---

[8] John Bolt, 'Editor's Introduction' in *RD* 1.11–19; 2.11–18; 3.10–17; 4.16–23.

[9] Eric Bristley, *Guide to the Writings of Herman Bavinck* (Grand Rapids: Reformation Heritage Books, 2008), 9–27.

[10] Ron Gleason, *Herman Bavinck: Pastor, Churchman, Statesman, Theologian* (Philipsburg: Presbyterian & Reformed Publications, 2010); cf. James Eglinton, 'Review' of Ron Gleason, *Herman Bavinck: Pastor, Churchman, Statesman, Theologian* in Scottish Bulletin of Evangelical Theology 29.1 (Spring 2011).

[11] Aside from that of Mackay, the sole English language work charting the nineteenth-century Netherlands' theological topography is Eldred Vanderlaan, *Protestant Modernism in Holland* (H. Milford: Oxford University Press, 1924). For non-English works, see Chantepie de la Saussaye, *La crise religieuse en Hollande – Souvenirs et impressions* (Leyde: De Breuk & Smits, 1860); Albert Réville, 'Les Controverses et les écoles religieuses en Holland' in *Revue des deux Mondes* (Paris, 1859); Christiaan Sepp, *Proeve eener Pragmatische Geschiedenis der Theologie in Nederland (1787–1858)* (Amsterdam: J.P. Sepp en Zoon, 1860); Allard Pierson, *Oudere Tijdgenooten* (Amsterdam, 1904); Jacobus Herderscheê, *De Modern-godsdienstige richting in Nederland* (Amsterdam: Van Holkema & Warendorf, 1904); Chantepie de la Saussaye, *Geestlijke Stroomingen* (Haarlem: Erven Bohn, 1907).

At various points in this book, the development of Bavinck's thought will be accounted for in relation to the key movements and schools of thought in the preceding two centuries of Dutch theology. As such, it is necessary to begin with a historical survey without which analysis of Bavinck's handling of the organic motif will prove considerably difficult. Although its subject matter is the theology of Bavinck, this book will make regular references to the key players in his thought world. Thus one must first establish the basic beliefs of the Heusdiaans, the Groningers and the Leiden theologians. One does not attempt to limit historical material to this opening chapter. Rather, subsequent chapters will also frame topical debates (ecclesiology, Scripture and so on) within their respective immediate historical contexts. Those smaller historical sketches, however, depend on and expand the initial broader historical overview provided in this chapter.

I. Who Was Herman Bavinck?

Noting in particular that Chapter 2 will offer a reinterpretation of Bavinck's own biography, it is necessary to provide the reader with a short retelling of his life. Born on 13 December 1854, in the Dutch town of Hoogeveen, Herman Bavinck was the son of Jan Bavinck, a German Reformed pastor. The second of eleven children, Herman was born into the highly conservative, separatist *Christelijke Gereformeerde Kerken*.[12] Having excelled throughout his early schooling, he enrolled as a student at the Theological School in Kampen, where his father was a professor. After one year, however, the young Bavinck made the daring decision to transfer to the aggressively modernist theological faculty at Leiden. This choice was made in search of a 'more scientific' theological training than could be offered at Kampen.[13]

Between 1874 and 1880, Bavinck studied under the likes of Johannes Scholten, Abraham Kuenen and Lodewijk Rauwenhoff at Leiden. There, he admired the scientific approach of his professors, though he often found himself in deep disagreement with their presuppositions and doctrinal conclusions. At this time, he also came under the influence of Abraham Kuyper, the rising star of a new wave of Dutch Calvinism. His *Christelijke Gereformeerde* pastor at Leiden, J. H. Donner, introduced him to Kuyper's Anti-Revolutionary Party. At Leiden, Bavinck wrote a doctoral thesis on the

---

[12] John Bolt, 'Editor's Introduction,' in Herman Bavinck, *The Last Things* (Grand Rapids: Baker Books, 1996), 10.

[13] Bremmer, *Herman Bavinck en zijn Tijdgenoten*, 20.

ethics of Ulrich Zwingli,[14] following which he sought ordination in the *Christelijke Gereformeerde Kerken*. Despite a deeply suspicious reception, he was admitted into the church and, in 1881, became pastor of the congregation in Franeker.

One year later, Bavinck was called to teach theology at Kampen, where he taught from 1883 to 1901. There, he wrote *Gereformeerde Dogmatiek*. He married Johanna Adrianna Schippers in 1888. During his time at Kampen, Bavinck and Kuyper were the key figures in the Union of the Reformed Churches in 1892. Following this Union, he accepted the post of theology professor at the Vrije Universiteit in Amsterdam.

This period in his life was marked by a broad and thorough engagement in the fields of politics (via the Kuyperian Anti-Revolutionary Party), philosophy, pedagogy and education. In 1920, after preaching at Synod, Bavinck suffered a heart attack. From this incident onwards, his health began to fail. He died on 29 July 1921.

II. Late Eighteenth- and Early Nineteenth-Century Dutch Theology

1. Mainline Theology pre-Groningen

At the turn of the nineteenth-century, various strands of Protestant theology are evident in the Netherlands. Rural life was dominated by a separatist brand of Calvinism drawing its confessional identity from the Heidelberg Catechism. The *Christelijke Gereformeerde Kerken* (Dutch Christian Reformed Church, also known as the *Afgescheidenen*), within which Bavinck was raised, stood in this tradition of conservative rural Calvinistic pietism.

In the Dutch cities, however, one finds differing developments. Prior to the rise of the Groninger school, mainline Dutch Protestantism generally regarded Christianity as a body of truths supernaturally revealed in Scripture. In contrast to the confessional Calvinism of the rural churches, however, mainstream theology often positioned itself against ecclesial dogma in favour of a closer biblicism: doctrines including the Trinity, a two-nature Christology and Calvinistic concepts of atonement and predestination were regularly opposed.

Dutch intellectual life, at this point, existed in a strange relationship to wider pan-European trends. Although the Dutch were aware of the philosophical revolution taking place in Germany, mainline theologians

---

[14] Herman Bavinck, *De Ethiek van Ulrich Zwingli* (Kampen: G. Ph. Zalsman, 1880).

seemed to express little interest in it.[15] This was perhaps the case due to their high view of supernatural, Biblical revelation. Roessingh posits this as the reason that Kant, Fichte, Schelling and Hegel made so little initial impact in the Netherlands.[16] While Schleiermacher's works were available in the Netherlands from 1830, the leading Dutch theological journal *Godgeleerde Bijdragen* remarked on the Dutch translation of his works: 'We consider it beneath the office of a Protestant teacher to translate such writings and to publish them without corrective annotations.'[17] Strauss' *Leben Jesu* received a lukewarm welcome, again due to the mainstream commitment to Biblical supernaturalism.[18] 'Whereas in many places in Europe after the Enlightenment theology attempted to determine its position vis-à-vis the new challenges, Dutch theology, exhausted by two hundred years of controversy, slept a deep supernaturalistic sleep.'[19]

Thus, before the advent of Groninger theology, one finds a mainstream theological tradition within which faith was an assent to a doctrinal system concerning the Christ, which necessitated the presence of a particular heart disposition.

2. The Groninger School: van Heusde, Pareau, van Oordt and Hofstede de Groot

Although Dutch Protestantism, until the rise of the Groninger School, existed in somewhat of a time lag, its intellectual life was eventually impacted by the paradigm shifts occurring outwith its borders. The locus of this impact moved between the university cities of Utrecht and Groningen.

Phillip Willem van Heusde, appointed professor of Greek and History at Utrecht in 1804, was among the first Dutch advocates of Schleiermacher, Lessing, Herder and the German *Vermittlungstheologie* (an important school of thought in nineteenth-century German Protestantism which attempted to wed the traditional Reformed confessions with modern science, philosophy and historical scholarship). He portrayed history as a process of humanity-wide education towards a morally ideal 'humanity'.[20] In sketching Bavinck's

[15] See also Simon De Vries, 'The Hexateuchal Criticism of Abraham Kuenen', in *Journal of Biblical Literature*, Vol. 82, No. 1, (March 1963), 32.

[16] K.H. Roessingh, *De moderne theologie in Nederland; hare voorbereiding en eerste period* (Dissertation, Groningen, 1914), 22–4.

[17] Cited in Roessingh, *De moderne theologie in Nederland*, 24.

[18] Cited in Roessingh, *De moderne theologie in Nederland*, 24–5.

[19] Hendrikus Berkhof, *Two Hundred Years of Theology* (Grand Rapids: Eerdmans, 1989), 97.

[20] Cited in Roessingh, *De moderne theologie in Nederland*, 35.

backdrop, van Heusde is a figure of immense significance, primarily for his influence on the founders of the Groningen school, and second for his effect on his nephew J.H. Scholten, the founder of the opposing Leiden school.

A gifted pedagogue, van Heusde attracted a considerable student following, known at the time as *Heusdiaans*. Between 1829 and 1830, three of van Heusde's students were promoted to professorships in the northern town of Groningen: the fabulist Louis Gerlach Pareau, Johan Frederik van Oordt and Willem Muurling. A fourth *Heusdiaan*, Petrus Hofstede de Groot, was appointed head of the Groningen Seminary. Hofstede de Groot was educated at Groningen rather than Utrecht and as such was not directly taught by van Heusde. However, while a student, he was given a manuscript copy of van Heusde's *Lectures on the History of Philosophy*, a book which marked him deeply. Van Heusde's reading of Plato was of particular importance to the *Heusdiaans*.[21] The driving sentiment conveyed to these men was that practical matters (in terms of Christian living and personal experience of Christ) are more important than doctrinal specifics: '*Niet de leer, maar het leven . . . Niet de leer, maar de Heer!*'[22] This emphasis is evident in the numerous fables popularized by Pareau: 'Two travellers rose at sunrise to make a journey together. Before setting out they began to dispute with one another as to whether the sun was incandescent only at its surface, or whether the incandescence went right to its centre. They discussed the question hotly until the sun had set, and so the day was lost.'[23] Pareau's central emphasis is that those who quibble over doctrinal nuances stand to miss out on the reality about which they debate.

In charting the Groninger school's rise to prominence, one notes the sense in which it carried on a precedent set by earlier mainstream theology: a stated unwillingness to look outwith the Netherlands for a basic theological identity. In the previous century, mainline Dutch theologians positioned themselves against the perceived Heidelberg and Geneva centrism of rural Calvinism. Theirs, it was asserted, was an indigenous Dutch appropriation of Christianity. The Groninger school took a similar direction, asserting that they were distinctly Dutch and needed not look abroad for theological direction. Mackay cites 'a sympathetic critic of the time':

It is not to the credit of our national Church that it should go for its spiritual milk and meat to Scotsmen and Englishmen, the French and the

---

[21] Mackay, *Religious Thought in Holland*, 50.
[22] English: 'Not doctrine, but life... Not doctrine, but the Lord!'
[23] Cited in Mackay, *Religious Thought in Holland*, 51–2.

Swiss. Foreign books and teachers give foreign twists to our piety. Even in
the kingdom of God nationality cannot be disregarded without impunity.
And although there is no distinction before God between Jew and Gentile, let every one remain as he is called: he who is called as a Dutchman,
a Dutchman let him remain.[24]

In 1842, Hofstede de Groot published a historical overview of Dutch
theology. This work asserted that the Brethren of Common Life, a
fourteenth-century sect established in the Netherlands by Geert Groote
(1340–84), represented a pure, Dutch theology. This indigenous faith,
Hofstede de Groot claimed, was replaced by the imposing alien force of
Calvinism. The Polish Reformer, Jan Łaski, as a non-Dutch theologian
lauded by the Groningers, was deemed acceptable by association as he was
a close friend of the Dutchman Erasmus and worked in the Dutch Churches
in Emden and London.[25]

In this sense, the Groninger theologians coincide with the period of
Restoration under King Willem I (1813–40), wherein Dutch culture
generally began seeking a keener self-identification in a new Europe.[26]
Within this context, the Groningen school seems to display a curious set of
double standards with regard to foreign ideas. Despite its aversion to much
Reformed theology (on the grounds of its non-Dutch origins), its intellectual
catalyst (via van Heusde) was undoubtedly German; Lessing, Herder and
Schleiermacher were van Heusde's major influences.[27] This influence was
passed on to the *Heusdiaans* who, like Herder and van Heusde, espoused a
fervent nationalism.[28]

Van Oordt, Pareau and Hofstede de Groote established the theological
journal *Waarheid en Liefde*[29] in 1837. The latter described its inception as
follows:

---

[24] Mackay, *Religious Thought in Holland*, 57. Frustratingly, in following the convention of his time,
Mackay does not reference this quotation. The sentiment was common to the Heusdiaans
and came from van Heusde's own insistence on interpreting an individual's behaviour and
actions as the effect of his nationality. Cf. Jasper Vree, *De Groninger godgeleerden. De oorsprongen
en de eerste periode van hun optreden (1820–43)* (Kampen: J.H. Kok, 1984), index s.v.

[25] Jan Łaski or John à Lasco (1499–1560) was a leading Polish reformer. The sole extant work
by Łaski is a catechism prepared under his direction. He gained interest in Germany and the
Netherlands in the 1840s, largely through the rise of Dutch nationalism as led by Hofstede
de Groot. See Polnischer Baron, *Humanist und europäischer Reformator Hrsg. v. Christoph Strohm*
(Tübingen: Mohr Siebeck, 2005).

[26] Berkhof, *Two Hundred Years of Theology*, 97.

[27] Roessingh, *De moderne theologie in Nederland*, 35; D.H. Kromminga, *The Christian Reformed Tradition, from the Reformation to the Present* (Grand Rapids: Eerdmans, 1943), 113.

[28] Kathleen Powers Erickson, *At Eternity's Gate: The Spiritual Vision of Vincent Van Gogh* (Grand
Rapids: Eerdmans, 1998), 17–18.

[29] English: Truth in Love.

On a certain Friday evening in the winter of 1833–34, we three professors, Van Oordt, Pareau and myself, were sitting together and talking over our lectures, a subject about which we were often at a loss and about which we used to consult one another. 'Yesterday it struck me with absolute clearness', said one, 'that history is properly the chief thing in Christianity, and that everything rests on what God has done and still does in and by Jesus Christ'.

'You mean', said the second, 'everything goes back to the revelation of God in Jesus Christ – thus St Paul expresses it. Fourteen days ago I saw that we must begin our theology with that'. Said the third, 'For three or four days I could not get on with my lectures at all till it flashed upon me like a light, "Not a doctrine of Paul or of Jesus is what we have to preach, but the Evangel, that is the glad tidings of a history of what God reveals and presents to us in His Son".' In such wise, more or less, we conversed. Who the first, the second, or the last speaker was I no longer remember, but only indeed this, that we now went deeper into a thought that for long had not been strange to us, but which at last and at the same time became quite clear to each of us, although on further discussion it appeared that it had come to one of us more by the way of exegesis, to another by that of history, and to the third by that of philosophy.[30]

Having established this shared vision, the Groningen school began propagating its views via *Waarheid in Liefde* and by organizing small discussion groups of pastors and theologians.[31]

The Groninger school marked a radical departure from its mainstream predecessor. Faith, it taught, was a total self-giving to God and that on the basis of an experience of his love. Although Hofstede de Groot explicitly attributes this change to Schleiermacher's influence, the Groningers saw fit to develop Schleiermacher's 'feeling of absolute dependence' into a *sensus dependentiae, sensus indigentiae, sensus amoris*.[32] Revelation thus moved from being a set of propositions given by Jesus (the previous mainline view) or about Jesus (the predominant position among rural Calvinists). Rather, revelation *was* Jesus Christ.[33] 'Christ came to make us over by his personal influence, to make humanity ever more conformed to the likeness of God. This, and not a satisfaction of the Divine justice, is the work of Christ.'[34]

---

[30] Cited in Mackay, *Religious Thought in Holland*, 59–60.
[31] Roessingh, *De moderne theologie in Nederland*, 26.
[32] Roessingh, *De moderne theologie in Nederland*, 15.
[33] Roessingh quotes Van Oordt, that revelation is 'his mission, his person, his history.' Roessingh, *De moderne theologie in Nederland*, 37.
[34] Vanderlaan, *Protestant Modernism in Holland*, 16; cf. Roessingh, *De moderne theologie in Nederland*, 38.

Groninger theology attempted to find a renewed Christocentrism in dogmatics, emphasizing that in the person and work of Christ, God is seen and known. This Christology takes an unusual and interesting shape. The Groninger theologians called for a recommitment to pre-Nicean Christology, claiming that before 325, the dominant orthodox view was a one-nature Christology, whereby Jesus has one nature which is simultaneously human and divine. Furthermore, while the Groninger school affirmed the pre-existence, miraculous birth and *imago Dei* status of Christ, it also denied his eternal existence.

The Groninger school's distinctive Christological formulation would ultimately prove decisive in Scholten's dissatisfaction with its overall dogmatics. This in turn led to the formation of the Leiden school in which Bavinck was educated.

In terms of ecclesiology, the Groningers were critical of both traditional Reformed and Lutheran ecclesiologies. Hofstede de Groot charged the Heidelberg Catechism (the confessional standard of the Dutch Reformed Church) with blurring the true meaning of the *ecclesia*:

'To understand the doctrine of the true Church, the word Church must first be explained. With the victory of the particularism of Calvinism at the Synod of Dort, insight into the meaning of the Church began to disappear. Luther did not see that separate Christians, each one for himself, can never realise the end of God in the appearance of Jesus Christ; that this can only be realised in the Communion of Saints, a doctrine which Luther did not understand.'[35]

In its ecclesiology, as Hofstede de Groot's *Theologica Naturalis* suggests, the Groningen school was heavily influenced by Jansensim. They laid a strong emphasis on spiritual community. Interestingly, the Groninger theologians chose to abandon the Reformed relationship between Old and New Covenants. Instead, they emphasized the New Covenant's attachment to the history of the church.

Much confusion has arisen in philosophy from not placing sufficiently in the foreground the fact that man is a social being, and can only become man in society. Man, as a solitary being upon a lonely island, is a creature of the imagination, not an actuality. Real men are born of parents, who care for them. They come into a small circle, gradually becoming wider,

---

[35] Hofstede de Groot, cited in Mackay, *Religious Thought in Holland*, 62–3.

of brothers and sisters, relations, neighbours, fellow-men, and, unless he lived in this constantly widening human society, the child would not become a man. In his mother's womb he lives the life of a plant, newly born that of an animal, and an animal he would remain were he not taken up into human society and there gradually formed into a man. The consciousness of the spiritual world, of which the child must become a member, would remain dormant in him if it were not awakened by seeing and hearing other men in whom this consciousness has become awake. It would sleep like the spark in the flint, which has not been struck by iron; like the flame in the oil, which has not been set alight by another flame. In man, viewed apart from society, we can look only for a capacity for the spiritual life. To find the beginning of the spiritual life we must thus go outside the individual, and seek for it in the spiritual society in which he lives.[36]

Just as the Groningen Christology sets the tone of its ecclesiology, this concept of church has a formative effect on its soteriology. Pareau's *Compendium Theologiæ Christianæ Moralis* demonstrates this relationship. Interpreting Christ's mission as being to establish a community committed to the spiritual and intellectual formation of men, the church's role and inherent soteriology are spelt out. The church is to strive for the development of Christ's divine-humanity in its human members.

3. The Réveil: Bilderdijk, Da Costa and van Prinsterer

While the Groningen school provoked a succeeding counter-movement in Scholten's Leiden theological stable, it also coexisted with a competing movement: the *Réveil*. The character of the *Réveil* is of considerable importance appropriating various aspects of Bavinck's immediate background.

Taking its name from its Swiss forerunner, the *Réveil* began to impact the Netherlands in the mid nineteenth-century. The *Réveil* has been described as a revivalist, 'sin-and-grace' brand of religion.[37] Due to the particular Calvinism of its early leader, Bilderdijk, the *Réveil*'s closest contemporary theological relation was the Heidelberg Catechism-led Calvinism of the Dutch countryside. However, the *Réveil* sprang up in an entirely different

---

[36] Hofstede de Groot, *Theologica Naturalis*, cited in Mackay, *Religious Thought in Holland*, 63–4.
[37] Vanderlaan, *Protestant Modernism in Holland*, 17.

social context: it was concentrated primarily in the cities, its leading lights being aristocrats, artists and intellectuals. In contrast to the intensely Dutch character of rural Calvinism, a significant proportion of the *Réveil*'s exponents were of non-Dutch extraction. While its own existence was relatively short-lived, its theological impact in urban areas (into the neo-Calvinist era) would be long lasting. The relative proximity of the *Réveil* and the more popular, rural, pietistic Calvinism is perhaps best accounted for by their shared roots: they are cousins, rather than siblings; the descendents of an earlier form of continental Calvinism. One was elitist; the other popular. However, their similarity was such that someone like Bavinck, whose background was rural pietism, could smoothly transition into the *Réveil*'s elitist context.

Willem Bilderdijk (1756–1831) was born into a family supportive of the *Huis van Oranje-Nassau*. Thus, his formative influences were strongly Calvinistic. His opposition to the Batavian Republic[38] led to a time in exile, first in Germany, then England. Eventually returning to the Netherlands, he began lecturing privately in Leiden, teaching law and history. In addition to his highly influential poetry, Bilderdijk's lectures drew a small group of acolytes, among them the Jewish poet Isaac Da Costa and the influential jurist and statesman Groen van Prinsterer.

Born in Amsterdam to parents of Portuguese Jewish ancestry, Isaac Da Costa (1798–1860) first encountered Bilderdijk's poetry while studying under Moses Lemans in Amsterdam. He then moved to Leiden where he joined Bilderdijk's inner circle. At Leiden he converted to Christianity. Through his poetry and theological writings, he spread the *Réveil* among the Dutch intelligentsia. The theological sentiments of Da Costa's poetry would go on to influence the later neo-Calvinist movement.[39]

Guillaume Groen van Prinsterer (1801–76) was a leading figure among the nineteenth-century Dutch aristocracy. He worked for a time as personal secretary to Willem I. The *Réveil*'s dissemination of Calvinism in the upper classes reached Groen van Prinsterer, through whom it had a lasting impact: when the *Réveil* itself had faded out, Groen van Prinsterer enthused what would become the Anti-Revolutionary Party (which Abraham Kuyper would formally establish in 1879, and with which Bavinck

---

[38] The Batavian Republic, which existed from 1795 to 1806, succeeded the Republic of the United Netherlands. See Jonathan Israel, *The Dutch Republic: Its Rise, Greatness and Fall, 1477–1806* (Oxford: University Press, 1998).

[39] van den Belt, for example, has demonstrated that Da Costa's doctrine of Scripture influenced Bavinck and Kuyper in their concept of organic inspiration as uniting Scripture's simultaneous humanity and divinity. Henk van den Belt, *Autopistia: The Self-Convincing Authority of Scripture in Reformed Theology*, (Leiden: University Press, 2006), 279.

would be heavily associated) with Bilderdijk's Calvinistic, pro-House of Orange vision.

As a theological movement, the *Réveil* positioned itself against the Groninger school. However, it should be stated that for a major player in a theological contest, the *Réveil* was at one level surprisingly untheological in character. Its theological output was not provided, for the most part, by specialist dogmaticians. Rather, it was the attempt of artists, poets and aristocrats to appropriate a largely conservative brand of Calvinism in an upper-to-middle class city-based environment. As could be expected for a small, elitist movement, the *Réveil* itself eventually waned. Its influence, however, outlived its own immediate momentum, as can clearly be seen in Groen van Prinsterer's role in the inception of the Anti-Revolutionary Party (which developed in conjunction with the neo-Calvinist theological revival).

4. The Leiden School: Johannes Scholten

The driving force behind Bavinck's *alma mater* Leiden school was Johannes Hendricus Scholten (1811–85).[40] As a student in Utrecht, Scholten lived with his famous uncle, van Heusde. Following his graduation, he spent two years working as the pastor of a rural congregation. His time as student and clergyman entailed firsthand experience of the various dominant schools of thought: the anti-Reformed bent of the *Heusdiaans*, the older mainline pre-Groninger theology of the Utrecht theological faculty and then the type of Calvinism deeply ingrained in rural Dutch life.

Examination of Scholten's progress at Utrecht reveals a growing disdain for mainline Dutch theology. His 1836 doctoral thesis makes this clear: mainline theology lacked a unifying principle, which Scholten found in the Christological revelation of divine love.[41] While a young minister, Scholten came under the influence of *Waarheid in Liefde*. Despite his initial warmth towards the *Heusdiaans*, he came to perceive a major Christological flaw in their theology.

This movement away from van Heusde's theology came to a head in 1840 when Scholten was appointed theology professor at the University of Franeker in the north-western province of Friesland. Interestingly, his student, Bavinck, would also go on to work in Franeker, albeit in the

---

[40] Scholten published accounts of his own theological development: *Herdenking mijner vijfentwintigjarige ambtsbediening*, (Leiden, 1865); and *Afscheidsrede bij het neerleggen van het hoogleeraarsambt aan de Universiteit te Leiden* (Leiden, 1881).

[41] Johannes Scholten, *Disquisitio de Dei erga hominem amore* (Trajecti ad Rhenum, 1836); see also Scholten, *Afscheidsrede*, 9.

pastorate rather than the academy. Scholten's choice of topic in his inaugural professorial address is telling: the lecture was entitled *The Duty of Avoiding Docetism*. It was a direct attack on Groninger Christology, which Scholten claimed was inherently Arian. Scholten also charged the rural Calvinists with defective Christology: it was alleged that they presented a less than fully human Christ. In contrast, Scholten's Jesus was presented as truly and fully human, sent to lead the human race towards his ideal humanity. Scholten taught that Christ is the one humanity can and must become like: '*nobis vero simul perfectâ voluerit [Deus] humanitatis imagine monstrare quo modo ipsi, et debeamus, et possimus ad divinae naturae similitudinem escendere.*'[12]

The sense in which humanity is dissimilar to Christ is that he is so by his own nature, whereas humanity becomes like Christ through Christ: 'ud quod ille *a se* sit, *naturâ suâ*, et vero *origine prorsus singulari*, id nos possimus et debeamus aliquando fiere; at vero non *a nobis*, non *proprio*, quod dicitur, *remigio*, sed unice per illum.'[13] In relation to the Groninger school, the early Scholten also maintains the virgin birth and pre-existence of Christ, though the latter topic receives little attention in his work.

By virtue of its academic composition (at this time, Franeker University was comprised only of its theological faculty) and low student numbers, Scholten's time at Franeker left much time for private study. In 1844, the Franeker faculty was closed, its building having been earmarked by the Dutch government as the site of a new psychiatric hospital. Scholten was initially reluctant to move elsewhere, but eventually was relocated to Leiden University where he remained throughout his working life. There, his opening lecture argued that Christianity demonstrated its divine origin *in animo humano*, and thus countered both the rationalism and supernaturalism of older mainline Dutch theology.

In sketching Scholten's appropriation of Reformed theology, two foci are of particular importance.

First, one finds his definition of the formal and material principles of the Reformed faith. Scholten lacked van Heusde's total aversion to historic Reformed theology. His drive was to examine the Reformed Church's historic confession of faith and the writings of the Reformers. In doing so, Scholten identified Scripture as the Reformed faith's formal principle: the church depends on divine self-revelation. This is followed by the material principle of unqualified divine sovereignty: one is utterly reliant on God for salvation

---

[12] Johannes Scholten, *Oratio de vitando in Jesu Christi historia interpretanda docetismo, nobili, ad rem Christianam promovendam hodiernae theologiae munere* (in *Annales Academi, 1839–40*, Hagae-Comitis, 1842), 265.

[13] Scholten, *Oratio de vitando in Jesu Christi*, 273.

by grace alone. During his time in the pastorate, Scholten was particularly impressed with the rural Calvinists' rigid commitment to predestination. Scholten's conviction was that Reformed theology, via this distinction, presents Christianity with greater clarity than its Lutheran or Roman Catholic alternatives. It seems fairly settled that Scholten's adoption of these principles was taken from Alexander Schweizer's *Die Glaubenslehre der evangelisch-reformierten Kirche*.[44] Scholten's *Leer der Hervormde Kerk* references Schweizer's work regularly. Indeed Berkhof goes as far as saying that 'Scholten, like Schweizer, set out to demonstrate that the theology of the Reformers, or the Reformed confessions, found its fulfilment in idealistic thought.'[45]

In this respect, one may clearly observe a high degree of consistency between Schweizer and his follower, Scholten. The distinction between 'material' and 'formal' principles first enters the Protestant theological vocabulary in the work of August Twesten, an early student of Schleiermacher. Twesten, writing in a Lutheran context, wrote of Scripture as Protestantism's 'formal principle', and justification *sola fide* as the 'material principle' of distinctly Lutheran theology.[46]

In *Die Glaubenslehre*, Schweizer, described elsewhere as 'arguably Schleiermacher's most gifted student,'[47] notes Twesten's earlier handling of Lutheran theology's 'material principle' as justification by faith alone. By contrast to this, he portrays the Reformed equivalent as 'absolute dependence upon God alone,' which his dogmatic formulation articulated as 'absolute predestination.'[48] McCormack has argued that, in Schweizer's theology, this material principle lacked an ultimate, all-controlling influence. 'It would have been very surprising indeed had Schweizer envisioned a *system* of doctrine derived more or less from a single material norm. The critical distance which he maintained from all doctrinal explanations of the religious consciousness would never have allowed such a move. And the truth is that he did not take that step.'[49]

[44] Alexander Schweizer, *Die Glaubenslehre der evangelisch-reformierten Kirche, Dargestellt und aus den Quellen belegt*, 2 vols. (Zürich: Orell, Füssli und Com, 1844–47).

[45] Berkhof, *Two Hundred Years of Theology*, 98.

[46] August Twesten, *Vorlesungen über die Dogmatik der evangelisch-lutherischen Kirche* (Hamburg: Perthes, 1826). The first historical analysis of this distinction was compiled by Albrecht Ritschl, 'Über die beiden Principien des Protestantismus; Antwort auf eine 25 Jahre alte Frage,' *Gesammelte Aufsätze* (Freiburg: J.C.B Mohrl, 1893), 234–47.

[47] Bruce McCormack, 'The Sum of the Gospel: The Doctrine of Election in the Theologies of Alexander Schweizer and Karl Barth,' *Toward the Future of Reformed Theology: Tasks, Topics, Traditions*, eds. David Willis-Watkins and Michael Welker (Grand Rapids: Eerdmans, 1999), 470.

[48] Schweizer, *Die Glaubenslehre der evangelisch-reformierten Kirche*, 1:38–43.

[49] McCormack, 'The Sum of the Gospel: The Doctrine of Election in the Theologies of Alexander Schweizer and Karl Barth,' 473–4.

As will be demonstrated, one cannot make a similar claim regarding Scholten, who boldly 'took that step'.

Second, Scholten's debate with Opzoomer over the issue of determinism profoundly impacted his theological system.[50] It moved his thought from idealism to empiricism, gave his doctrine of God a distinctly monistic flavour and ingrained his predestinationism with starkly anti-supernatural lines. The change brought on Scholten was central in the development of the Leiden school within which Bavinck was educated, and against which he would later write.

When examining the *Réveil*'s theology, Scholten understood its major emphases (a theology of atonement, the Trinity and Jesus' deity) to be misplaced. He argued that the *Réveil* had supplanted the Reformed tradition's material principle of predestination in grace. In doing so, he claimed that the *Réveil* had fundamentally misappropriated Reformed theology.[51]

In this light, Scholten's understanding and definition of 'Reformed' is somewhat unusual. Clearly, Scholten was a highly committed theist. Particularly as he shifted from idealism to empiricism in the aftermath of his debate with Opzoomer, an omnicausal deity provided Scholten with a convincing reason for assenting with the prevailing determinism of contemporary natural science. Theism was a suitable foundation for a mechanical worldview. A critical reading of Scholten might suggest that his particular principle of determinism provided the hermeneutic with which he then formed a doctrine of God, rather than allowing God's self-revelation to shape the relationship of God's will to cosmic history.[52] Such a claim finds momentum in Scholten's own theological development. Particularly as he moved towards empiricism, his determinism adopted a rigid, anti-supernaturalist pose. In tandem with this, his doctrine of God became less Trinitarian and more monistic.[53] Such an outcome fits neatly with Scholten's earlier assertion that the specifics of God's being (in particular his triunity) are less important than the material principle of predestination.[54]

Outwith the bare formal and material principles of Scripture and predestination, which comprise the heart of Scholten's Reformed

[50] Berkhof, *Two Hundred Years of Theology*, 98–103.
[51] Scholten, *De leer der Hervormde Kerk*, 18–20.
[52] Scholten's statement that his doctrine of God is reached by 'reflection grounded upon observation [of the cosmos]' ('*bespiegeling gegrond op waarneming*', *De leer der Hervormde Kerk*, 4:lxi) also hints at this verdict.
[53] This fact was not lost on Bavinck, who critiqued Scholten for this very point: Herman Bavinck, *RD* 2.43. See also Herman Bavinck, *Philosophy of Revelation* (London: Longmans, Green and Co., 1909), 46. Hereafter *PR*.
[54] Scholten, *De leer der Hervormde Kerk*, 18–20.

Christianity, little else in the Reformers' own theology needs to be retained if one is to remain in their tradition. On the grounds that it is inconsistent with the principle that God predestines everything and that this must be done in grace, Scholten argues that Calvin was wrong, among other things, to maintain a belief in hell. He makes similar claims regarding soteriology and previous Reformed doctrines of sin and forgiveness, consistently arguing that such doctrines contradict the two aforementioned supreme principles of the Reformed faith.[55] At the core of this thought is that from its inception, the Reformed faith, even in certain aspects of the works of Calvin and Luther, has contained much that contradicts its own material and formal principles, and as such must be fundamentally reworked. The Leiden school's assertion was that it had brought this revision. Its rigorously naturalist, mechanical, theistic determinism was, Scholten claimed, the purest expression of the essential Reformed faith.

It must be noted that aside from broadly similar commitments to revelation and predestination, Scholten's understanding of 'Reformed' has relatively little in common with the Reformers or substantial sections of the subsequent Reformed tradition. When one examines Calvin's own hierarchy of truths, the true doctrine of God takes ultimate priority, following which he lists the theology of the gospel.[56] Calvin's priorities were somewhat different from those of Scholten. Vanderlaan offers the somewhat cynical assessment that 'because Calvinism is deterministic, and Scholten also is a determinist, therefore Scholten thinks himself a true Calvinist.'[57]

Considerable Trinitarian and Christological differences highlight that the Leiden school offered a radical reinterpretation of Reformed theology.[58] Establishing this fact is central in understanding Bavinck's aims as a former student of this school. Indeed, it sets the backdrop for Bavinck's appropriation of the Reformed tradition in *Gereformeerde Dogmatiek*.

One notes such an emphasis as present in Bavinck's post-Leiden letters.[59] A significant element in Bavinck's writing (particularly as regards his organic motif), it will be seen, is his redefinition of Reformed theology *contra* Scholten. Taking this approach to Bavinck and Scholten is hardly

[55] Scholten, *De leer der Hervormde Kerk*, 18–20.
[56] John Calvin, *Institutes of the Christian Religion*, IV.i, 12.
[57] Vanderlaan, *Protestant Modernism in Holland*, 31.
[58] The primary critic of this revision in Scholten's day was Daniel Chantepie de la Saussaye (1818–74).
[59] Bavinck to Snouck, 24 November 1880, in *Een Leidse vriendschap* (Baarn: Ten Have, 1999), Jan de Bruijn and George Harinck, eds., 75–6.

speculative: Leiden Professor Abraham Kuenen, speaking as Scholten's colleague and Bavinck's former teacher, once quipped that 'Leiden is Scholten and Bavinck was Kampen.'[60]

5. The Higher Education Act (1876)

In examining the context in which Bavinck's theology develops, one also acknowledges the influence of debate on the place of theology in the university. Bavinck was born into a context where the basic right of theology to exist within the academy was called into question. In response to the pan-European Revolutions of 1848, the Dutch Parliament adopted a new, liberal constitution in October 1848. This constitution placed the Dutch government under considerable pressure to replace the theology departments in its universities with religious studies faculties.

Bavinck, who entered higher education at Kampen in 1873 before moving to Leiden one year later, became a student at the climax of this struggle. In 1876, midway through his Leiden years, the Higher Education Act was passed. The net effect of this legislation was that the Dutch universities were to retain the name 'theology', but the content of their teaching was to become 'religious studies'. Bavinck's own recollection of this environment focuses on its uncertainty regarding theology's nature and possibility:

> The reason for this odd development was that the state did not wish to relinquish its influence in the training of ministers for the Dutch Reformed Church (*Nederlands Hervormde Kerk*) while at the same time *the synod* [of the NHK] *was unable or unwilling to create its own institution for the training of its ministers.* The result was a strange mixture of incompatibles lacking all integration and unity of conception. Some of the subjects taught remind one of the old theology programs; others clearly belong to the field of religious studies. This unfortunate development also places the professors who must lecture in these departments in a difficult situation.[61]

The significance of this movement can scarcely be underemphasized in developing a reading of Bavinck's theology. Reasserting both the possibility

[60] Abraham Kuenen cited by Henry Elias Dosker, 'Herman Bavinck' in Herman Bavinck, *Essays on Religion, Science and Society* (Grand Rapids: Baker Academic, 2008), 16.

[61] Herman Bavinck, 'Theology and Religious Studies', in *Essays on Religion, Science and Society*, John Bolt, ed., Harry Boonstra and Gerrit Sheeres, trs. (Grand Rapids: Baker Publishing Group, 2008), 53.

and place of theology forms a major emphasis in his *Prolegomena*.[62] Indeed, in responding to the 1876 Act, Bavinck called for nothing less than 'a fundamental revision of the present-day concept of science.'[63] In 1892 he published *Godgeleerdheid en godsdienstwetenschap* ('Theology and the Scientific Study of Religion(s)').[64] In 1902, Bavinck's inaugural professorial address at the Vrije Universiteit Amsterdam was entitled *Godsdienst en godgeleerdheid* ('Religion and Theology').[65] This was clearly a career-spanning concern for Bavinck, and in this light one must read his Dogmatics as a striving for the reassertion of theology in post-Enlightenment Europe.

III. Neo-Calvinism: Herman Bavinck and Abraham Kuyper

No account of Bavinck's historical theological backdrop would be complete without reference to Abraham Kuyper (1837–1920), one of Scholten's most prominent students and, later, the figurehead of the neo-Calvinist movement with which Herman Bavinck was so heavily involved. Harinck memorably writes: 'When mentioned together, we take the names of Abraham Kuyper and Herman Bavinck not as the name of two individuals but as a brand name. Kuyper and Bavinck belong together like Goldman and Sachs or Mercedes and Benz. Together they stand for neo-Calvinism.'[66]

Through the work of Scholten's successor, LWE Rauwenhoff,[67] the Leiden school came to emphasize a particularly ethical focus in dogmatics. Kuyper's theological adolescence was spent learning Scholten's brand of Reformed theology via Rauwenhoff's ethical lens.[68] 'At Leyden Abraham Kuyper had been the ardent pupil of Scholten, inspired by his knowledge of Reformed theology and his determination to raise it, through fresh interpretation, to

---

[62] *RD* 1.36–58. 'In the Netherlands, in 1876, following the ideas of Tiele and Rauwenhoff, a division was instituted at state universities between the science of religion, which would be taught by the university, and the dogmatic and practical disciplines, which would be taught under the auspices of the church. . . . In the Netherlands this is the direction that has been taken by modern theologians for many years already and is embodied in the Higher Education Act of 1876.'

[63] *RD* 1.37.

[64] Herman Bavinck, 'Godgeleerdheid en godsdienstwetenschap' in *De vrije kerk* 18 (1892), 197–225.

[65] Herman Bavinck, *Godsdienst en godgeleerdheid* (Wageningen: Vada, 1902).

[66] George Harinck, 'Herman Bavinck and Geerhardus Vos,' *Calvin Theological Journal* 45 (2010), 18.

[67] The most thorough recent summary of Rauwenhoff's theology is P. L. Slis, *L. W. E. Rauwenhoff (1828–89): apologeet van het modernisme – Predikant, kerkhistoricus en godsdienstfilosoof* (Kampen: Kok, 2003).

[68] George Puchinger, *Abraham Kuyper: De Jonge Kuyper (1837–67)* (Franeker: Weaver, 1987).

"the height of the modern age".[69] He enrolled at Leiden in 1855, graduated *summa cum laude* in philosophy in 1858 and earned a doctorate in 1862.[70] Kuyper followed his father into the ministry of the *Hervormde Kerk*. Relatively early on, Kuyper's theological trajectory changed considerably. Various factors contributed to this about-turn: his earlier research on the pre-Scholten Reformed tradition (principally in the works of John Calvin and Jan Łaski[71]), exposure to an alternative understanding of the Reformed faith in his early rural parish ministry and a personal crisis of faith leading to an experience of spiritual 'rebirth'.

In sketching the rise of neo-Calvinism, the state of Calvin studies in Kuyper's youth should be noted. Kuyper became a student when modern Calvin study was at its earliest stage. Remarkably, Beza's *Ioannis calvini vita* (1575) remained the only published Calvin biography until Friedrich Perthes' *Das Leben Johann Calvins des grossen Reformators* (1835). By Kuyper's time, the single most important work on Calvin was Henry's 2,200-page volume on Calvin (1844).[72] While Kuyper was an undergraduate, the first baccalaureate theses on Calvin were written at the University of Strasbourg.[73] One thus finds Kuyper (followed shortly by Bavinck) entering theological study just as Calvin studies was emerging as an exciting discipline in its own right. However, the Dutch theological scene lagged behind Germany and France in this regard. The premier Dutch Calvin biography was P.J.L. Huet's *Iets over Calvyn*,[74] a popular-level work based on somewhat limited sources. Prior to Kuyper's work, only two doctoral theses on Calvin were written in the Netherlands, and this interest was limited to Utrecht University.[75] The theses, supervised by Professors Vinke and Royaards, used only Dutch and

[69] Berkhof, *Two Hundred Years of Theology*, 109.

[70] Abraham Kuyper, *Disquisitio historico-theologica, exhibens Johannis Calvini et Johannis à Lasco de Ecclesia Sententiarum inter se compositionem* (Den Haag en Amsterdam, 1862).

[71] The young Kuyper, an avowed liberal, stressed a low ecclesiology. However, his essay on Calvin and Łaski shows the change in his view from church as outmoded and involuntary to the climax of God's plan for the cosmos. This essay marks the entry point of 'organic' language into Kuyper's writings. See Vree and Zwaan, *Abraham Kuyper's Commentatio (1860), The Young Kuyper about Calvin, a Lasco, and the Church, I: Introduction, Annotations, Bibliography and Indices*, 57.

[72] A bibliographic summary of Calvin research until 1850 is found in Frederik Lodewijk Rutgers, *Calvijns invloed* (Den Haag, 1901), 46–7.

[73] Charles Théodore Gérold, *La Faculté de théologie et le Séminaire protestant de Strasbourg (1803–72). Une page de l'Histoire de l'Alsace* (Strasbourg: Librairie Istra, 1923), 180.

[74] J.L. Huet, 'Iets over Calvyn,' *Nieuw christelijk maandschrift, voor den beschaafden stand* 5 (1831), 617–57; 6 (1832), 69–111; 7 (1833), 207–40.

[75] D.G. Escher, *Disquisitio de Calvino, librorum N.T. historicorum interprete* (Utrecht: R. Nathan, 1840); F.J. Sibmacher Zijnen, *Specimen historico-dogmaticum, quo Anselmi et Calvini placita de hominum per Christum a peccato redemtione inter se conferuntur* (Schoonhoven: S.E. van Nooten, 1852).

German sources and as such were limited in quality. Immediately pre-Kuyper, the wave of Calvin studies received distinct reception in the leading Leiden and Groningen schools.

In the north, the Groningers rejected Calvin's views on the unity of Scripture, atonement and predestination. They did, however, laud his Pneumatology.[76] No works devoting exclusive attention to Calvin came out of the Groninger school.

In the west, as has already been described, the Leiden school enthusiastically latched onto the idea of predestination and adapted it into a rigid brand of mechanical determinism. What should be emphasized at this point is that when Kuyper was a student, Scholten's understanding of Calvinism was by no means universally accepted: Calvin studies was a theological growth industry. Indeed, the epithet 'Calvinism' was, at this point, without a conclusive definition in the Netherlands.

The young Kuyper was initially unimpressed with Scholten's dogmatics classes. 'As far as one can make out, not one professor of theology really charmed him in that first year, nor could the dogmatician Scholten. Although Kuyper together with other students was received by Scholten at his home on at least two occasions for the customary cup of tea, no special relationship developed.'[77]

Thus when one finds Kuyper embarking on an essay competition on the ecclesiology of Calvin and Łaski,[78] it should come as little surprise that although he was Scholten's student, he did not merely accept Scholten's definition of Calvinism. Rather, Kuyper embarked on in-depth study of the original texts. A brief glance at Kuyper's early research on Calvin hints at the dynamic nature of this new field and, accordingly, highlights the path that Bavinck was soon to follow in the fledgling neo-Calvinist school of thought.

His early work on Calvin was not limited to the resources available in Leiden or, for that matter, the appropriation of Calvin taught there. Kuyper conducted research trips to Utrecht, Haarlem, Amsterdam and The Hague. The only major university library not visited in Kuyper's initial search for

---

[76] Jasper Vree, 'Hofstede de Groot en de armenverzorging door vrouwen. Een hoofdstuk uit de geschiedenis van de Groninger inwendige zending,' G. Van Halsema Thzn et al., eds., *Geloven in Groningen. Capita selecta uit de geloofsgeschiedenis van een stad* (Kampen: J.H. Kok, 1990), 218.

[77] Jasper Vree and Johan Zwaan, *Abraham Kuyper's Commentatio (1860): The Young Kuyper about Calvin, a Lasco and the Church, I. Introduction, Annotations, Bibliography and Indices* (Leiden: Brill, 2005), 21.

[78] In Kuyper's time, the only available biography of Łaski was J.F. Bertram's *Historia critica Johannis à Lasco* (Aurich: H. Tapper, 1733).

Calvin-related material was Groningen. He also began to investigate access to works on Calvin in Germany (Frankfurt am Mein, Hamburg and Dresden) and France (Strasbourg). In 1859, Kuyper became aware that a dissertation on Calvin had been written at Strasbourg University. He wrote to Edouard Reuss,[79] the New Testament Professor at Strasbourg, requesting a copy of this work. Reuss complied quickly, sending Kuyper a copy of the dissertation in question along with nine other theses of which Kuyper had been wholly unaware. The impact of this on Kuyper was considerable. The quality of Kuyper's research and involvement with Reuss marked his arrival as a major player in the rapidly expanding area of Calvin studies. Indeed, Kuyper blazed a trail followed by Bavinck: in order to portray either theologian accurately, one must consider them at the crest of a new wave of rigorous Calvin scholarship. (With regard to Bavinck's theological identity and the nature of his organic motif, this point is of particular relevance: intensive engagement with Calvin led to his disagreement with Scholten on the content of Calvinism. Set in this light, Bavinck's short work *Johannes Calvijn* becomes particularly interesting).[80]

One biographical point that should not be omitted is the acknowledgement that the eight months of intensive research invested by Kuyper in this study led to a period of nervous exhaustion following the competition. A six-month spell in a spa at Wiesbaden followed the news that he had won the competition.[81] Kuyper thus began his ministry having already suffered burnout.

In addition to this, Kuyper's early ministry took place at a time when the implementation of Scholten's vision began to falter. Having initially spread quickly via popular-level works such as Conrad Busken Huet's *Questions and Answers: Letters about the Bible*[82] the Leiden school's momentum ground to a halt in the 1870s. During the 1860s, a significant number of its early exponents resigned their pastoral charges. Four years after the publication of *Questions and Answers*, C.B. Huet left the ministry in favour of a career in journalism.[83] In 1866, he published a pamphlet stating that ministers of like theological disposition who remained within the church were guilty of dishonesty.[84]

[79] Cf. A. Caquot, 'Reuss et Renan,' *Revue d'Histoire et de Philosophie Religieuses* 71 (1991), 437–42.
[80] Herman Bavinck, *Johannes Calvijn* (Kampen: Kok, 1909).
[81] James D. Bratt, 'Raging Tumults of the Soul: The Private Life of Abraham Kuyper,' *Reformed Journal* No. 1 (November 1987), 9.
[82] Conrad Busken Huet, *Vragen en antwoorden; brieven over den bijbel* (Haarlem, 1858).
[83] Hederscheê, *Modern-godsdienstige richting*, 136.
[84] Conrad Busken Huet, *Ongevraagd advies in de zaak van Pierson tegen Réville c.s.* (Haarlem, 1866).

Allard Pierson, a high-profile minister in Rotterdam, left his charge in 1865. His resignation was accompanied by the pamphlet *Letter to my Last Church*.[85] The remainder of his career was spent teaching literature, aesthetics and art history in Heidelberg and Amsterdam.

In the following decade, the Leiden school's line of questioning first became 'what can be done to enthuse the clergy and laity alike with this theology?' before shifting to 'can the clergy's religion also be that of the laity?'[86] The Dutch ecclesiastical scene became a fractured environment. Under the leadership of Philip Reinhart and Petrus Hermannus Hugenholtz, the *De Vrije Gemeente* seceded in 1877 from the *Hervormde Kerk* in Amsterdam. The *Vereeniging van Vrijzinning-Hervormden* (The Liberal Reformed Union) formed in Leiden. The *Protestantenbond* also came into existence at this time.

As the Leiden school's impact fractured, it began to voice serious concerns as to its own relevance and workability. The young Kuyper first looked to its principal critics, Alexandre Vinet, Daniel Chantepie de la Saussaye and Johannes Hermanus Gunning. In 1863, Kuyper became minister of the *Hervormde Kerk* in Beesd. At this point, his relationship with his father was somewhat strained. The two had clashed on various issues of confessional commitment within the church. The following year, he met the *Réveil* statesman, Groen van Prinsterer, who encouraged his continued engagement with Calvin. In the face of Kuyper's ideological departure from his father, Groen van Prinsterer became something of a second father to him. At the same time, his experience of the different appropriation of Calvinism in the *volkskerk* profoundly affected Kuyper. The simple faith of Pietje Balthus, a farmer's wife, marked him deeply.

The 1880s saw Kuyper at the forefront of significant developments in both church and academy. These developments involved Herman Bavinck directly.

In 1880, Kuyper founded the *Vrije Universiteit Amsterdam*. He was quickly installed as its professor of theology and first rector. Recognizing the talents of the *Christelijke Gereformeerde Kerken*'s young Dr Bavinck, Kuyper quickly set about recruiting him for the *Vrije Universiteit*. Indeed, he made two failed approaches to Bavinck (in 1881, just over a decade before the 1892 Union of Churches, and again in 1895, after the Union) before he finally accepted the post in 1902.

This was also a time of major ecclesiastical upheaval in the Netherlands. Again, Kuyper was at the centre of this, and Bavinck was also directly

[85] Allard Pierson, *Brief aan mijn laatste gemeente* (Arnhem, 1865).
[86] A.M. Brouwer, *De moderne richting* (Nijmegen, 1904), 132.

involved. The Amsterdam Consistory of the *Hervormde Kerk*, of which Kuyper
was a member, began to make insistences regarding the confessional
subscription of its members. Due to this, some eighty Amsterdam presbyters,
including Kuyper, were suspended in 1885. Following a failed ecclesiastical
appeal, Kuyper's group (which numbered approximately two hundred
congregations) became known as the *Dolerenden*, literally the 'grieving
ones'. Seeing no future within the *Hervormde Kerk*, Kuyper's *Doleantie* group
left the State Church in 1886 and began to operate independently while
seeking ecclesiastical union with Bavinck's *Christelijke Gereformeerde Kerken*.
In 1892, the *Gereformeerde Kerken in Nederland* became the fruit of this
movement of schism-into-union. Thus by the early 1890s, one finds Bavinck
and Kuyper as members in the same denomination. Within a few years, they
were also colleagues at the same university.

This complex web of factors dovetails into Kuyper's role at the forefront
of the neo-Calvinist movement in which Herman Bavinck appears.

IV. 'The Brief Triumph of Neo-Confessionalism'

The unique historical story of the Netherlands meant that Bavinck and
Kuyper appeared as the figureheads of a neo-Confessional revival somewhat
out of step with similar trends in other European countries. While similar
neo-Confessional movements had bloomed elsewhere in the 1820s and
1830s, the Dutch revival occurred a half-century late. Berkhof accounts for
this in terms of the late arrival of modernism in the Netherlands: 'Here this
theology was consciously forged, next to and after modernism and the
theology of mediation, as a third response to the intellectual challenge
arising from the Enlightenment. That is what gave it a vitality and scope
which is usually not typical of confessionalism elsewhere. Besides, it was a
powerful inspiration in the political and cultural awakening of the Calvinistic
segment of the population which in these years achieved a strong position
in the modern world.'[87]

The uniqueness of the neo-Calvinist movement is worth noting: before
ecclesiastical conflict brought Dutch systematic and public theology to a
virtual standstill, the movement fronted by Bavinck and Kuyper represented
the zenith of a confessional emphasis that would go unmatched until the
aftermath of World War I.

---

[87] Berkhof, *Two Hundred Years of Theology*, 113.

V. The Context of Reformed Dogmatics

When one begins to outline the major events of Kuyper's life, it becomes difficult to proceed without also making frequent explanations of Bavinck's role and thus stray into the reproduction of Bavinck's biography.[88] Such is not the intention of this chapter. Rather, its aim is captured in Picasso's earlier cited words to Brassaï: in understanding the works of an artist, one must know when he produced them, how, why and in which circumstances. As such, one finds Bavinck's major legacy to theology, the *Reformed Dogmatics*, appearing at the end of two centuries of struggle over the true identity of Reformed Christianity. Clearly, various competitors have claimed to be Calvin's theological offspring: the *Réveil* theologians, the Heusdiaans, Scholten and now Kuyper.

In such circumstances, that Bavinck attaches the descriptor *Gereformeerde* to his four tomes of dogmatic theology is highly telling. He is fully cognisant of his own historical–intellectual context. To Bavinck's own mind, *Gereformeerde* Dogmatiek is just that. He is entering the ring with a clear intention; he is also laying claim to the Reformed tradition.

In context, the production of a *dogmatiek* is also somewhat significant. Vanderlaan's survey of Dutch Protestant modernist theology ends before the neo-Calvinists appear and thus he makes no mention of Bavinck. His closing paragraph notes that in the various moves from Groningen to Leiden, the discipline of systematic theology had suffered a great deal. He closes with the following fascinating remark: 'But no modernist produces a *dogmatiek*. Some feel that on a "modern" basis, with authority gone, no generally acceptable system of dogmatics can be written. And yet, if some new Schleiermacher should arise, to set all religious thought once again on a new foundation, who knows whether the Dutch modernists may not yet enjoy a renaissance of systematic theology?'[89]

In the light of history, the resurrection of *dogmatics* in Dutch theology was soon to occur. However, this much anticipated dogmatician arose in an entirely different theological stable. The 'new Schleiermacher' was the son of a separatist manse, the student of Scholten but the theological mouthpiece of neo-Calvinism.

---

[88] For a helpful statement on why Bavinck was drawn to the Kuyperian movement, see John Bolt, 'Grand Rapids between Kampen and Amsterdam,' *Calvin Theological Journal* 38 No. 2 N. 2003, 267.

[89] Vanderlaan, *Protestant Modernism in Holland*, 122.

It would seem that the purpose of the first volume of Reformed Dogmatics, *Prolegomena,* is to rediscover the lost art of systematic, Reformed theology. Most interesting is that Bavinck's strivings to resurrect the science of *gereformeerde dogmatiek* are so consistently peppered with references to the 'organic'. The distinctly neo-Calvinistic relationship between this dogmatic task and the organic motif, which will thus form the subject of this book, is suggested in Kuyper's Fourth Stone Lecture:

> The subject-matter of the several sciences must be grouped under one head and brought under the sway of one principle by means of theory or hypothesis, and finally Systematics, as the queen of sciences, comes forth from her tent to weave all the different results into one organic whole. . . . The question about the origin, interconnection and destiny of everything that exists cannot be suppressed; and the *veni, vidi, vici* wherewith the theory of evolution with full speed occupied the ground in all the circles, inimical to the Word of God, and especially among our naturalists, is convincing proof of how much we need unity of view.[90]

[90] Abraham Kuyper, *Lectures on Calvinism* (Grand Rapids: Eerdmans, 1931), 113.

Chapter 2

How Many Herman Bavincks?

I. Introduction[1]

This book provides a new reading of Herman Bavinck's use of the organic motif in theology. As such, its first substantial (and most important) conversation partner is Jan Veenhof, whose seminal publication *Revelatie en Inspiratie*[2] is generally regarded as the benchmark for work on Bavinck's use of the organic. With a few notable recent exceptions, secondary material on Bavinck defers to Veenhof's interpretation of this aspect of Bavinck's theology. However, as will soon become apparent, this book advances a considerably different general reading of Bavinck's theology which, in turn, leads to a major departure from its specific application to the organic motif.

Although Chapter 3 will offer a critical evaluation of Veenhof's reading of Bavinck on a specific topic (the organic motif), it is first necessary to describe and evaluate the basic assumption through which he reads Bavinck. In this instance, the general shapes the particular and, as such, one must critique the former before the latter.

II. Towards a New 'General' Reading of Bavinck

Bavinck's personal biography is an unusual one. As the son of a separatist manse, the student of modernist theologians and the iconoclastic writer of *Gereformeerde Dogmatiek*, the dogmatician who later became a highly active politician and educational theorist, his theological species has proven rather difficult to classify. The riddle of how this theologian could somehow exist between so many apparent extremes has given the bulk of

[1] An earlier version of this chapter has been published as James Eglinton, 'How Many Herman Bavincks? *De Gemeene Genade* and the "Two Bavincks' Hypothesis"', *Kuyper Center Review Vol. 2: Revelation and Common Grace*, ed. John Bowlin (Grand Rapids: Eerdmans, 2011), 279–301.
[2] Jan Veenhof, *Revelatie en Inspiratie* (Amsterdam: Buijten & Schipperheijn, 1968).

Bavinck studies, Veenhof's work included, a very particular shape. In short, the normative reading has been of Bavinck as a bipolar figure: he is seemingly a Jekyll and Hyde theologian who vacillates between moments of 'orthodoxy' and 'modernity' without ever resolving his own basic crisis of theological identity. The habit has been to speak of 'two' Herman Bavincks.

The 'two Bavincks' hypothesis rests on a particular interpretation of his personal narrative: it combines the factors of his conservative upbringing, liberal university education, employment as a reformed dogmatician, involvement in politics, philosophy, psychology and education, and various events from his old age (the most famous being the sale of his theological library[3] and dying statement: 'My dogmatics avail me nothing, nor my knowledge, but I have my faith and in this I have all'[4]). This hypothesis is not a simple recognition of 'orthodox' and 'modern' elements in Bavinck's theology, the presence of which can scarcely be ignored. In a qualified sense, one may speak of a 'duality' in Bavinck's thought.[5] A. Anema, one of Bavinck's colleagues at the Vrije Universiteit, on noting that Bavinck was both a 'Secession preacher and a representative of modern culture', once remarked: 'That was a striking characteristic. In that duality is found Bavinck's significance. That duality is also a reflection of the tension—at times the crisis—in Bavinck's life. In many respects it is a simple matter to be a preacher in the Secession Church, and, in a certain sense, it is also not that difficult to be a modern person. But in no way is it a simple matter to be the one as well as the other.'[6]

The 'two Bavincks' interpretation of his biography is that Bavinck never reconciled the basic duality of orthodoxy and modernity. Unlike Anema's careful remark that it is not easy to be both orthodox and modern, the hypothesis asserts that for Bavinck, this ultimately proved an impossible task. For Bavinck, the greatest of crises had no great solution, and thus the trend has been to speak of two Bavincks rather than one.

This caricature has, for many decades, provided a hermeneutical lens through which Bavinck's particular nuances have been interpreted. The net effect of this bipolar reading has been the division of Bavinck's work

---

[3] Hepp reports Bavinck as having said: 'I have no further need of them.' Hepp, *Dr. Herman Bavinck*, 317–18.

[4] Dosker, 'Herman Bavinck', 21.

[5] John Bolt provides a thorough overview of this 'duality' in 'A Man Between Two Worlds', *The Imitation of Christ Theme in the Cultural-Ethical Ideal of Herman Bavinck* (PhD dissertation, Toronto, University of St Michael's College, 1982), 53–9.

[6] Cited in Veenhof, *Revelatie en Inspiratie*, 108. Cf. F. H. von Meyenfeldt, 'Prof. Dr. Herman Bavinck: 1854–1954 "Christus en de Cultuur"', *Polemios*, IX (15 October 1954).

wherein certain sections of his theology have become the property of his 'orthodox' followers, and others the territory of his 'modernist' disciples.

The basic conviction of this book is that Bavinck's theological vision is considerably more sophisticated and united than the normative reading makes out. As will be put forward, the 'two Bavincks' reading overlooks the central theme of his work: divine tri-unity leads to an overriding concern for synthesis, which, although not conceptually synonymous with the organic motif, is associated with and regularly expressed by it. Re-reading Bavinck in this light (which, in turn, requires a dramatic reappraisal of the aforesaid motif) provides a solution to the *de facto* apartheid which has been erected in the realm of Bavinck studies. As will be demonstrated, Bavinck turns to the organic motif when explaining the sense in which the archetypal unity of the Godhead brings a sense of coherence to all other reality. As such, one of the great misfortunes of Bavinck studies is that the organic motif has been misunderstood for so long as a symptom of disunity, rather than the primary analogy and agent of unity in the creation.

This chapter is thus intended to frame the remainder of this book. It first surveys the current field of Bavinck studies in order to highlight the current dependence on the 'two Bavincks' model. Having done so, it highlights the inherently problematic nature of the hypothesis. In developing this theme, it then demonstrates various significant flaws behind the 'two Bavincks' reading and notes that the wider world of Bavinck studies is beginning to move away from its basic assumptions on Bavinck's alleged incoherence. Acknowledging that Veenhof's reading of the organic motif rests on this model, the chapter develops the proposal that a new reading of the organic motif and a new (united) interpretation of Bavinck go hand in hand. Fresh study of the organic motif, one hopes, will shed much light on the sense in which there was one Bavinck, rather than two.

III. The 'Two' Bavincks

Writing on the multifaceted nature of Bavinck's personal history, John Bolt has claimed that Bavinck, most unfortunately, lends himself to this caricaturing. (It should be observed, as will be subsequently explained, that Bolt's position on the 'two Bavincks' has changed considerably in the course of recent debate.) 'We must begin by reminding ourselves that any consideration of Herman Bavinck's influence has to start with the annoying acknowledgment that there is not just one but rather *two* Bavincks. Radically different people and agendas could and did appeal to Bavinck as the authority for their views.'[7]

Central to Veenhof's portrayal of Bavinck is also that there are 'two Bavincks' and 'two poles' in his thought.[8] Veenhof's influence on the wider handling of Bavinck has been considerable; indeed, the bipolar portrayal of Bavinck has become normative. This is particularly evident when one surveys the use of Bavinck's name in recent debates on the doctrine of Scripture. In this context, Henk Vroom writes: '[A] time bomb lay under Bavinck's view of Scripture. He combines two opposing lines: that of absolute authority and the broad, unshakeable certainty of faith on the one hand and openness in the search for the true meaning of texts and their correct application in modern life on the other. For this reason later generations could choose which of Bavinck's lines they wished to follow. Among Bavinck's students some followed one line of thinking, and others followed another.'[9]

Typical of recent presentations of Bavinck's life and theology is Malcolm Yarnell's 'Herman Bavinck, Reasonably Reformed'.[10] Writing that the 'two major aspects' of his theological foundation are philosophy and Scripture, Yarnell makes the claim that 'Bavinck's enigmatic, shifting and often contradictory treatment of these two aspects of his theological foundation, or "two poles", has resulted in the conjecture that there were "two Bavincks". The "first Bavinck" is a Reformed and theological churchman, while the "second Bavinck" is a modern and progressive academic.'[11]

On this foundation, Yarnell produces an overview of Bavinck's theology through the 'two Bavincks' lens.

The claim so commonplace within Bavinck scholarship (as exemplified by Yarnell) is that his theology, to a greater or lesser extent, is self-contradictory to the point of being impossible to replicate. Rather, one must select 'which Bavinck' to follow. While Vroom's claim is at the extreme end in this debate, the invocation of his name in debates on Scripture consistently present Bavinck as an incoherent figure, particularly in vociferous claims that he is both strongly opposed to and highly supportive

---

[7] John Bolt, 'Grand Rapids between Kampen and Amsterdam: Herman Bavinck's influence and reception in North America', 263–64.

[8] Veenhof, *Revelatie en Inspiratie*, 108–11.

[9] Henk Vroom, 'Scripture Read and Interpreted: The Development of the Doctrine of Scripture and Hermeneutics in Gereformeerde Theology in the Netherlands', *Calvin Theological Journal*, 28 No. 2 (1993), 363.

[10] Malcolm B. Yarnell, *The Formation of Christian Doctrine* (B & H Publishing Group: Nashville, 2007), 49–59.

[11] Yarnell, *The Formation of Christian Doctrine*, 50. Note Yarnell's reliance on Veenhof's 'two poles' imagery.

of Warfield's theology.[12] On this topic, Yarnell refers to 'contradictions in Bavinck with regard to the priority of Scripture and reason [which] form an almost schizophrenic picture'.[13]

It should be acknowledged, however, that the 'two Bavincks' model is not restricted to the interpretation of Bavinck on Scripture. Indeed, it is used in a paradigmatic fashion throughout his writings. Brian Mattson, another recent critic of the 'two Bavincks' reading, highlights that Eugene Heideman's *The Relation of Revelation and Reason in E. Brunner and H. Bavinck* attempts to discover 'which Bavinck', the 'biblical' Bavinck or the 'idealist, scholastic' Bavinck, is responsible for various sections of Reformed Dogmatics.[14] As will be seen, the most obvious recent examples of this are the appeals to 'two Bavincks' with regard to the two kingdoms theology (VanDrunen) and the organic motif (Veenhof).

Bolt's reluctant acceptance of the 'two Bavincks' hypothesis rests on an oft-quoted observation from the work of Gerrit Berkouwer: 'Professor Berkouwer was keenly aware of that when in his final, large theological autobiography he observed that Bavinck was particularly susceptible to being "annexed" by contemporary devotees for their own purposes. Berkouwer judges that it is difficult to overcome this danger "because Bavinck's theology contains so many irreconcilable themes in tension".'[15]

As such, one is left with the 'orthodox' Bavinck and the 'modernist' Bavinck. The former is the son of the Secession and bulwark of theological conservatism; the latter is the bold theological freethinker and darling of those who align themselves against Old Princeton. To nuance Bolt's position somewhat, he regards this caricature as exaggerated and claims that the 'good, progressive modernist Bavinck' was 'invented by Valentijn Hepp; celebrated by G.C. Berkouwer and his students; and, finally, shamelessly

---

[12] For 'Bavinck against Warfield', see Donald McKim and Jack Rogers, *The Authority and Interpretation of the Bible* (San Francisco: Harper & Row, 1979); and Andrew T.B. McGowan, *The Divine Spiration of Scripture: Challenging Evangelical Perspectives* (Inter-Varsity: Downers Grove, 2007). For 'Bavinck with Warfield', see Richard Gaffin, *God's Word in Servant-Form* (Greenville: Reformed Academic Press, 2008).

[13] Yarnell, *The Formation of Christian Doctrine*, 51.

[14] Brian Mattson, *Restored to our Destiny* (unpublished PhD thesis, University of Aberdeen, 2008), 8; cf; Eugene Heideman, *Relation of Revelation and Reason* (Sheboygan Falls, Wisconsin: Van Gorcum & Comp. N.V. – Dr. H.J. Prakke & H.M.G. Prakke, 1959), 131–2, 138, 142, 144, 156–7, 177–9, 183, 189fn.1.

[15] Bolt, 'Grand Rapids between Kampen and Amsterdam: Herman Bavinck's influence and reception in North America', 265. The full Dutch reference is as follows: 'Het gevaar van een beschrijving en beoordeling van Bavincks levenswerk is, dat men hem annexeert voor eigen inzichten. Het is niet onmogelijk boven dat annexatie-gevaar uit te komen, doordat in het werk van Bavinck allerlei onweersprekelijke motieven zichtbaar worden.' G. C. Berkouwer, *Zoeken en Vinden: Herinneringm en Ervanngm* (Kampen: Kok, 1989), 55.

exploited by more recent Gereformeerden such as Harry Kuitert.'[16] Bolt is
also cynical of the trend of 'setting the scholastic Bavinck over against the
good biblical, Christocentric, kerygmatic, Bavinck and then using the latter
to sit in judgment on the former.'[17]

Although Bolt paints a deliberately stereotyped bipolar Bavinck, he
nonetheless notes:

> The portrait I have just sketched of the two Bavincks—the fundamental-
> ist scholastic and the good progressive modern man—is of course, in its
> exaggeration, a cartoon, a caricature. Yet, there is plenty of evidence to
> warrant talking about a duality in Bavinck, and we cannot understand the
> developments in twentieth-century Dutch Reformed theology apart from
> the conflicting appeals made to these two sides. Let me state it more mod-
> estly and moderately: The two sides of Herman Bavinck the theologian
> reflect a pull between the academic theologian (*wetenschappelijke theoloog*)
> and the churchly dogmatician (*kerkelijke dogmaticus*).[18]

Thus, while Bolt is sensitive to speak of 'duality' rather than 'bipolarity', he
nonetheless regards the caricature as containing a grain of truth. Although
Bolt finds the practice of setting Bavinck against himself somewhat
distasteful, the alleged existence of this grain of truth renders this distaste a
personal preference rather than a point in principle. It is inconsistent to
accept the fundamental basis of the 'two Bavincks' hypothesis (whether that
be labelled as duality or bipolarity) while denying the subsequent right to
pit one Bavinck against the other. Indeed, Yarnell's portrait of the bipolar
Bavinck makes heavy use of Bolt's statement and, ignoring Bolt's plea for
restraint from exaggerated caricatures, proceeds to write about Bavinck in
the unfortunate language of 'schizophrenia'.[19]

Although Veenhof, Vroom and Bolt accept the basic core of this portrait
(albeit with differing levels of reluctance), none formally make the explicit
claim that Bavinck was thus an inherently inconsistent figure. Evidently, such
a claim is central to Yarnell's presentation of Bavinck. However, Yarnell is by
no means the only person to push the 'two Bavincks' model to this extent.

---

[16] Bolt, 'Grand Rapids between Kampen and Amsterdam: Herman Bavinck's influence and
reception in North America', 266.

[17] Bolt, 'Grand Rapids between Kampen and Amsterdam: Herman Bavinck's influence and
reception in North America', 268.

[18] Bolt, 'Grand Rapids between Kampen and Amsterdam: Herman Bavinck's influence and
reception in North America', 267.

[19] For Bolt's reaction to Yarnell, see John Bolt, 'Bavinck's Use of Wisdom Literature in Systematic Theology', *Scottish Bulletin of Evangelical Theology*, 29.1 (Spring 2011), 5–8.

David VanDrunen's 'Natural Law and the Two Kingdoms in the Thought of Herman Bavinck' asserts that the reality of the 'two Bavincks' requires that he be read with segregationist hermeneutics.[20] VanDrunen's claim is that Bavinck fails to present a unified concept of the Christian's role between church and culture. He writes: 'Though a complete account is more complex, a good general argument can be made, I believe, that his defense of the natural law and two kingdoms categories belongs to the orthodox Bavinck and his advocacy of themes such as grace restoring nature and the kingdom as leaven belongs to the modern Bavinck.'[21]

VanDrunen's paper perhaps represents the apex of this 'annexation': one is now encouraged not simply to discover 'which Bavinck wrote which section' (*à la* Heideman), but instead to set Bavinck against himself (or rather, to play the 'orthodox' Bavinck against his 'modernist' alter ego). In following Vroom's critique, VanDrunen numbers himself among the 'orthodox' Bavinck-students, choosing 'one line' of Bavinck's thinking while rejecting the other. Although he provides perhaps the most extreme recent example of this reliance on the 'two Bavincks' model, the bulk of recent Bavinck scholarship (*à la* Yarnell) on the doctrine of Scripture operates on the same assumption of Bavinck's basic, perpetual crisis of theological identity.

IV. The General Affects the Particular

Left unchecked, the 'two Bavincks' model produces a type of theological apartheid within Bavinck studies, the effect of which is that those who appreciate his work must interpret every area of his theology as belonging to one of his alter egos. To use VanDrunen's reading, it seems that Bavinck's 'two kingdoms' theology has no real import for the 'modernist' Bavinck reader. The conviction that one cannot read Bavinck holistically has become deeply entrenched.

It seems hard to deny that the community busy with the interpretation of his work has segregated his thought and basic theological identity. The same is true, as will be demonstrated, regarding Veenhof's reading of Bavinck's organic motif via the 'two Bavincks' hermeneutical lens: the motif, one is led to assume, belongs exclusively to Bavinck's 'modern' disciples.

---

[20] David VanDrunen, 'The Kingship of Christ Is Twofold: Natural Law and the Two Kingdoms in the Thought of Herman Bavinck', *Calvin Theological Journal* (April 2010), No. 45, Vol. 1, 162.

[21] David VanDrunen, 'The Kingship of Christ Is Twofold: Natural Law and the Two Kingdoms in the Thought of Herman Bavinck', 162, footnote 75.

This policy of segregation has had a most undesirable, paralysing effect on the field of Bavinck studies. Whenever one strain of Bavinck devotees finds a section in his work which contradicts their basic working assumptions (and which would therefore challenge their presentation of him), it can be conveniently dismissed as the writings of the 'other Bavinck'. As it presents the Bavinck reader with the need to allocate each of his thoughts, sentences, paragraphs and notions to one of the two Bavincks, this hermeneutical partisanship considerably hinders the constructive reading of his work. In short, it requires that one read him with the unfailing presupposition that these ideas can form no harmonious unity. Such a presupposition will markedly affect the reading which will follow. Its presuppositions pressure the reader to 'discover' the hallmarks of internal division throughout Bavinck's work.

V. The 'Two Bavincks' Model and the Organic Motif

As has already been acknowledged, the 'two poles' model is central to Veenhof's reading of Bavinck.[22] That Veenhof interprets Bavinck through this lens has a considerable impact on his understanding of the organic motif's place in Bavinck's theology. Noting that in Veenhof's account, the organic motif comes to Bavinck from Hegel, Schelling, the History of Religions School and the Dutch Ethical theologians,[23] one is left to conclude that the organic motif therefore belongs to 'one Bavinck' rather than the other: the 'modernist' Bavinck.

Bavinck has organic thoughts, one is led to believe, only in his 'modernist' moments. The motif occurs when Bavinck's Hegelian, Leiden-influenced side surfaces. Consequently, the organic motif is the property of one particular strand of Bavinck's followers. It thus becomes an aspect of Bavinck's internal division, rather than the primary agent of synthesis in his worldview.

As will be demonstrated in the next chapter,[24] Veenhof's assertion of an unbroken conceptual continuum between Bavinck's motif and German Idealism, the Ethical Theologians *et al.* is dangerously flawed and requires considerable revision. Prior to critiquing his reading of the particular (the organic motif), one must first provide an alternative reading to the basic dichotomy assumed in *Revelatie en Inspiratie*. It should be made clear that in

---

[22] Veenhof, *Revelatie en Inspiratie*, 108–11.
[23] Veenhof, *Revelatie en Inspiratie*, 267–8.
[24] See Chapter 3.

challenging Veenhof's allocation of the organic motif to the 'modern' Bavinck, this book is not a crude attempt to reclaim the motif for the followers of his 'orthodox' alter ego. Rather, this chapter questions the existence of 'two Bavincks' altogether. The case will be made that there is only one Herman Bavinck and that one ought to re-read the organic motif in this light.

The 'two Bavincks' hypothesis will be challenged on two fronts: first, recent opposition to the hypothesis will be acknowledged and, second, Bavinck's final rectorial address delivered in Kampen (*De Gemeene Genade*, 1894) will be used to critique the fundamental assumptions of the hypothesis.

VI. The 'One Bavinck': The Recent Direction of Bavinck Studies

The foremost recent critique of the 'two Bavincks' model comes from Nelson Kloosterman.[25] He recognizes that while Veenhof and Berkouwer perceive 'tensions' in Bavinck's thought, neither sees a consequent incoherence in Bavinck's work. Kloosterman also offers an alternative translation of the Berkouwer citation[26] upon which Bolt's account of Bavinck's 'duality' rests: 'The danger present in describing and evaluating Bavinck's life-work is that one might annex him for one's own insights. It is, however, not impossible to escape that annexation-danger since various undeniable themes become manifest in Bavinck's work.'[27]

Berkouwer's statement takes on an entirely different hue when one notes that the Dutch word translated by Bolt as 'irreconcilable' (*onweersprekelijk*) should actually be rendered 'incontestable' or 'undeniable'. Viewed in context, it seems that although Berkouwer emphasized the fear that one might annex aspects of Bavinck's thought for one's own ends, he also quelled this worry: if one recognizes the 'various undeniable themes' of Bavinck's thought, it becomes possible to avoid annexation. In short, Berkouwer's claim seems to be that the 'two Bavincks' model will only emerge if one does not first grasp the nature of the diverse central themes of his worldview

[25] Nelson D. Kloosterman, 'A Response to "The Kingdom of God Is Twofold": Natural Law and the Two Kingdoms in the Thought of Herman Bavinck by David VanDrunen', *Calvin Theological Journal* (April 2010), Vol. 45, No. 1, 174–5.

[26] 'Het gevaar van een beschrijving en beoordeling van Bavincks levenswerk is, dat men hem annexeert voor eigen inzichten. Het is niet onmogelijk boven dat annexatie-gevaar uit te komen, doordaat in het werk van Bavinck allerlei onweersprekelijke motieven zichtbaar worden.' Berkouwer, *Zoeken en Vinden*, 55.

[27] Kloosterman, 'A Response to "The Kingdom of God Is Twofold": Natural Law and the Two Kingdoms in the Thought of Herman Bavinck by David VanDrunen', 175.

and, one logically assumes, the nature of their overall unity. 'In other words, respecting the *coherence* of Bavinck's own thought will prevent us from the danger of succumbing to the danger embedded in the popular approach of isolating and identifying one's own point of view with one or another "strand" in Bavinck – a danger that was not altogether avoided, regrettably, in VanDrunen's conference paper. In summary, although one can identify various tensions within the thought of Herman Bavinck, this is inadequate warrant for the claim that there existed two Bavincks, i.e., two irreconcilable strands of thought within Bavinck's theology.'[28]

Indeed, such an assertion is supported by Berkouwer's own twofold summary of Bavinck's lifework: catholicity and synthesis.[29] Berkouwer's perspective on Bavinck was not of a theologian wrought with 'irreconcilable themes in tension', but rather of a man committed to the synthesis of 'various undeniable themes'.

Bolt's response to this has been to state as follows:

> Kloosterman then does the cause of Bavinck scholarship a great service (though at the cost of some embarrassment to yours truly) by correcting my translation of G.C. Berkouwer's claim that 'Bavinck's theology contains so many *onweersprekelijke* motieven' which I erroneously translated as '*irreconcilable* themes' rather than as '*undeniable* themes'. Kloosterman is quite correct in observing that Berkouwer is not speaking of people '*with opposing views* appealing to Bavinck, but rather about the danger that *Berkouwer himself* faced' in appealing to Bavinck for one's own agenda. Berkouwer continues by saying that it was possible to overcome any such danger because there are *undeniable* (not *irreconcilable*) themes in Bavinck that are clearly visible. . . . In summary, although one can identify various 'tensions' within the thought of Herman Bavinck (as one can for every theologian, including John Calvin!), this is inadequate warrant for the claim that there existed 'two Bavincks', i.e., two irreconcilable strands of thought within Bavinck's theology.[30]

That Bolt has affirmed this new translation of Berkouwer's dictum (thus consequentially affirming that the correct translation gravely undermines

---

[28] Kloosterman, 'A Response to "The Kingdom of God Is Twofold": Natural Law and the Two Kingdoms in the Thought of Herman Bavinck by David VanDrunen', 175.

[29] Berkouwer, 'Katholiciteit. H. Bavinck', in *Zoeken en Vinden*, 40–70.

[30] John Bolt, 'Bavinck Society Discussion # 1: The VanDrunen-Kloosterman Debate on "Natural Law" and "Two Kingdoms" in the Theology of Herman Bavinck' (published online via the Bavinck Institute: http://bavinck.calvinseminary.edu/wp-content/uploads/2010/06/Discussion_1_VanDrunen-Kloosterman_debate.pdf), 21.

the 'two Bavincks' hypothesis) is a development in Bavinck studies that should not go unnoticed. In short, this admission that the bulk of work on Bavinck has thus far rested on a faulty presupposition necessitates a new reading of Bavinck.[31]

It is also significant that Kloosterman's insistence on the coherence of Bavinck's theological vision is shared by the likes of George Harinck, Henk van den Belt and Brian Mattson. Harinck's reading of Berkouwer,[32] while not a direct critique of the 'two Bavincks' model, nonetheless mirrors that of Kloosterman: he presents a Bavinck who synthesizes diverse themes, rather than a Bavinck swamped by undesirable dualism. Given Bavinck's ecclesiastical and educational background, Harinck finds this urge for catholicity as somewhat unsurprising.

> At that time, [Bavinck's] dogmatic and philosophical work formed a new expression of Christian belief in relationship to modern culture, whereby rather than the words *heathenism* and *antithesis* giving the relationship colour, he used the words *synthesis* and *catholicity*. . . . Bavinck's life shows the measure to which this theme of religion and modernity and his synthetic aim in church and science was tied up with his own experiences. . . . That longing for unity . . . was the *Leitmotiv* of Bavinck's life. Also in science, he did not think of himself as a critic, not a cool analyst; he primarily looked for synthesis among his friends as well as in his faith and scholastic work.[33]

Henk van den Belt's assessment of Bavinck's theology similarly notes the essentially synthetic nature of his theological method. 'He approached theological issues in a synthetic rather than antithetic manner and searched for the catholic elements.'[34]

---

[31] Yarnell's work on Bavinck, for example, cites Bolt's earlier work on the 'two Bavincks' and, on that basis, allocates the various sections of Bavinck's work to 'the first' and 'the second' Bavincks: 'This is why John Bolt has referred to two Bavincks. In the same work, *Prolegomena*, the first Bavinck writes in a way that prefigures Barth's declamation of natural theology. . . . In the same work, *Prolegomena*, the second Bavinck writes two chapters directly on theological foundations, but both chapters interact with philosophy more than with Scripture.' Yarnell, *The Formation of Christian Doctrine*, 51.

[32] George Harinck, '"Something that must remain, if the truth is to be sweet and precious to us": The Reformed Spirituality of Herman Bavinck', *Calvin Theological Journal*, 38 (2003), 250.

[33] Harinck, '"Something that must remain, if the truth is to be sweet and precious to us": The Reformed Spirituality of Herman Bavinck', 250, 254.

[34] van den Belt, Autopistia: The Self-Convincing Authority of Scripture in Reformed Theology, 250.

When one considers the broad trends in the theologies of Bavinck and Kuyper, one major terminological difference quickly becomes apparent. While Kuyper regularly spoke in the language of antithesis between Christian and non-Christian cultures, Bavinck did not. A common critique of Kuyper's thought is that it posits an uneasy tension between the closely related concepts of antithesis between Christian and non-Christian world-views and common grace.[35] The same accusation has not been made of Bavinck. This is no doubt due to the fact that while Bavinck and Kuyper, as will be explained, share the same core of antithesis (as between sin and grace), Bavinck develops the sin–grace antithesis into the grace-restores-nature synthesis (thus creating quite a different dynamic in terms of the Christian's role in relation to non-Christian culture).

VII. Two Speeches and the 'Two Bavincks'

There are two key speeches given by Bavinck which cast considerable doubt on the 'two Bavincks' model. These speeches were given in 1882 and 1894: years which mark his arrival at and departure from the Theological School in Kampen.

Upon his appointment as Dogmatics Professor in Kampen, Bavinck's opening address was entitled 'The Science of Holy Theology' (*De wetenschap der Heilige Godgeleerdheid*). His opening salvo spelt out the conviction that orthodoxy (*heilige godgeleerdheid*) and the modern world (as represented by *wetenschap*) belong together. As Harinck carefully notes, this lecture did not refer to the modern theology of his Leiden education. Rather, Bavinck chooses the adjective 'holy' deliberately: 'This speech was not about piety but rather about *science*; he did not mean the modernistic theology but holy theology.'[36] The historic, richly catholic theology he found so lacking in the works of Scholten and Rauwenhoff was rooted in the past but continued to merit inclusion in the present. In Bavinck's estimations, theology's basic character is marked by an ever-relevant sanctity. This lecture prompted Abraham Kuyper to remark: 'Now this is really scientific Reformed Theology. Here the first principles are again correctly set forth, here a road is staked out which may lead to an excellent development. . . . I have hardly

[35] Sean Michael Lucas, 'Southern-Fried Kuyper? Robert Louis Dabney, Abraham Kuyper and the Limitations of Public Theology', *Westminster Theological Journal* 66, (2004), 198.
[36] Harinck, '"Something that must remain, if the truth is to be sweet and precious to us": The Reformed Spirituality of Herman Bavinck', 255.

ever read a treatise with such undivided attention, from start to finish, as this inaugural.'[37]

The material found in this opening professorial address provides the foundation for Bavinck's later defence of theology as a scientific discipline in Reformed Dogmatics. That his time at Kampen begins on such a note, signalling that one can be historically orthodox and a full player in the modern intellectual context, should raise suspicion against the 'two Bavincks' hypothesis which operates on the premise that such a unity was a frustrating impossibility to Bavinck.

In 1894, Bavinck accepted the post of Theology Professor at the Vrije Universiteit Amsterdam. His closing speech at Kampen, by this point a rectorial rather than professorial address, was on the topic of 'Common Grace' (*De Gemeene Genade*).[38] While 'The Science of Holy Theology's' insistence that theological orthodoxy belongs in the modern world undermines the 'two Bavincks' hypothesis somewhat, the fundamental assertions made by Bavinck in 'Common Grace' pose a far more obvious problem to the caricature.

Common grace was not a new topic for Bavinck; he had already touched upon it in his earlier 1888 publication 'The Catholicity of Christianity and the Church'. However, he chose the Kampen address to return to this theme with exclusive attention. As will be demonstrated, the specific nuances of the neo-Calvinist understanding of common grace are of considerable import in how one must critically read much secondary literature on Bavinck's theology.

It is appropriate to describe common grace as a broad neo-Calvinist emphasis, rather than a passing fad for Bavinck alone, as it features heavily in the works of Bavinck's colleague, Abraham Kuyper. Bavinck's publications on common grace were released in the 1880–90s, and this momentum was carried into the early twentieth-century by Kuyper, who released the mammoth three-volume work *De Gemeene Gratie* (1903–4).[39] At a deeper level, a worldview centred on common grace was foundational to the entire Kuyperian vision for Christianity's engagement with its host culture. Conceptually then, it is of nothing less than paradigmic significance. If one can show that this paradigm, shared by Bavinck and

---

[37] Abraham Kuyper in *De Heraut* (21 January 1883), quoted by Dosker, 'Herman Bavinck', 16.

[38] Herman Bavinck, *De Algemeene Genade: Rede gehouden bij de overdracht van het Rectoraat aan de Theologische School te Kampen op 6 Dec. 1894* (Kampen: G. Ph. Zalsman, 1894). This lecture has been translated into English and is available as Herman Bavinck, 'Common Grace', *Calvin Theological Journal*, 24 No. 1, April 1989, 35–65, tr. Raymond C. Van Leeuwen.

[39] In writing about common grace, Bavinck favours the term *genade*, whereas Kuyper prefers *gratie*.

Kuyper, is distinctly out-of-step with the 'two Bavincks' model, the model must be reassessed.

In order to demonstrate the problem posed to the 'two Bavincks' model by Bavinck's idea of *de gemeene genade*, the background of this common grace emphasis must be described. In 1879, Pope Leo XIII published the encyclical *Aeterni Patris*[40] which marked a considerable growth in neo-Thomistic theology. Leo's prior tenure as Cardinal of Perugia (as Cardinal Pecci) was marked by his fervour for Medieval Scholasticism. Having judged that, in modernist thought, reason was being elevated far beyond faith, he called for a neo-Thomistic revival whereby faith and reason would be related along the basic natural and supernatural distinctions earlier advocated by Aquinas. This belief that a return to Thomas would put an end to the problems of modernist theology's influence on Roman Catholicism continued when he became Pope: hence *Aeterni Patris.*[41]

The renaissance of Thomism within the Roman Catholic Church was one of the major movements in nineteenth-century theology; Bavinck's theology must be read with sensitivity to this fact.

Although Leo believed the problems posed by modernity would be solved by a return to Medieval Scholasticism, Bavinck maintained that such a manoeuvre would create more difficulties than solutions. In *De Gemeene Genade*, he critiques Medieval and neo-Thomism. Both movements, he claims, are riddled with a series of (what Bavinck sees as unbiblical) dualisms: religion as *natural* and *supernatural*, doctrinal articles as *mixed* and *pure*, the human being *in a natural state* and *with the superadded gifts* and so forth.

VIII. *Aeterni Patris,* Common Grace and the Two Bavincks

Bavinck's dissatisfaction with *Aeterni Patris* centres on the antithesis between sin and grace, which Bavinck regards as central to the Christian faith. In Leo's system, this has been replaced with a non-antithetical dualism between natural and supernatural (thus grace elevates, rather than restores, nature). Conceptually, antithesis and non-antithetical dualism perform distinct

---

[40] Leo XIII, *Aeterni Patris* (Inst. Surdo-mutorum, 1879).
[41] This development forms the backdrop to various emphases in Bavinck's work. For example, Leo XIII supported the neo-Thomistic association of mystery and doctrine (within this concept, a doctrine might be rationally counter-intuitive, but it must nonetheless be accepted as a 'pure' rather than 'mixed' article, as such doctrines are inherently mysterious). Bavinck reacts against this neo-Thomistic strain by detaching 'mystery' from 'doctrine' and reattaching it to 'God'. Although the theology proper of Reformed Dogmatics begins with the statement that 'mystery is the lifeblood of dogmatics', this is only so because God is mysterious and he is the exclusive content of dogmatics. Cf. *RD* 2.29.

functions. The former requires a choice between two mutual exclusivities. One must be selected on the grounds that it denies the other. *Either* sin *or* grace must be chosen because grace is *for* God and sin is *against* God. For Bavinck, there are no other options.

Although, as has been previously noted, Bavinck prefers the language of synthesis over that of antithesis, his conception of Christianity nonetheless rests on this crucial antithesis. Christianity, for Bavinck, has an essentially antithetical foundation. This antithetical core does not, however, mean that its essence is one of unbridled antithesis. Post-creation, humankind chose not to be *pros ton theon*; it embraced the wrong side of the antithesis. Consequently, nature became corrupt, following which the Triune God began working in grace towards its restoration.[42] In short, the rudimentary principle of antithesis, followed by the axiom of 'grace restores nature' means that while Bavinck's Christianity is established on an antithetical foundation, its overall structure is nonetheless one of synthesis. Indeed, synthesis is the consequence of antithesis: grace restores nature to bring us to the right side of the antithesis.[43]

The dualistic patterns of *Aeterni Patris* make no such demands. Rather, they allow the Christian to choose between natural and supernatural theology, secular or sacred lives and so on. 'According to the viewpoint of Rome, there exist in the divine mind two conceptions of man [man *in puris naturalibus* and man having received the *donum superadditum*] and thus also a double moral law, two sorts of love and a twofold destination or goal.'[44]

Bavinck claims that the centrality of this non-antithetical dualism within neo-Thomism consistently produces Christians who either flee the world or conform to it. 'This juxtaposition of a natural and a supernatural order

---

[42] See Hielema, *Eschatological Understanding of Redemption*, 175; Veenhof, *Revelatie en Inspiratie*, 347 ff.; Bolt, *Imitation of Christ Theme*, 104.

[43] As such, one must be careful to nuance the potentially simplistic caricature of Bavinck and Kuyper as, respectively, 'synthetic' and 'antithetic'. Both share the same starting point of antithesis between sin and grace. Indeed, this antithesis is the basis for all of Bavinck's later thought on 'grace restores nature' (synthesis). When one notes Bavinck's relation between synthesis and antithesis, it is natural to question whether his thought process evinces a latent Hegelianism. However, it seems insufficient to make the unqualified assertion that Bavinck is therefore Hegelian. The content of Bavinck's antithesis and synthesis seems, initially at least, to be decidedly distinct from the Hegelian thesis–antithesis synthesis. In the Hegelian model, the thesis is brought together with its antithesis via the reconciliation of their common ground, and this in order to create a wholly new proposition. For Bavinck, the antithesis between sin and grace is such that the two are irreconcilable: the antithesis can only be undone by doing away with sin. As such, the process of synthesis is that of grace restoring nature, which is to say that grace brings nature back to its unfallen state (to use Hegelian terminology, the original *thesis*), rather than to synthesize both sin and grace together into some new proposition.

[44] Bavinck, 'Common Grace', 45.

explains the remarkable phenomenon that Rome has always reared two
types of children and has tailored Christianity more or less to suit all men
without exception.'[45]

In describing the first of these 'two types of children', Bavinck argues that
the decidedly non-pessimistic Roman Catholic view of the 'natural' man
legitimizes contentment with the merely natural life and, by its consequent
encouragement to rely on reason rather than revelation, leads to nominal
Christianity, secularism and ultimately atheism.

> But Rome also rears another class of children. There exist idealistic, mysti-
> cal people who are not content with the natural, who thirst for something
> higher and better. These reach up to the destination of a supernatural
> life, which God has made possible through the church. To reach this
> goal, the natural life is an unprofitable hindrance. It is not sinful *per se*
> but is nevertheless an impediment. . . . The origins of monasticism in
> many respects still remain obscure. But the spirit of this movement has
> come to permeate the whole Roman Catholic system. The supernatural
> is an order all its own, highly exalted above and cut off from natural life.
> He who would serve in the first order must, so far as possible, put to death
> the second.[46]

His argument is that those who espouse non-Reformed theology either
capitulate into their surrounding culture or beat a hurried retreat from it.
Most interesting is that a strikingly similar paradigm is central to the bipolar
critique of Bavinck's own thinking. The 'two Bavincks' hypothesis asserts that
he ranged from wanting to blend into the modernist Leiden school to wishing
that he could retreat into the intellectual monastery that was the world of pre-
Enlightenment Reformed theology. In essence, the hypothesis is that Bavinck
simply cannot decide which path to tread: that of intellectual world-flight or
of intellectual world-conformity. In critiquing *Aeterni Patris*, Bavinck argues
that Reformed theology (by its antithetical core, distinctive understanding of
the covenants, the *imago Dei* and the nature–grace relationship) provides an
alternative to world-flight and world-conformity. On either side of neo-
Thomisim's dualism, the world goes unsanctified, as the Christian light either
goes out (the choice to be 'natural') or is hidden under a monastic bushel
(the choice to be 'supernatural'). The only way to break out of this paradigm
is by forming a worldview centred on common grace.

---

[45] Bavinck, 'Common Grace', 48.
[46] Bavinck, 'Common Grace', 48.

Furthermore, Bavinck offers a scathing critique of Thomism's influence on Protestant Christianity. He traces the world-conformity movement as stemming from the Socinians to the Remonstrants and, in turn, to the Dutch anti-supernaturalism espoused by Scholten *et al.* It seems fairly evident that the Leiden school was, in Bavinck's eyes, guilty of much world-conformity. Protestant world-flight, he writes, was nurtured in Anabaptist circles and came to strongly influence separatist movements across Europe. Indeed, its reach extended to the Reformed Church:

> Similarly, in pious circles, certain traits kept coming up which called to mind the old Anabaptism. The scorning of the letter of Scripture and the elevation of the inner light of the Holy Spirit; the preference for impromptu edifying discourses along with a denigration of the office of minister of the Word; the belittling of the objective ordinances of God for church and covenant, for the sacraments and offices; the preference for closed societies; the rejection of art, scholarship, science, culture, and all the goods of earthly life, and the spurning of the vocation that rests upon us in family, business, and the state—all these are fruits not of healthy Reformation but of the unsound Anabaptist tradition.[47]

No doubt Bavinck is critiquing certain aspects of his own separatist heritage. Evidently, he had little appetite for isolationist theology.[48]

That he focuses on this alternative to world-conformity and world-flight at various key moments in his theological career (indeed, his intent in the opening and closing speeches at Kampen was undoubtedly to impress upon his students the conviction that *holy theology* belongs in the modern scientific world) poses heavy problems to the caricature which undergirds the 'two Bavincks' model. It seems incredulous that Bavinck, who so carefully articulated the centrality of common grace in Reformed theology's non-conformist, active participatory role in the modern world, would nonetheless be trapped in the unrelenting identity crisis assumed by those who advocate the 'two Bavincks' hypothesis.

The same aversion to dualism and its effects on theology was evident in Bavinck's contribution to the Union of the Reformed Churches in 1892.[49] Prior to this the theological institutions represented by Bavinck and Kuyper

---

[47] Bavinck, 'Common Grace', 54.

[48] J.D. Tangelder, 'Dr. Herman Bavinck 1854–1921: Theologian of the Word', *Christian Renewal* 19 (2001), 14–51.

[49] Herman Bavinck, 'The Reformed Churches of the Netherlands', *Princeton Theological Review* 8 (1910); Hendrik Bouma, *Secession, Doleantie and Union: 1834–92*, tr. Theodore Plantinga (Neerlandia, Alberta: Inheritance Publications, 1995).

(respectively, the Theological School at Kampen and the Vrije Universiteit Amsterdam) had operated separately. With ecclesiastical union came the question of how these institutions should be related. In this context, Bavinck published a great deal of material on educational reform.[50] His fear was that Amsterdam and Kampen would be polarized and that, to borrow the terminology of *De Gemeene Genade*, one would flee from the modern world while the other would conform to it. In *The Theological School and the Free University*, Bavinck argued for an 'organic union' of the two institutions. Much to his disappointment, the Synod disagreed and instead designated Kampen the site of 'practical' ministry training and Amsterdam the locus of 'scientific' theology.[51] It should be noted that Bavinck's sentiments in *The Theological School and the Free University* are highly consonant with his earlier paper, *Theology and Religious Studies* (*Godgeleerdheid en godsdienstwetenschap*), which was published at the time of the Union.

In an almost prescient fashion, Bavinck marks the Union of the Reformed Churches by highlighting their need to break from the dualistic heart of the Higher Education Act (1876). He alleged that the Act, in annexing the heart to the pietists and the head to the modernists, had rendered theological education a shambolic experience for both sides: 'The result was a strange mixture of incompatibles lacking all integration and unity of conception.'[52] Unsurprisingly, he was left dismayed by the post-Union rejection of his *The Theological School and the Free University* in favour of adherence to the Higher Education Act. Although the division between Kampen and Amsterdam is concerned with the dichotomization of theory and practice, rather than that between nature and grace, it remains a highly useful analogy in this context.

IX. Biographical Interpretation

One should note that the strong case for a new reading of Bavinck's theology is consistent with an existing alternative reading of Bavinck's biography. Indeed, the interpretation of his life which undergirds the 'two Bavincks' approach to his theology is by no means uncontested.

The development of his Amsterdam-era role as a politician, for example, need not be interpreted as Bavinck having given up on theology's relevance.

---

[50] See Herman Bavinck, *Education and Theology* (*Opleiding en theologie, 1896*); *The Office of 'Doctor' [in the Church]* (*Het doctorenambt*, 1899); *Erudition and Scholarship* (*Geleerdheid en wetenschap*, 1899); *The Authority of the Church and the Freedom of Science* (*Het recht der kerken en de vrijheid der wetenschap*, 1899) and *The Theological School and the Free University* (*Theologische School en Vrije Universiteit*, 1899).

[51] For Bavinck's assessment, see 'The Reformed Churches of the Netherlands', 457–8.

[52] Herman Bavinck, 'Theology and Religious Studies', 53.

Indeed, when one takes stock of various other facts, this suggestion seems most unlikely. For all of his political involvement, Bavinck continued to teach theology and serve the church. He was Professor of Systematic Theology at the Vrije Universiteit until his death in 1921. It was when speaking at the Synod in Leeuwarden in 1920 that he suffered the heart attack which signalled the end of his effective personal contribution within both spheres.

Furthermore, recent research has demonstrated that while writing *Gereformeerde Dogmatiek* in Kampen, Bavinck was also busy preparing a companion volume *Gereformeerde Ethiek*.[53] He was deeply concerned with the application of theology in every sphere of life. Unfortunately, Bavinck never finished writing Reformed Ethics and as such it remained an unpublished, unknown work for many years. The presence of different extant ethics manuscripts either written by Bavinck or compiled by his ethics students[54] during his Kampen years highlights that his time in Kampen aimed at both dogmatics and ethics. For Bavinck, the production of Reformed Ethics was no afterthought. It was an essential companion activity while writing Reformed Dogmatics. According to his own ideal, the true dogmatician cannot express dogmatics in its entirety without engaging in ethics.[55]

It seems most likely that *Gereformeerde Ethiek* never saw the light of day as Bavinck had yet to settle on its final form when he moved to the Vrije Universiteit. In comparing Bavinck's own early manuscript to the later ethics manuscripts compiled by Kampen students from his ethics classes, there is an evident desire to restructure the work. When Bavinck arrived at the Vrije Universiteit, his new colleague, the ethicist Wilhelm Geesink, was already busy preparing a neo-Calvinist Reformed Ethics.[56] Viewed in that

---

[53] Dirk van Keulen, 'Herman Bavinck's *Reformed Ethics*: Some Remarks about Unpublished Manuscripts in the Libraries of Amsterdam and Kampen', *The Bavinck Review* 1 (2010), 25–56; and 'Herman Bavinck on the Imitation of Christ', *Scottish Bulletin of Evangelical Theology* 29 (2011), 28–9.

[54] Reinder Jan van der Veen, *Gereformeerde Ethiek. Acroam. van: Prof. Dr. H. Bavinck* (originally 327 pages in two volumes, the first of which has been lost); Cornelis Lindeboom, *Gereformeerde Ethiek – Dictaat van Prof. Bavinck*; cf. van Keulen, 'Herman Bavinck's *Reformed Ethics*: Some Remarks about Unpublished Manuscripts in the Libraries of Amsterdam and Kampen', 29.

[55] 'Dogmatics describes the deeds of God done for, to and in human beings; ethics describes what renewed human beings now do on the basis of and in the strength of those divine deeds. In dogmatics human beings are passive; they receive and believe; in ethics they are themselves active agents. . . . Dogmatics is the system of the knowledge of God; ethics is that of the service of God. The two disciplines, far from facing each other as two independent entities, together form a single system; they are related members of a single organism.' *RD* 1.58.

[56] Willem Geesink, *Gereformeerde Ethiek*, 2 vols. (Kampen: Kok, 1931); While there are minor differences between Bavinck and Geesink as ethicists, their approaches are substantially the same as neo-Calvinist ethicists.

light, his failure to complete a volume on ethics is understandable, though perhaps unfortunate.

However, one must acknowledge that his many forays into these other spheres were carried out in the spirit of this *dogmatiek*-into-*ethiek* movement. His numerous publications on education were in opposition to the increasing secularization of the Dutch school system.[57] In recognition of his contribution to the development of Christian education, many Dutch schools were named after him.

In politics, Bavinck aligned himself with Kuyper's Anti-Revolutionary Party, a Party with origins in the earlier *Réveil* movement and wholly committed to a Calvinistic worldview.[58] In this capacity, he sought to approach society from a Christian perspective.[59] The notion that Bavinck entered politics because he doubted the relevance of Reformed theology is distinctly out of step with the direction taken by Bavinck as a politician. In fact, his political involvement seems founded on the conviction that Reformed theology is of pressing relevance to modern life.

The statement 'My dogmatics avails me nothing',[60] made post-heart attack (when asked if he feared dying), should not be read as expressing loss of belief in the said theology. Rather, as Bristley helpfully counsels, 'He was not disparaging his work, but only confessed what he had affirmed all along.'[61] On this dictum, Hendricksen has argued: 'The statement simply means that a system of doctrine, however necessary and valuable, is of no avail in and by itself. It must be translated into Christian living. There must be genuine faith in the Triune God as manifested in Jesus Christ.'[62]

It has been recently argued that Hepp's portrayal of Bavinck's old age despair is somewhat exaggerated.[63] Certainly when Hepp's picture of this

---

[57] See Herman Bavinck, *Principles of Education* (*Paedagogische Beginselen*, 1904); *Training of the Teacher* (*De opleiding van den onderwijzer*, 1914); *Education of Adolescents* (*De opvoeding der rijpere jeugd*, 1916) and *New Education* (*De nieuwe opvoeding*, 1917). For a thorough analysis of Bavinck's contribution to Christian education, see Cornelius Jaarsma, *The Educational Philosophy of Herman Bavinck* (Grand Rapids: Eerdmans, 1935).

[58] McKendree R. Langley, *The Practice of Political Spirituality: Episodes from the Public Career of Abraham Kuyper, 1879–1918* (Jordan Station, ON: Paideia Press, 1984).

[59] His various publications from this time are highly indicative of this fact: see Herman Bavinck, *The Imitation of Christ in Modern Life* (*De navolging van Christus in het moderne leven*, 1918); *The Christian Family* (*Het Christelijke huisgezin*, 1908); and *The Role of Woman in Modern Society* (*De vrouw in de hedendaagsche maatschappij*, 1918). In the final work, Bavinck fought for women's suffrage.

[60] Dosker, 'Herman Bavinck', 21.

[61] Bristley, *Guide to the Writings of Herman Bavinck*, 26.

[62] William Hendriksen, preface to Herman Bavinck, *The Doctrine of God* (Edinburgh: Banner of Truth, 1977), 5.

[63] Bolt, 'Grand Rapids Between Kampen and Amsterdam: Herman Bavinck's Reception and Influence in North America', 266.

period is compared with that of Bremmer, it appears rather out of proportion.[64]

The aim of this brief excursus into the interpretation of Bavinck's biography is simply to demonstrate that the portrait of his (allegedly disjointed) multifaceted career, through which his writings are read as the work of a Jekyll and Hyde theologian, is by no means a settled one.

X. Bavinck's Identity Crisis

When surveying Bavinck's biography, particularly the letters exchanged with friends in his Leiden period, it is apparent that Bavinck, in his student days, underwent something of a crisis of faith. Between the polar extremes of his Secessionist upbringing and the radical modernism of the Leiden school, the young Bavinck spent a portion of his university life in what can fairly be called a theological identity crisis. 'He had many a bitter struggle at Leiden. Keuenen especially, with his "heart of gold", was his idol among his professors. I remember his letters of that period, his description of serious doubts and questionings and battles; but all these struggles only tested and purified his faith.'[65]

It was commonly known in the *Christelijke Gereformeerde Kerken* that while at Leiden, the young Bavinck became unsure of his assent to the Thirty-Seven Articles (the Dutch Creed). Indeed, when he accepted the call to the pastorate in Franeker, his friend Henry Elias Dosker wrote to him: 'I was astonished to read in the papers of your acceptance of the call of Franeker. Why? Because of the struggles, through which you passed as described in your last letter? Have the 37 articles become plainer or more acceptable than before? Knowing your character I must accept that as the most plausible explanation and I do thank the Lord for this victory of faith.'[66]

In a slightly similar pattern to that of Kuyper, Bavinck's short time in the pastoral ministry marked his departure from the theology learned at Leiden. As the following letter to his friend Christiaan Snouck Hurgronje makes plain, although he became unconvinced of the Leiden school's theology, the earlier student-era crisis of faith came at a longer-term experiential cost.

Their contemplations on Scripture aside, Kuenen and Scholten have not had much influence on me, if by that you mean losing my faith and

---

[64] Bremmer, *Herman Bavinck en zijn Tijdgenoten*, 263–6.
[65] Dosker, 'Herman Bavinck', 15.
[66] Dosker to Bavinck, 12 February 1881. Bavinck Archives.

taking on theirs. But they have indeed had (and it could be no other way) an influence on the power and manner with which I embrace those truths. That naïve and childlike faith, with its unlimited trust in the truth as it has been instilled, you see, has been lost; and that is a great deal; in that way their influence has been great and strong. Now I know that I can never regain that. That said, I find it good and am thankful for losing it. In that innocence there was much that was untrue and had to be purified. But still, there is that naïve (and I know no better word) something, that is good, that is a consolation; something that must remain if the truth is to stay sweet and precious to us. Sometimes, very rarely (as where can you find the rock solid faith of yesteryear in our day and age?), I meet some people in my congregation who have just that, who fare so well by it and are so happy. Now, I can't help but wish that I believed as they did, so happy and joyous, and then I feel that if I were so, I could *preach*, animated, warm, always full of conviction about what I say; then I could be useful. I would be alive, living for others. But I know full well that this is in the past, it is no longer possible.[67]

That Bavinck himself saw this identity crisis as confined to his student days is apparent during his correspondence with Hurgronje.

Having left Leiden, many things in the modern theology and worldview look different to me than when I was so strongly under the influence of Scholten and Kuenen. I learned much in Leiden, but I have unlearned much too. The latter could partly have had negative effects on me; I am starting to recognize them more and more. The time in which the convictions of our youth were thrown into crucible of critique is now over. What

---

[67] De Bruijn and Harinck, eds., *Leidse vriendschap*, 81. Dutch original: 'Kuenen en Scholten hebben op mij (behalve in de Schriftbeschouwing) niet veel invloed gehad, als ge daaronder verstaat het verliezen van geloofswaarheden en het aannemen van andere, van de hunne. Maar zij hebben wel (hoe kon het anders) invloed gehad op de kracht en de wijze, waarmee ik die waarheden omhels. Het naïve van het kinderlijk geloof, van het onbegrensd vertrouwen op de mij ingeprente waarheid, zie, dat ben ik kwijt een dat is veel, heel veel; zoo is die invloed groot en sterk geweest. En nu weet ik wel, dat ik dat nooit terugkrijg. Zelfs vind ik het goed en ben ik er waarlijk en oprecht dankbaar voor, dat ik heb verloren heb. Er was ook in dat naive veel, wat onwaar was en gereinigdmoest worden. Maar toch, er is in dat naïve (ik week geen beter woord) iets, dat goed is, dat wel doet; iets dat blijven moet, zal de waarheid ons ooit zoet en dierbaar wezen. En als ik dan soms – heel enkel, want och, waar is het rotsensterke geloof van vroeger tijd nog in onze eeuw? – in de gemeente nog enkele menschen ontmoet, die dat hebben en er zoo wel bij zijn en zoo gelukkig, nu, ik kan niet helpen, maar dan wenschte ik weer te gelooven als zij, zoo blij en zoo vrolijk; en dan voel ik, als ik dat had, en ik kon dan zoo preeken, bezield, warm, altijd ten volle overtuigd van wat ik zei, dan kon ik nuttig zijn; zelf levend, zou ik leven voor anderen. Maar ik weet wel, dat is voorbij; dat is thans niet meer mogelijk.'

matters at this moment is to be faithful to the convictions we now have and to defend them with the weapons that are at our disposal.[68]

Although the year in Franeker convinced Bavinck that Scholten was not the true inheritor of the Reformed tradition, his reaction was not to practice intellectual world-flight. Rather, he remained open to the questions posed by the modern world and firmly believed that the Reformed tradition, as he understood it, was historic catholic Christianity's greatest hope in the modern age. Such is evident from the opening address given by Bavinck in Kampen. The year in Franeker shaped the convictions so evident in 'The Science of Holy Theology' (*De wetenschap der Heilige Godgeleerdheid*). In that sense, the young Bavinck emerged from this one period of genuine confusion with a single, resolved identity, as a Reformed theologian combating what Zylstra calls 'moribund formal orthodoxy, on the one hand, and an evasive pietism, on the other.'[69]

XI. Conclusion

The strange irony of the 'two Bavincks' hypothesis is that it requires one to read his theology with a dualistic hermeneutic: just as *Aeterni Patris* legitimizes the choice to be a 'natural' or 'supernatural' believer, and as the late nineteenth-century Dutch Reformed Church legitimized the choice to study 'practical' or 'scientific' theology, the likes of Vroom and VanDrunen legitimize the choice of 'which line of Bavinck's thinking' one wishes to follow. The implication is thus that Bavinck's theology necessitates precisely the kind of dualism that *De Gemeene Genade* and *The Theological School and the Free University* so forcefully repudiate.

As Harinck was well argued, this is a choice Bavinck never felt in his own life. 'Yet, he refused to take the consequences that he had to *choose* between faith and science [one might say, between orthodoxy and modernity]. All

---

[68] Bavinck to Snouck, 24 November 1880, in De Bruijn and Harinck, eds., *Leidse vriendschap*, 75–6. Dutch original: 'Nu ik uit Leiden weg ben, en de moderne theologie en de moderne wereldbeschouwing wat anders in de oogen zie, dan toen ik zoo sterk onder den invloed van Kuenen en Scholten stond, nu lijkt mij veel weer heel anders toe dan waarin het mij toen voorkwam. Ik heb in Leiden veel geleerd, maar ook veel verleerd. Dat laatste kan ten deele schadelijk voor mij gewerkt hebben, maar meer en meer begin ik dat schadelijke ervan in te zien. Het tijdperk, waarin onze van vroeger meegebrachte overtuigingen in den smeltkroes der kritiek geworpen zijn, is voorbij. 't Komt er nu op aan, de overtuigingen, die wij thans hebben, trouw te zijn en ze te verdedigen met de wapenen die ons ten dienste staan.'

[69] Henry Zylstra, 'Preface', in Herman Bavinck, *Our Reasonable Faith* (Grand Rapids: Baker Book House, 1956), 10.

his theological work can be regarded as a refutation of the duality of faith
and culture, which was, given his secessionist background, so familiar to
him and for which a meeting with modern theology offered such an
opportunity. This rejection of duality, which he knew from the Secession
and from Leiden, was a decisive step in Bavinck's spiritual development and
became characteristic of his Reformed spirituality.'[70]

Evidently the bulk of scholarship on Bavinck has, for the best part of five
decades, operated on a far from unshakeable foundation.[71] A new reading
of Bavinck, one in line with Kloosterman's correct translation of Berkouwer
(and which, consequently, does not read him through a bipolar lens but
rather allows that it may well be possible to avoid the danger of annexation),
is warranted. Initially at least, the organic motif has tremendous potential
in highlighting the sense in which one may speak of a single Herman
Bavinck. The following chapter will engage with Veenhof's particular
application of the 'two Bavincks' model to the motif. In being freed from
this hypothesis, sufficient leverage is created in order to explore whether a
new reading of the motif might further such an exploration. Despite
Veenhof's annexation of the motif to the 'modern' Bavinck and his followers,
it will be argued that Bavinck uses the motif when reflecting on the
archetypal unity of the Godhead, which enables the dogmatician to conceive
of cosmic unity-in-diversity. Thus Chapter 3 will attempt to move away from
Veenhof's reading of the organic motif, following which Chapter 4 will
move into Bavinck's doctrine of God.

---

[70] Harinck, '"Something that must remain, if the truth is to be sweet and precious to us": The
Reformed Spirituality of Herman Bavinck', 252.
[71] The current state of Bavinck studies is reminiscent of the common reading of the Scottish
theologian John Baillie. In that case, an article by Donald Klinefelter asserted that Baillie
had become neo-orthodox in the 1930s, only to revert into pre-Barthian liberalism after this
(Donald Klinefelter, 'The Theology of John Baillie: A Biographical Introduction', *Scottish
Journal of Theology* 22 (1969), 419–36). This perception of Baillie remained normative until
the release of David Fergusson's 'John Baillie: Orthodox Liberal', which demonstrated that
Baillie had not been neo-orthodox in the 1930s, and became progressively more Barthian
(rather than pre-Barthian liberal) towards the end of his career (David Fergusson, 'John
Baillie: Orthodox Liberal', *Christ, Church and Society: Essays on David Baillie and John Baillie*
(London: T & T Clark, 1993), ed. David Fergusson, 140).

Chapter 3

Bavinck's Organic Motif

'He views theology as an organism always expanding, so long as the fullness of the Word is not exhausted. God, not religion, is the object of theology.'[1]

I. Introduction

As was shown in the previous chapter, the bulk of work on Bavinck over the last four decades has operated on the premise that his thought is inherently untenable: hence the normalized speech of 'two Bavincks'. However, noting that this model presently stands on the brink of collapse, it has become imperative to find the basis (if one exists) upon which one may speak of a united theological worldview in his writings.

The organic motif is thus chosen for its considerable promise as an agent of unity in Bavinck's thought. Under the previous reading, this would have been impossible: Veenhof's application of the general 'two Bavincks' model to the motif, as will be explained, rendered it the property of the 'modernist' stream of Bavinck's disciples. However, having begun to interpret Bavinck without the presupposition of inevitable internal discord, it is hoped that the organic motif, used by Bavinck to express the notion of triniform unity-in-diversity, might provide answers to the quest for a united Bavinck.[2]

That the motif plays a crucial role in his approach to theology is beyond doubt. Even the most casual reading of Bavinck's work quickly reveals the regularity with which he uses organic language, imagery and concepts. The motif is central to one of the most important and provocative statements in *Reformed Dogmatics*: 'In Christ, in the middle of history, God created an organic centre; from this centre, in an ever widening sphere, God drew the

---

[1] Dosker, 'Herman Bavinck', 23. Cf. Abraham Kuyper, *Sacred Theology* (Lafayette: Sovereign Grace Publishers, 2001), 264.
[2] An earlier version of this chapter was published as James Eglinton, 'Bavinck's Organic Motif: Questions Seeking Answers', *Calvin Theological Journal*, 45 no. 1 April 2010, 51–71.

circles within which the light of revelation shines. . . . Presently the grace of
God appears to all human beings. The Holy Spirit takes everything from
Christ, adding nothing new to revelation. . . . In Christ God both fully
revealed and fully gave himself. Consequently also Scripture is complete; it
is the perfected Word of God.'[3]

Here, Bavinck draws together various theological loci (revelation,
pneumatology, an account of history, redemption, Scripture) and centres
them on the person of Christ, who stands as an 'organic centre' to the
overarching plans of the Triune God in the cosmos. Elsewhere, he writes:
'For if the knowledge of God has been revealed by himself in his Word, it
cannot contain contradictory elements or be in conflict with what is known
of God from nature and history. God's thoughts cannot be opposed to one
another and thus necessarily [form] an organic unity.'[4]

In probing the workings of this theological system, one immediately faces
a set of questions which must be answered: What does Bavinck mean by
organic, and from where do these organic concerns come? Without
answering these pertinent questions one can scarcely lay claim to a nuanced
understanding of Bavinck's work. Indeed, without deliberate definition,
the various parts of Bavinck's dogmatic system cannot be related with any
assurance or specificity. In reliance upon the 'two Bavincks' model, Veenhof
has provided a set of answers to these questions which, it will be seen, have
been forcefully shaken by the failure of their hermeneutical presuppositions.
These questions, then, must be posed again without the influence of the
'two Bavincks' framework.

Noting Bavinck's dictum that 'the imperative task of the dogmatician is to
think God's thoughts after him and to trace their unity,'[5] it becomes clear that
Bavinck views the dogmatician as an inherently organic thinker. Indeed, if
God's thoughts truly come together in an organic fashion, one can neither
think these thoughts nor trace their unity without probing this organic
motif.

Although it has not previously been the focus of exclusive attention,
Bavinck's use of the organic has been noted in various doctoral theses.[6] It is
also the subject of an excursus in Veenhof's *Revelatie en Inspiratie.*[7] Veenhof's

---

[3] *RD*, 1.383.
[4] *RD*, 1.44. The English translation *Reformed Dogmatics* contains a typographic error in this
sentence ('from' in place of 'form').
[5] *RD*, 1.44.
[6] Brian Mattson, *Restored to our Destiny* (PhD dissertation, University of Aberdeen, 2008), 42–9;
Bolt, *The Imitation of Christ Theme*; Syd Hielema, *Herman Bavinck's Eschatological Understanding
of Redemption* (ThD dissertation, Toronto: Wycliffe School of Theology, 1998), 59–60.
[7] Veenhof, *Revelatie en Inspiratie*, 250–68.

account of Bavinck's organic idea has, until now, been the industry standard.[8] While the stellar contribution of *Revelatie en Inspiratie* to the development of Bavinck studies is beyond doubt, its handling of the organic motif has recently been called into question and thus has thrust the topic to the forefront of Bavinck studies.[9] Perhaps the distinctive feature of this book, of course, is that it doubts the 'two Bavincks' hypothesis common to much secondary material on Bavinck (Veenhof's work included). As it has already disputed the legitimacy of a 'two poles' and 'two Bavincks'[10] caricature as the basis for which to generally interpret Bavinck's theology, it comes as no surprise that one will also move to critique the specific application of the 'two Bavincks' model made by Veenhof in exploring Bavinck's organic motif. Indeed, if the 'two Bavincks' hypothesis is holed below the waterline, as recent developments in Bavinck studies would suggest, a new normative reading of this crucial motif (which does not depend on a dualistic hermeneutic) is necessary.

In attempting to provide such a reading, this chapter will place Veenhof's description of Bavinck's use of the organic in dialogue with the normative cross-disciplinary accounts of wider organic trends, before attempting critical engagement with both. One hopes that this engagement will yield clear answers to the aforementioned questions.

Although both Veenhof's reading of the motif, and the motif's new interpretation as advanced in this book, will be outlined in greater detail in the main body of this chapter, it is perhaps useful for the sake of initial clarity if both are succinctly outlined at this point. In Veenhof's reading, the 'modern' Bavinck turns to various schools of thought (German Idealism, the History of Religions school and the Ethical Theologians) from whom he borrows the organic motif. Veenhof posits that the term is used more or less homogeneously by these schools, and that Bavinck (and Kuyper), accordingly, used organic terminology 'in the universal sense of the time'. When one reads Bavinck's use of the motif, therefore, one finds that the

---

[8] John Bolt, 'The Trinity as a Unifying Theme in Reformed Thought: A Response to Dr George Vandervelde', *Calvin Theological Journal*, 22 No. 1 (April 1987), 94; Ron Gleason, 'The Centrality of the *Unio Mystica*', 356; Louis Praamsma, 'Review of *Revelatie en inspiratie: De Openbarings en Schriftbeschouwing van Herman Bavinck in vergelijking met die der ethische theologie*,' *Westminster Theological Journal* (32 no 1 N 1969), 100; Gerben Heitink, *Practical Theology* (Kok: Kampen, 1993), 71; Henk Vroom, 'Understanding the Gospel Contextually,' *Contextuality in Reformed Europe: The Mission of the Church in the Transformation of European Culture* (Amsterdam: Editions Rodopi, 2004), eds. Christine Lienemann-Perrin, Hendrik Vroom and Michael Weinrich, 43–4.

[9] James Eglinton, 'Bavinck's Organic Motif: Questions Seeking Answers', *Calvin Theological Journal* (April 2010), Vol. 45, No. 1, 51–71.

[10] Veenhof, *Revelatie en Inspiratie*, 108–11.

'modern' Bavinck is a neo-Hegelian deeply at odds with other significant sections of his own theological identity.

This book will argue, however, that Bavinck's organic motif has a somewhat different source – a richly Trinitarian doctrine of God as received by the Patristic and Reformation traditions – and that it accounts for the triniformity so abundant throughout all created reality. God as archetypal (triune) unity-in-diversity is the basis for all subsequent (triniform) ectypal cosmic unity-in-diversity. Whenever one finds Bavinck handling these concepts, he consistently makes use of the organic motif.

II. Veenhof's Account

Veenhof's 1968 thesis devotes some twenty pages to Bavinck's recurrent organic motif. Two general points should be noted regarding Veenhof's influential description. First, he concedes that the organic motif has ancient origins. Second, he holds that Bavinck's use of this motif also has a more recent history: it is the direct successor of the organicism developed by German Idealism.

Conceptually, he notes, organicism's heritage stretches back into antiquity. In this ancient context, theological organicism occurs primarily through reflection on the divine economy. Moving forward two millennia, however, one finds the same story progressing into the era of the nineteenth-century world of Schelling and Hegel. Veenhof's conclusion is that Bavinck (and his neo-Calvinist contemporary, Abraham Kuyper) inherited the organic idea from three sources: Schelling's Idealist philosophy, the history of religions school and the Ethical theologians.[11] His final sentiment is that 'Kuyper and Bavinck employed the concepts of "organism" and "organic" in the universal sense of the time.'[12] As such, the organic motif is annexed to the thought of the 'modern' Bavinck. It is apparently disconnected from his 'orthodox' alter ego and is of little significance to those who choose this 'line of Bavinck's thinking'. The motif, according to Veenhof, reflects the perpetual disunity of Bavinck's mind.

The general hermeneutic with which Veenhof reads specific sections of Bavinck's work has already been critiqued. One will not cover the same ground in this chapter. Rather, his particular handling of the organic motif

---

[11] Veenhof, *Revelatie en Inspiratie*, 267–8.
[12] Veenhof, *Revelatie en Inspiratie*, 268.

will be placed under scrutiny. In this context it is perhaps most important to note that Veenhof's work seems to rest on two presuppositions. First, it is assumed that the history of organicism (from antiquity to the nineteenth-century) is a single development possessing a certain degree of homogeneity. The essence of organicism, he posits, has a 'universal sense'. Second, it makes the related assumption that Bavinck's organic idea is best defined by study of the historical–etymological, cross-disciplinary development of organicism.

III. Generalist Intellectual Histories of Organicism

When Veenhof's account is placed in conversation with generalist intellectual–historical accounts of organicism, interesting results are yielded. Indeed, one quickly comes to see that while Veenhof's account provides much valuable information, it nonetheless evinces the same interpretative flaws as many of its generalist counterparts.

General intellectual histories of Western thought, tracing its development from antiquity to the modern day, have portrayed the history of organicism as broadly univocal.[13] Beginning in the ancient world, one finds an Aristotelian understanding of cause and effect which takes shape and holds sway through the medieval era. However, the Enlightenment (and particularly the advent of Newtonian physics) changes this understanding of movement in the physical world. Scientific determinism begets philosophical offspring, and a generation of mechanical thinkers comes to prominence between the seventeenth and eighteenth centuries. The limits of this mechanical worldview become apparent in the mid eighteenth-century, and the collapse of mechanism prompts the return and development of organicism, the modern avatar of the ancient thought system found in Plato's cosmos-as-*macroanthropos*[14] and the Apostle Paul's church-as-*corpus*.[15]

---

[13] Compare Veenhof's history with that of Louis Dupré, *The Enlightenment and the Intellectual Foundations of Modern Culture* (Yale University Press: London, 2004); George Mead, *Movements of Thought in the Nineteenth Century* (University of Chicago Press: Chicago, 1972); Frederick Beiser, *Hegel* (Routledge: New York, 2005); Jagdish Hattiangadi, 'Philosophy of biology in the nineteenth century', in *Routledge History of Philosophy Volume VII: The Nineteenth Century* (Routledge: London, 1994), ed. C.L. Ten; Roland Stromberg, *European Intellectual History Since 1789* (Prentice-Hall: New Jersey, 1986).

[14] Plato, *Timaeus* (30d, 33b).

[15] 1 Corinthians 12:14.

IV. Engagement with Veenhof's Account

Veenhof's claim is that, having begun with Aristotle and Kant, the ancient
organic idea has undergone a long process of development, appearing in
the nineteenth-century via Hegel and Schelling, and then passing into
Bavinck's theology.[16]

As has already been noted, Veenhof posits a degree of uniformity and
homogeneity spanning the history of organicism. When Aristotle and Hegel
talk in organic terms, it is alleged, they are describing substantially the same
thing, albeit in a different stage of its development. In addition to this, Veenhof's methodology attempts to define Bavinck's use of language through the
historical usage of the said terminology. The underlying assertion is that one
should define a term in relation to its etymological and conceptual history,
rather than seek definition by its immediate contextual usage.

In this light, Veenhof's analysis of Bavinck's organic motif bears a striking
resemblance to the aforementioned generalist history of organicism. Both
analyses seem to imply that organicism is essentially a vast but singular
movement. Its exponents apparently have enough in common that one
should use organicism's generic history to define its specific applications.
Thus Bavinck is explained by Schelling, who is defined (albeit by negation)
by Newton, who is, in turn, negatively explained by Aristotle.

Noting the high degree of similarity between Veenhof's analysis and
generalist histories of organicism, one must ask how Veenhof's thesis fares
when brought into conversation with the primary critics of general organicist histories.

Van Eck is among the foremost challengers of the accepted organicist
historical accounts.[17] Writing on the application of organicism to architecture
and the arts, van Eck's call is for a 'clear break with the majority of the
existing literature on organicism . . . the prevalent opinion about the
connections between organicism and philosophy must be substantially
revised.'[18] Her extensive critique has two main points. First, the generalist
historical portrait of organicism, centring on its development in the build
up to and reaction against the Enlightenment, is inherently wrong. 'Until
now, most studies devoted to organicism posited a significant change in the

---

[16] Veenhof, Revelatie en Inspiratie, 252–66.

[17] Caroline van Eck, *Organicism in nineteenth-century architecture: An inquiry into its theoretical and philosophical background* (Architectura & Natura Press: Amsterdam, 1994). See also Charles I. Armstrong, *Romantic organicism: from idealist origins to ambivalent afterlife* (New York: Palgrave Macmillan, 2003).

[18] van Eck, *Organicism in nineteenth-century architecture*, 32.

end of the eighteenth-century, when developments in natural philosophy led to the rise of biology and the realisation of a fundamental difference between living, or organic nature and dead, or inorganic matter.'[19]

Second, this Enlightenment-centric reading of organicist history is flawed because it misguidedly presupposes the existence of organicism as a singular, generic phenomenon. Central to van Eck's thesis is the claim that organicism is a broad, non-uniform term lacking in universally applicable definition.

V. Veenhof and van Eck in Conversation

In developing a trialogue between van Eck's critique, the mainstream history of organicism and Veenhof's appropriation of Bavinck's organic idea, three points stand out.[20]

First, the Enlightenment-centric history of organicism, upon which Veenhof's thesis rests, is deeply flawed. Assigning this crucial place to one event implies an essential uniformity as inherent to organicism: it asserts that all organicism, before and after the Enlightenment, can be reduced to the influence of a single historical event. Van Eck's claim is that an Enlightenment-centric history of organicism is incongruent with the facts of history: she finds that post-Enlightenment artistic organicism, for example, grew out of the Vitruvian tradition of the Renaissance.[21] Particularly through her use of the Renaissance figure Alberti, she demonstrates that artistic organicism, from the Medieval period onwards, does not fit into the Enlightenment-centric model.[22]

It seems that van Eck is justified in beginning a critique of generic historical accounts of organicism by denying the place of the Enlightenment as organicism's defining moment. Bearing in mind that Veenhof's account of Bavinck traces his organicism to Schelling (and this on the premise that German Idealism's organicism was a reaction to the post-Enlightenment

---

[19] van Eck, *Organicism in nineteenth-century architecture*, 21.

[20] As she writes on the relationship between Schelling and architecture, van Eck is a useful conversation partner: van Eck, *Organicism in nineteenth-century architecture*, 24, 114–5, 124, 130, 186.

[21] van Eck, *Organicism in nineteenth-century architecture*, 21. As such, van Eck's account of architectural organicism is Vitruvian, rather than Enlightenment-centric. She maintains, nonetheless, that hers is not an all-encompassing study of generic organicism. Her focus is on organicism in the realm of art and architecture. Within this sphere, the Renaissance, rather than the Enlightenment, takes central place. The significance of this claim is that it moves the discussion away from the notion of the 'organic' having a 'general sense of the time' (*à la* Veenhof).

[22] van Eck, *Organicism in nineteenth-century architecture*, 49–67.

mechanism caused by Newton), van Eck's critique has considerable implications for Bavinck studies. Those who understand Bavinck's organic motif as primarily the product of the Enlightenment's various conceptual revolutions may well be misreading him.

Second, van Eck rests a denial of organicism's generic history on the refutation of its generic definition. If marked diversity of definition can be demonstrated among noted organicists, it becomes difficult to maintain that they nonetheless are exponents of a single system with one history.

If organicism is not a uniform process moving through a chain of historical events, it logically follows that there can be no single cross-disciplinary definition of organicism. If van Eck is correct, a paradigm shift becomes necessary in all studies of organicism; Bavinck-related scholarship included. Indeed, if her critique is just, studies of Bavinck's organic motif which presuppose and rest upon a generic history and definition of organicism quickly appear not simply outdated, but factually incorrect.

Post-Enlightenment intellectual life is riddled with organicism. Samuel Coleridge (1772–1834) set a trend for organicist poetry which was followed by John Ruskin and Isaac Williams.[23] In addition to Idealist organicism, many cross-disciplinary examples stand out. Alois Hirt (1759–1839) was the first to use the term *organisch* in the realm of architecture.[24] The debate between Georges Cuvier and Etienne Geoffroy Saint-Hilaire at the Parisian Académie des Sciences in 1830 centred on the use of organicism in science.

The existence of pre-Enlightenment organicism is also beyond doubt. Even excluding the ancient organicism (of which Veenhof writes), strongly organic elements can be seen in the Early Renaissance period. In 1452, Alberti, of whom van Eck makes much use,[25] wrote: '[J]ust as the head, foot, and indeed any member must correspond to each other and to all the rest of the body in an animal, so in a building, and especially a temple, the parts of the whole body must be so composed that they all correspond

---

[23] 'The spirit of poetry, like all other living powers . . . must embody in order to reveal itself; but a living body is of necessity an organized one; – and what is organization, but the connection of parts to a whole, so that each part is at once end and means!' Samuel Coleridge, *Coleridge's Criticism of Shakespeare: A Selection* (London: Athlone Press, 1989), ed. R.A. Foakes, 52.

[24] 'One may consider every work of architecture as an organic whole, consisting of primary, secondary and contingent parts, which stand in definite volumetric relationship to each other. In the case of organic bodies nature herself has determined the relations of the parts to each other in accordance with individual ends. In case of buildings, man is the determinator.' Alois Hirt, *Die Baukunst nach den Grundgesätzen der Alten* (1809), 13.

[25] van Eck, *Organicism in nineteenth-century architecture*, 41–67.

one to another, and any one, taken individually, may provide the dimensions of all the rest.'[26]

The notion that such diverse figures as Aristotle, Alberti, Hirt, Hegel, Ruskin, Cuvier and Saint-Hilaire, in speaking of the organic, were essentially describing the same thing, is hard to sustain. It seems van Eck is correct; organicism possesses neither generic history nor univocal definition. Different people, writing in different contexts on behalf of different disciplines often mean different things despite their use of the same (or similar) nomenclature.

Mattson argues that Veenhof's thesis is flawed in precisely this respect: it operates on the basis that Bavinck's organic motif can be defined by the use of similar terminology in different disciplines and contexts. '[Veenhof's thesis] attempts to explain the meaning of the language, as used by Kuyper and Bavinck, by tracing its historical and philosophical background. While a fascinating study in its own right, from Aristotle to Kant, the Romantics and, finally, Hegel and Schelling, it is nevertheless to engage in the genetic fallacy. That is, one does not explain the meaning of words by tracing their historical origins.'[27]

Citing Bavinck's critique of post-Enlightenment philosophy's relationship to Reformed theology, Mattson makes a strong case that Bavinck himself was against such a hermeneutic: 'No doubt between these two mighty movements of modern history certain lines of resemblance may be traced. But formal resemblance is not the same as real likeness, analogy as identity.'[28]

Third, if the currently accepted history of organicism requires fundamental revision, the sense in which one goes about defining a particular contextual appropriation of organicism must follow suit. This is particularly relevant to Bavinck studies: the interpretation of Bavinck built on a now discredited generic history cannot be maintained. With what, however, should one replace the old hermeneutic? Mattson's suggestion is that Bavinck, in order to find the organic idea, needed look no further than his own Reformed orthodox scholastic tradition. Tentatively, he writes of 'the possibility that the source of Neo-Calvinism's organic metaphor is not primarily 19th century German philosophy at all, but rather a fresh appropriation of its own tradition. Granted, the overall climate of the 19th century certainly provided its own situational motivations for using the terms, but it is at least possible that Kuyper and Bavinck were

---

[26] Alberti, *De re aedificatoria* (1452), VII.5 (Alberti [1991], 199).
[27] Mattson, *Restored To Our Destiny*, 43.
[28] *PR*, 4.

speaking to the critical issues of their day out of resources internal to their own historical-theological tradition. In fact, this hypothesis makes for a far more satisfying account.'[29]

VI. Engagement with Mattson's Critique

Mattson's thesis, an eschatological reading of Bavinck, does not dwell at length on this topic. However, he makes four brief claims which must be scrutinized and merit expansion.

First, he argues, Veenhof's account sits awkwardly with Bavinck's own frequent antagonism towards Hegel and Schelling.[30] Moving away from Veenhof's thesis removes the tension it posits between Bavinck's open aversion to Idealism and his apparent latent dependence on it.

Second, Veenhof fails to account for why Bavinck traces a historical lineage from Cocceius to Schelling, via Bengel, Böhme, Oetinger and Beck,[31] and fails to identify himself with them.[32] The linkage of Böhme's mysticism to Bavinck's organicism is important in Veenhof's analysis.[33] In this respect, one may add that Veenhof's work represents the start of a tradition within which Bavinck and Kuyper are portrayed as 'semi-mystics' writing 'in a manner reminiscent of the *Zeitgeist* of Neo-Idealism'.[34] However, as Mattson acknowledges, Bavinck singularly fails to identify his own organic concerns with Böhme's mysticism.

To the contrary, Bavinck charges Böhme's 'mystical theosophy' with fuelling the growth of nineteenth-century pantheism.[35] The argument that Bavinck stands as Böhme's inheritor at the turn of the twentieth-century seems incongruent with Bavinck's own critique of Böhme's mysticism. In the work of Frederik van Eeden (1860–1932), one finds a Dutch intellectual more obviously indebted to Böhme. Van Eeden, a socialist utopian, wrote of the cosmos in organic terms and was openly influenced by Böhme.[36] However, when one compares the responses to Böhme's mysticism and the

---

[29] Mattson, *Restored To Our Destiny*, 45.

[30] Mattson, *Restored To Our Destiny*, 45.

[31] Veenhof draws this as the line along which organicism developed in German Idealism and was transmitted to Bavinck: Veenhof, *Revelatie en Inspiratie*, 253.

[32] *RD*, 1.1, 64.

[33] Veenhof, *Revelatie en Inspiratie*, 257.

[34] John Vander Stelt, 'Kuyper's Semi-Mystical Conception' in *Philosophia Reformata: Orgaan van de Vereniging voor Calvinistische Wijsbegeerte* 38ᵉ Jaargang 1973, 186, 190.

[35] *RD*, 3.211.

[36] Frederik van Eeden, *The Bride of Dreams* (Teddington: The Echo Library: 2009), tr. Mellie von Auw, 149.

respective eschatologies of Bavinck and van Eeden, it becomes hard to sustain claims of a genetic relationship between Böhme's mysticism and Bavinck's organic motif.

Third, Mattson suggests that reading Bavinck's organic idea as rooted in historic Reformed orthodoxy accords with Bavinck's own rejection of the Hegelian core of his Leiden education.

Fourth, he argues that the relationship of Bavinck to Geerhardus Vos (who strained to differentiate his own use of the organic from that of German Idealism[37]) also points towards Reformed scholasticism as the source of Bavinck's organic idea.

Veenhof's account of the organic motif seems somewhat lacking. Indeed, Mattson's critique makes this plain. One must ask, however, whether Mattson's proposal represents a workable replacement. His conclusion is that '[i]t is therefore simply not necessary for Kuyper and Bavinck to enlist the aid of German Idealism to form their concept of the "organic," because it is already latent in their own tradition. This is not to say that 19th century philosophical preoccupation with teleological concepts of history play no role; it likely provided them the motivation to draw on these internal resources to provide a biblical and Reformed answer to what they viewed as the pantheistic and evolutionary thought-forms of their day. In a word: Kuyper and Bavinck did not speak from their times to their tradition; they spoke from their tradition to their times.'[38]

Like van Eck, Mattson demonstrates the failure of generic historical definitions of organicism. This prompts the following suggestion: the best person to define his use of a term is that person. A term's meaning is deduced primarily from its immediate use in context, rather than its original etymology or historic usage.[39] Indeed, on this point, James Barr inadvertently demolished the foundations of Veenhof's account decades before Mattson's critique came into being.[40]

In asking what Bavinck means by 'organic', it seems odd to begin with Aristotle. One should instead first inquire whether Bavinck ever consciously defined his usage of the word. The same principle applies to movements and disciplines. When probing how the broader neo-Calvinist movement

---

[37] Geerhardus Vos, 'The Idea of Biblical Theology,' *Redemptive History and Biblical Interpretation* (Philipsburg: Presbyterian & Reformed Publishing, 2001), 15–18.

[38] Mattson, *Restored To Our Destiny*, 49.

[39] Mattson, *Restored To Our Destiny*, 43.

[40] James Barr, *The Semantics of Biblical Language* (London: Oxford University Press, 1961), 107–100, 158–60; also see Moisés Silva, *Biblical Words and Their Meaning: An Introduction to Lexical Semantics* (Grand Rapids: Academie/Zondervan, 1983), 35–51.

understood its frequent organic references, one must begin the search for a neo-Calvinist statement on the subject. The viability of Mattson's suggestions depends on whether Bavinck's self-understanding of the organic motif is demonstrably grounded in Reformed orthodoxy.

VII. The Immediate Context of Bavinck's Organic Motif

In looking to avoid the pitfalls of Veenhof's account, the search to define Bavinck's organic motif changes its starting point. Veenhof's order will be reversed: one will move from Bavinck to Aristotle, rather than Aristotle to Bavinck. In that light, the search for a definition begins with Bavinck himself and looks for Bavinck's own writings and theological context to clarify the sense in which he uses organic language, concepts and metaphors.

VIII. Mechanism in Dutch Theology: Scholten and Rauwenhoff

As was noted in Chapter 1, Bavinck emerges at a fascinating time. The backdrop to his story is a complex web of historic, intellectual, linguistic, ecclesiastical and educational factors. Trying to separate these influences is no easy task. However, some feeling for the various factors is necessary in grasping Bavinck's own *Sitz im Leben*. Understanding the particular brand of Reformed theology taught by Scholten and Rauwenhoff at Leiden, Bavinck's *alma matter*, is of considerable importance.[41]

Central to the development of theological mechanism in the Netherlands is Bavinck's former professor Johannes Scholten. Scholten's theology was deterministic, anti-supernatural and monistic. His *Leer der Hervormde Kerk* displays the starkly deterministic nature of his theology. Scholten's worldview can perhaps be fairly labelled as theistic mechanism.[42] A well-publicized debate with Cornelis Willem Opzoomer was pivotal in Scholten's development in this regard. His mature theology coupled absolute predestinationism with the scientific and philosophical determinism of the previous century. As such, his theology made no allowances for special revelation or the miraculous. His basic *modus operandi*, stemming from the

---

[41] For an introduction to Scholten and Rauwenhoff, see Chapter 1, 18–23.

[42] This is further demonstrated in his interactions with S. Hoekstra (Johannes Scholten, *Vrijheid in verband met zelfbewustheid, zedelijkheid, en zonde* (Amsterdam, 1858)) and in his work *The Free Will* (*De vrije wil*, (Leiden: P. Engels, 1859), 257–62).

omnicausality of God, was uninterrupted cause and effect.[43] 'It is in discussing this . . . that Scholten indicates his argument for theism, thus: From the existence and character of nature we are led to believe in a Cause, which as contrasted with nature, its effect, must be infinite, perfect, and self-existent; if infinite and perfect, then one, omnipresent, eternal, and almighty. From the order observed in nature we conclude that this Cause is understanding – a thinking Being, a Spirit.'[44]

Within this system of absolute determinism, God is the Cause and the reason of all else existing as predetermined effect.

In portraying Scholten as an inherently mechanistic thinker, this work consciously departs from an existing assessment of Scholten as having espoused an organic worldview. The most recent work to make this claim is Henk van den Belt's *Autopistia*. Van den Belt asserts that Bavinck's organic thinking came from Scholten, who 'adhered to an organic worldview and rejected a mechanical worldview.'[45] One does note, however, that on this point, van den Belt's reading of Scholten is entirely dependent on that of Veenhof,[46] whose reading of Scholten, in turn, leans heavily on the thesis of Brillenberg Wurth.[47] It should come as no surprise that Scholten, as a nineteenth-century European intellectual, occasionally employed organic imagery in writing.[48] However, the mere presence of organicist language does not mean that one thus automatically has an anti-mechanist worldview. Within the framework of Darwinian evolution, for example, one finds much nineteenth-century organic imagery. However, the 'organism', in this context, is essentially a machine.[49] It is, thus, a logical fallacy to assert that Scholten's use of organic imagery means he has therefore rejected mechanism. In fact, the only concrete assertion that can be made with this fact is that Scholten used organic imagery, and therefore Scholten could belong to almost any nineteenth-century stream of thought. A wider survey of Scholten's writings makes plain that his use of the organic motif was firmly within a closed, mechanical system. Even if Scholten denied that he was a mechanist by *name*, he almost certainly held to a worldview that was mechanical in *nature*.

---

[43] Berkhof, *Two Hundred Years of Theology*, 102.
[44] Vanderlaan, *Protestant Modernism in Holland*, 33.
[45] van den Belt, *Autopistia*, 277, footnote 157.
[46] Veenhof, *Revelatie en Inspiratie*, 260.
[47] Gerrit Brillenburg Wurth, *J.H. Scholten als systematisch theoloog* ('s-Gravenhagen: Van Haeringen, 1927).
[48] Johannes Scholten, *Geschiedenis der godsdienst en wijsbegeerte* (Leiden: Akademische Boekhandel van P. Engels, 1863), 365, 369, 374, 381.
[49] Bavinck's critique of mechanical organicism is found in *Christelijke Wereldbeschouwing*, 61.

Bavinck, as has already been stated, studied under Scholten. The two were personally acquainted. Bavinck's letters to Snouck Hurgronje are peppered with references to Scholten's lectures, and also note Bavinck as having read his *Leer der Hervormde Kerk*.[50]

The new 'modernist' movement established by Scholten via his opening address at Franeker[51] and his *Leer der Hervormde Kerk* was continued by Rauwenhoff. Despite the former's move into ethical theology, Scholten's brand of mechanical theism continued and marked the piety of nineteenth-century Dutch Protestants.[52]

Landwehr's biography of Bavinck notes the presence and international reputation of both Scholten and Rauwenhoff during Bavinck's university years.[53] Bavinck's friend Henry Elias Dosker made similar observations. 'Doctor J.H. Scholten was still there, the founder of that new system of Reformed theology, of which reason, determinism and monism were the main pillars. But Scholten was beyond his prime and no longer swayed the hearts of the students as of yore; his was a setting sun.'[54]

The mere fact that Scholten's immediate influence within the theology faculty was diminishing by Bavinck's time, of course, does not mean that one may assume his monistic determinism to be of no concern to Bavinck. Indeed, quite the opposite is true. Scholten's sun was setting, but it had not yet fully gone down: Bavinck was exposed to his brand of theological mechanism and made great efforts to counter it. The frequent interactions with Scholten's works in *Reformed Dogmatics* make plain that Bavinck saw him as a threat.

Bavinck was aware that Scholten was in some respects influenced by Hegel.[55] In a discussion of ontology, he writes: 'Philosophy, the pure science, specifically logic, is the description of God's being as such. It understands the Absolute in its appropriate correspondent form as thought – in the form of a concept. Along these Hegelian lines, by purifying and deepening the concepts, many thinkers (e.g., Strauss, Biedermann, Ed. von Hartmann, Scholten) attempted to get even closer to transcendent reality.'[56]

---

[50] Bavinck to Snouck Hurgronje, 7 January 1878: 'Ik heb doorgelezen Scholtens *Hervormde Kerk*.' De Bruijn and Harinck, eds., *Een Leidse Vriendschap*, 36.

[51] Mackay, *Religious Thought in Holland*, 88–9.

[52] This is seen in his discussion of prayer in *De vrije wil*, 257–62.

[53] J. Landwehr *Prof. Dr. Herman Bavinck* (Kok: Kampen, 1921), 9.

[54] Dosker, 'Herman Bavinck', 15.

[55] *RD*, 2.43. Elsewhere, Bavinck highlights aspects of Scholten's methodology as Hegelian; Herman Bavinck, 'The Essence of Christianity', in *Essays on Religion, Science and Society*, 39. For a further analysis of Scholten (as a representative of Dutch modernism) as Hegelian, see De Vries, 'The Hexateuchal Criticism of Abraham Kuenen', 33, footnote 7.

[56] *RD*, 2.43.

However, he then distinguishes Scholten's Hegelian aspects from other interpretations of Hegel. 'But in the case of others, Hegel's philosophy led to a totally different outcome. They made the claim that a sense-related representation could never be overcome in the idea of God and therefore ended up in atheism. Feuerbach said that the personal God was nothing other than the essence of humans themselves, and theology nothing but anthropology.'[57]

Thus, one has the immediate context of Bavinck's theological education. His professors presented a worldview marked by deliberate, rigorous mechanism, and an Idealist interpretation of the Reformed tradition with which Bavinck profoundly disagreed.

Such an account is no mere speculation; Bavinck explicitly writes of mechanism's growth in the eighteenth-century,[58] forming the tradition in which Scholten and Rauwenhoff stood. Undoubtedly, his use of the organic was developed to combat the theological appropriation of post-Enlightenment mechanism. In that sense, it is important to frame the development of mechanistic paradigms in the aftermath of the Enlightenment. Insofar as he presents Bavinck's organic motif as developing in protest of this movement, Veenhof is correct.

The debatable aspect of Veenhof's thesis is whether Bavinck used German Idealism, rather than his own Reformed heritage, to do so.

IX. Bavinck's Definition of the 'Organic'

A logical implication of Mattson's critique is that the best placed person to define Bavinck is, invariably, Bavinck himself. Clearly, 'organic' language is a major feature of German Idealism.[59] It is also commonplace in the history of religions school and the Dutch Ethical theologians. The advent of Darwinism, with its notion of the organism in evolution, also significantly overlaps the rise of neo-Calvinism. 'It cannot be denied that the simultaneity of Neo-Calvinism's "organic" emphasis with these wider cultural and intellectual movements is indeed striking. What accounts for this? Are

---

[57] *RD*, 2.43.

[58] 'But in the eighteenth century a gradual change took place. Its way was prepared by Deism, and it emerged for the first time clearly and plainly in Baron d'Holbach's *Système de la nature*, published in 1770, which has rightly been called the bible of materialism. The naturalism it promulgated – which, judging by the time in which the work appeared – was not the fruit of an exact science but the product of a philosophic worldview.' Herman Bavinck, 'Christianity and Natural Science', in *Essays on Religion, Science and Society*, 100–1.

[59] Beiser, *Hegel*, 80.

Kuyper and Bavinck influenced by these trends? If so, the question arises whether they are self-consciously co-opting the language or whether they are somewhat unwitting "children of their time".[60]

It is fair to conclude that Bavinck, a careful and deliberate thinker, would be aware of this. Failure to clearly define the substance of his organic emphasis *contra* Hegel and Schelling would be, in context, a tacit admission that his organic concerns are rooted in an Idealist worldview.[61] The obvious question thus becomes, did Bavinck define his use of 'organic'?

If this question can be affirmatively answered, Bavinck's own definition becomes essential in appropriating the sense in which he uses 'organic' thinking. Returning to the provocative quote given at the outset of this chapter,[62] Bavinck's definition will shed much light on the entirety of his theological system. Indeed, it may provide the basis by which a single theological vision may be spoken of in Bavinck's work.

Tapping into Bavinck's self-conscious formulation of the 'organic' is also of import in examining his critique of Idealist philosophy. Broadly speaking, Bavinck and Hegel are committed organicists. Do they think organic thoughts in substantially the same way?

Both scholars attempt to be rigorously organic in style and substance. Hegel's organicism leads to monism and understands the *telos* of organicism in that light. His organicism is also closely related to his overall panentheistic concerns.

For Hegel, organicism also plays a central role in his absolute idealism. Both fundamental aspects of absolute idealism, its monism and idealism, ultimately presuppose organicism. Monism, in the anti-dualistic sense, is based upon the philosophical organicist thesis that the mental and physical, the ideal and real, are only different stages of development or degrees of organization of a single living force. Idealism rests upon the organicist doctrine that everything in nature and history conforms to a purpose or an end.[63] Does Bavinck's use of the organic resemble this?

---

[60] Mattson, *Restored To Our Destiny*, 42–3.

[61] Mattson hypothesizes that Geerhardus Vos, also a frequent exponent of organicism, keenly felt this potential for misunderstanding; Mattson, *Restored To Our Destiny*, 48, footnotes 151–2.

[62] *RD*, 1.383. 'In Christ, in the middle of history, God created an organic centre; from this centre, in an ever widening sphere, God drew the circles within which the light of revelation shines. . . . Presently the grace of God appears to all human beings. The Holy Spirit takes everything from Christ, adding nothing new to revelation. . . . In Christ God both fully revealed and fully gave himself. Consequently also Scripture is complete; it is the perfected Word of God.'

[63] Beiser, *Hegel*, 81.

In his 1904 work *Christelijke Wereldbeschouwing*[64] Bavinck defined the sense in which he uses the term 'organic'. That Bavinck felt the need to provide this definition strongly suggests that he is not the uncritical inheritor of Schelling and Hegel.

In *CW*, he asserts that, at the most basic level, only two worldviews exist: the theistic and the atheistic.[65] Bavinck associates a mechanical worldview with the latter, and thus demonstrates his dissatisfaction with the theistic mechanism of his Leiden Professors Scholten and Rauwenhoff. The notion of a closed-system universe operating solely by uninterrupted cause and effect (in essence, a mechanical cosmos) is, for Bavinck, irreconcilable with Christian theism. A worldview founded on a Trinitarian doctrine of God must move towards a non-mechanical interpretation of the universe.

'There is a most profuse diversity [in the cosmos] and yet, in that diversity, there is also a superlative kind of unity. The foundation for both diversity and unity is in God. . . . Here is a unity that does not destroy but rather maintains diversity, and a diversity that does not come at the expense of unity, but rather unfolds it in its riches. In virtue of this unity the world can, metaphorically, be called an organism, in which all the parts are connected with each other and influence each other reciprocally.'[66]

In this definition, Bavinck provides four guiding principles within his organic worldview.[67]

First, the created order is marked by simultaneous unity and diversity.[68] This is essential if God is Triune. As the universe itself is a general revelation of God, it must reflect his identity as three-in-one. Reality therefore becomes somewhat triniform: life is a unity of different parts. Perceiving the Trinitarian contours of created reality is of huge importance to Bavinck: 'The Christian mind remains unsatisfied until all of existence is referred back to the triune God, and until the confession of God's Trinity functions at the centre of our thought and life.'[69] Consciously Trinitarian thinkers see life in the light of the Triune God. Organic thinking begins by seeing the

---

[64] Herman Bavinck, *Christelijke Wereldbeschouwing* (Kampen: Kok, 1904). English: *The Christian Worldview*, hereafter referred to as *CW*.

[65] *CW*, 51; 'eigenlijk zijn er dus maar twee wereldbeschouwingen, de theïstische en de atheïstische.'

[66] *RD*, 2.435–6.

[67] In addition to this, Hielema has produced a helpful summary of the broad characteristics of Bavinck's organic thinking; Hielema, *Herman Bavinck's Eschatological Understanding of Redemption*, 59–60.

[68] *CW*, 50; 'Dan alleen komt èn de eenheid èn de verscheidenheid, zoowel het zijn als het worden tot zijn recht, als wij de mechanische en dynamische wereldbeschouwing door de organische vervangen.'

[69] *RD*, 2.330.

universe as the general revelation of God's Trinity. A highly similar thought occurs in Kuyper's *Sacred Theology*.[70]

A theological concern lies at the core of Bavinck's organicism. He wants a Trinitarian appropriation of reality. One may say that for Bavinck, a theology of Trinity *ad intra* requires a cosmology of organicism *ad extra*. Viewed against the backdrop of Scholten's theistic mechanism, one notes that Bavinck found fault with Scholten's doctrine of God, claiming it was more monistic than Trinitarian.[71] It is hardly surprising that having tried to begin from a more thoroughly Trinitarian foundation, Bavinck would go on to form a substantially different worldview.

Bavinck claims that his organic motif begins with reflection on the divine economy. Veenhof recognizes that ancient theological organicism presents in the same context. It is unfortunate that his account places such a strong accent on the influence of Schelling, while failing to explore the relationship between Trinitarian theology and organic cosmology.

However, one may say that Hegel's organicism also develops out of a theological concern. In *The Spirit of Christianity*,[72] his motivation for organic thinking appears to be John 1:1–4. The bare fact of theocentric intentions, however, does not by itself render Bavinck's use of the organic as therefore Hegelian. As will be seen, Bavinck's theocentric starting point is Trinitarian, whereas Hegel's is monistic; and furthermore, his *telos* is non-reductionist, whereas that of Hegel is quite different.

Second, unity precedes diversity.[73] Here, Bavinck is attempting to clarify that 'unity in diversity' is orderly. God creates a singular cosmos. Having spoken time and space into being, he then works to fill this single cosmos with diversity: distinguishing the earth from the celestial bodies, separating land from sea and creating different species of animals. However, in the relationship of unity to diversity, Bavinck's claim is that unity comes first. This precedence finds its cause in God himself. He develops this emphasis in *RD*.[74]

An example of this principle is found in the application of the organic motif to ecclesiology: 'In the first place, therefore, the ingathering of the

[70] Kuyper, *Sacred Theology*, 204. 'In all organic life unity in the germ is first, from which multiplicity spreads itself.'

[71] *RD*, 2.115.

[72] G.W.F. Hegel, 'The Spirit of Christianity and its Fate', *Early Theological Writings*, tr. T. M. Knox (Chicago: Chicago University Press, 1948), 182–301; ed. Herman Nohl, *Hegels' Theologische Jugendschriften* (Frankfurt: Minerva, 1966), 182–301.

[73] *CW*, 51; 'gaat volgens de organische beschouwing het geheel aan de delen, de eenheid aan de veelheid voorafgaat.'

[74] *RD*, 2.435–6.

elect must not be conceived of individualistically and atomistically. The elect, after all, have been given eternally to Christ, are included in the covenant, have all been born in due time from Christ as the body with all its members are all born from the head, and made partakers of all his benefits. The church is an organism, not an aggregate; the whole, in its case, precedes the parts.'[75]

The notion that, within an organism, the whole precedes the parts is also found in Idealist organicism.[76] Both were reacting against the mechanistic notion that the parts come first.

Third, the organism's shared life is orchestrated by a common idea.[77] Again, this combats the idea that 'unity in diversity' is disorderly. Although bodily organs perform different functions, they also work in synchrony to run the same body. In a healthy body, the distinctive organs complement, rather than counter, each other. Here, Bavinck cements the idea that unity in diversity is quite unlike the chaos of multiformity.

Finally, Bavinck crystallizes his organic thinking by noting its teleological definiteness.[78] The organism has a drive towards its goal. The organism, in all its unity and diversity, has been made for the glory of the Triune God. Rather than being well represented in the reduction of the organism's parts into a single, monad-like state, the Trinity is glorified as the organism maintains simultaneous unity and diversity. Interestingly, Bavinck critiques Darwinism as being both 'mechanical' and 'anti-teleological'.[79] The close proximity drawn by Bavinck between the organic motif and the *telos* was noted by Dosker. 'Doctor Bavinck strenuously upholds the central and organic conception of revelation. It occupies a definitely teleological position; it reveals to us the coming of God to humanity, forever to dwell with humankind.'[80]

---

[75] *RD*, 3.524.

[76] G.W.F. Hegel, *The Science of Logic* (Amherst: Prometheus, 1989).

[77] *CW*, 57; 'Zij zijn zelve, niet door uitwendigen dwang, maar innerlijk, in haar eigen wezen, aan gedachte gebonden'; 66, 'Maar al deze onderscheidene schepselen met hunne verschillende substanties, ideeën, krachten en wetten zijn volgens de organische beschouwing opgenomen in één groot geheel en aan een hoogste doel dienstbaar.'

[78] *CW*, 65; 'De organische wereldbeschouwing is daarom ten slotte ook door en door teleologisch, niet in den platten zin van het rationalisme, dat den verstandsmensch als maatstaf en doel van alle dingen beschouwd, maar in dien verheven zin, welken de Schrift ons kennen doet, en waarnaar al wat is door God en tot Zijne eere bestaat. . . . De teleologie is niet met de causale, maar wel met de mechanische beschouwing in strijd, want deze kent geene natuur dan de lichamelijke, geene substantie dan de stof, geen kracht dan de physische en daarom ook geene ander oorzaak dan de mechanische. . . . Maar de organische wereldbeschouwing neemt de schepping, gelijk zij zich geeft, in hare eindelooze verscheidenheid van substantiën en krachten, van oorzaken en wetten.'

[79] *PR*, 12.

[80] Dosker, 'Herman Bavinck', 23.

The last point highlights the major difference between organicism according to Idealism and the neo-Calvinists, between Hegel and Bavinck. Hegel's system operates around a panentheistic doctrine of God. He is concerned with the *Hen kai Pan*. The becoming of God is not just reflected but is actually worked out in the cosmos: it starts as an ontological singularity, differentiates itself into various parts and then integrates these parts into a united whole. One might say that for Hegel, the cosmos is organic because God is organic. More precisely perhaps, God is *in* the cosmos, and both are together in this organic paradigm.[81]

Bavinck, however, differs from this considerably. While he describes many things as 'organic', the notable exception to this pattern regards God himself. The deliberate intent of Bavinck's system, it seems, is to consistently describe the creation as organic and the Creator as Triune. Ontologically, Bavinck posits a rigid separateness between God and the cosmos.[82] The ontology of one does not naturally merge with the other.[83] Bavinck is neither pan- nor panen-theistic.[84] The introduction and conclusion to his organic thought reflect this. Its genesis is not pantheistic, nor is its *telos* monistic. Rather, its goal is to maintain unity and diversity in perpetuity, and that to the glory of the Father, the Son and the Holy Spirit; three eternally coexistent persons in one Godhead.

In relating his doctrines of God and creation to a wider worldview, Bavinck makes a telling statement which reflects the four points given in *CW*. Writing against the cosmologies of Idealist pantheism and Enlightenment mechanism, he claims:

> Scripture's worldview is radically different. From the beginning heaven and earth have been distinct. Everything was created with a nature of its own and rests in ordinances established by God. . . . The foundation of both diversity and unity [point one, unity-in-diversity[85]] is in God. It is

---

[81] 'Both are the same, *becoming*, and although they differ so in direction they interpenetrate and paralyse each other. The one is *ceasing-to-be*: being passes over into nothing, but nothing is equally the opposite of itself, transition into being, coming-to-be. This coming-to-be is the other direction: nothing passes over into being, but being equally sublates itself and is rather transition into nothing, is ceasing-to-be. . . . Each sublates itself in itself and is in its own self the opposite of itself.' G.W.F. Hegel, ed. Stephen Houlgate, *The Hegel Reader* (Oxford: Blackwell Publishing, 1998), 193.

[82] *RD*, 2.30, 158–9.

[83] *RD*, 2.154.

[84] *RD*, 2.111. 'Moreover, with a view to pantheism, which equates the being of God with that of the universe, it is even supremely important to stress the fact that God has a nature of his own, that he is an independent being, whose essence is distinct from that of the universe.'

[85] *CW*, 50.

he who created all things [point two, unity precedes diversity[86]] . . . who continually upholds them in their distinctive natures, who guides and governs them in keeping with their own increated energies and laws, and who, as the supreme good and ultimate goal of all things, is pursued and desired by all things in their measure and manner [point three, the organism's members are driven by a common ideal]. Here is a unity that does not destroy but rather maintains diversity, and a diversity that does not come at the expense of unity, but rather unfolds its riches [point four, the organism's *telos*[87]]. In virtue of this unity the world can, metaphorically, be called an organism, in which all the parts are connected with each other and influence each other reciprocally.[88]

The strange irony of Veenhof's 'two Bavincks' inspired portrayal of the motif is its insistence that the motif, as the property of the 'modern' Bavinck, is a symptom of disunity. Bavinck's own definition of the motif is that it is a profound agent of unity.

X. Bavinck on Cause and Effect

It is worth noting that while the organic motif suited his needs in responding to the mechanical and monistic theology of the Leiden school,[89] his reaction to mechanism was not antithetical.

In his rejection of the mechanistic life and worldview, however, Bavinck acknowledged that the mechanical explanation of the world had a rightful place, but not in the exclusive sense in which it had been embraced.[90] His 1911 article 'Christianity and Natural Science' demonstrates the rationale behind this critique. 'The mechanical explanation of nature is not science but a specific viewpoint among the practitioners of science who are intent on drawing all these phenomena of organic life within the circle of physics, chemistry, and engineering (mechanics) in order to explain them in a purely mechanical and merely quantitative fashion.'[91]

The issue at hand is how one understands God and the cosmos. One's views of the divine and the general revelation of the divine are intertwined.

---

[86] *CW*, 51.
[87] *CW*, 65.
[88] *RD*, 2.435–6.
[89] Bremmer, *Herman Bavinck en zijn Tijdgenoten*, 37–76.
[90] Gleason, 'The Importance of the "Unio Mystica" in Dr. Herman Bavinck's Theology', 5.
[91] Bavinck, 'Christianity and Natural Science', 101.

'God's unity,' he writes, 'brought about the unity of the world.'[92] Misinterpreting God as monistic, Bavinck claims, leads to the misappropriation of the cosmos as exclusively mechanical.[93] Again, one returns to the hypothesis that trinity *ad intra* leads to organicism *ad extra.*

Bavinck saw a degree of mechanism as necessary within an orthodox theology of nature: 'the first and the second article of the Apostles' Creed are mutually related. Nature is a mechanism in which everything moves according to a fixed order, measure, and number.'[94]

The mechanism Bavinck opposes is typified by Ernst Haeckel.[95] Central to Bavinck's viewpoint is: 'Christianity gave to the newer natural science the realisation that nature, however mechanically it may operate, is subject to the spirit and that the whole world is an instrument, an apparatus, for the realisation of an eternal divine plan.'[96]

Bavinck's response to mechanism reflects his nature as a synthetic, rather than strictly antithetical, thinker. Refusing to reject mechanism outright, he rather assigns it a limiting nuance and relocates it within the wider scheme of his organic paradigm: to a certain degree, the cosmos operates mechanically, but this operation is carefully reinterpreted by Bavinck. His notion of mechanism lacks the absolute finality of Haeckel.

XI. The Organic Motif in Wider Neo-Calvinism

By 'organic', Bavinck sees the cosmos as a unity in diversity, whereby unity precedes diversity, and wherein the parts cooperate towards a shared ideal culminating in a non-reductionist *eschaton.* This theological appropriation

---

[92] Bavinck, 'Christianity and Natural Science', 99.
[93] Compare Bavinck's critiques of mechanistic science ('Christianity and Natural Science', 97–102) and theistic mechanism (*RD*, 2.115). For a similar viewpoint, see the later neo-Calvinist Herman Dooyeweerd's assessment of the mechanical worldview: 'But when one conceives of the other distinct aspects of reality – such as the organic, the logical, the historical, etc. – in terms of mechanical motion, then the unrealistic picture of the classical science ideal results. One is then predisposed to think that all other sciences must operate according to the methods of mechanical physics, believing that organic processes, emotional feeling, the historical development of culture, logical processes, economic processes, and so forth must be scientifically approached and explained as processes of mechanical motion which are determined entirely within the chain of cause and effect. . . . The classical ideal of science does not take into account the *order of reality* set by God the creator. In this order we detect the great diversity of aspects, each with its own irreducible nature and law, which proclaims the astonishing richness and harmony of God's creative wisdom. The classical science ideal rejects this great diversity in the order of reality.' Herman Dooyeweerd, *Roots of Western Culture: Pagan, Secular, and Christian Options* (Toronto: Wedge Publishing Foundation, 1979), 173.
[94] Bavinck, 'Christianity and Natural Science', 97.
[95] Ernst Haeckel, *Riddle of the Universe* (Buffalo: Prometheus Books, 1992), 180–2.
[96] Bavinck, 'Christianity and Natural Science', 97.

of the organic motif, for Bavinck, reflects the creation's essential triniformity: like its Creator, it is characterized by profound unity-in-diversity.

Is Bavinck's definition of the organic shared within the wider neo-Calvinist movement?

In the era of Kuyper and Bavinck, Dutch neo-Calvinism consciously positioned itself against the uniform tendencies of their post-Revolution, post-Enlightenment social context. They did so via the axiom of 'unity and diversity', which was usually expressed in their language of the 'organic'. 'Unity and diversity' was, within the neo-Calvinist movement, a deliberate intellectual effort. In their specific desire to preserve diversity (by uniting diverse elements, rather than remove their distinctives and reduce diversity to uniformity), the neo-Calvinists were concerned precisely to facilitate, rather than remove, the tension between distinct elements in a system.

Why did Bavinck, and the wider neo-Calvinist movement, see unity as so conceptually distinct from uniformity? Perhaps the most useful demonstration of this distinction is found in Kuyper's 1864 speech 'Uniformity: The Curse of Modern Life'.[97] This speech marked a key moment in the development of the Anti-Revolutionary Party, which ultimately led to Kuyper's election as Prime Minister of the Netherlands in 1900.

Kuyper begins with a profound hamartiological insight: sin is inherently without creative power. Rather it apes and distorts that which God has created. He portrays sin as God's parodist. 'Sin always acts so: it puts the stamp of God's image on its counterfeit currency and misuses its God-given powers to imitate God's activity. Itself powerless, without creative ideas of its own, sin lives solely by plagiarising the ideas of God.'[98]

As the speech progresses, Kuyper claims that the model by which God builds his kingdom is centred on unity-in-diversity. 'In God's plan vital unity develops by internal strength precisely from the diversity of nations and races.' Sin's parody of this divine plan, he asserts, takes the guise of uniformist reductionism[99]; 'but sin, by a reckless levelling and the elimination of all diversity, seeks a false, deceptive unity, the uniformity of death.'[100] (A highly similar association between uniformity and death is found in Bavinck's work.[101])

[97] Abraham Kuyper, 'Uniformity: The Curse of Modern Life', *Abraham Kuyper: A Centennial Reader*, ed. James Bratt (Eerdmans: Grand Rapids: 1998), 19–44.
[98] Kuyper, 'Uniformity: The Curse of Modern Life', 22.
[99] Kuyper uses the terms 'true uniformity' and 'false uniformity', and 'uniformity' and 'unity' interchangeably. The pairs convey the same meaning.
[100] Kuyper, 'Uniformity: The Curse of Modern Life', 23.
[101] *RD*, 1.367 ff. See also Mattson, 'A "Bath of Deadly Uniformity"', *Restored to our Destiny*, 30–40.

Kuyper's rhetoric focuses on the various aspects of Continental uniformity in the aftermath of the French Revolution. At the levels of architecture, fashion, age-appropriate behaviour, the distinction between masculine and feminine, and language, he charged Europe with becoming a bland, homogenized continent. 'So here we are. Everything has to be equalised and levelled; all diversity must be whittled down. Differences in architectural style must go. Age differences must go. Gender differences must go. Differences in dress must go. Differences in language must go. Indeed, what doesn't have to go if this drive toward uniformity succeeds? For what I have said so far is barely a beginning of the indictment against uniformity.'[102]

Clearly, Kuyper has a paradigmic dislike for what has been more recently called 'world cliché culture'.[103] In direct opposition to this trend for uniformist reductionism, neo-Calvinism valued the uniting of diverse parts while maintaining their distinctives. As his train of thought develops, Kuyper chooses one word to encapsulate this unity-in-diversity worldview: organic. 'There, in a word, lies the profound difference distinguishing the spurious unity of the world from the life-unity designed by God.'[104]

During Bavinck's adolescence, the fledgling neo-Calvinist movement was articulating its worldview as organic (*contra* mechanical) and uniting (*contra* unifying). Can one find supporting evidence from within neo-Calvinism, as it develops, which supports the hypothesis that Kuyper, and then Bavinck, took these concepts from their own Reformed orthodox heritage?

As was previously noted, Kuyper's organic motif has elsewhere been referred to as a 'semi-mystical' and 'neo-Idealist'.[105] Can one substantiate the claim that Kuyper's use of the organic is a rehashed mix of mysticism and Idealism? Such a hypothesis fails to account for the development of Kuyper's theology within his own lifetime, as was seen in Chapter 2's discussion of his developing Calvinist ecclesiology.[106]

Josef Bohatec's article 'The Organic Idea in Calvin's Thought', written in the 1926 neo-Calvinist publication *Antirevolutionaire Staatkunde*,[107] provides

---

[102] Kuyper, 'Uniformity: The Curse of Modern Life', 32.

[103] David Wells, *No Place For Truth: Or Whatever Happened to Evangelical Theology* (Leicester: Inter-Varsity Press, 1993), 53–92.

[104] Kuyper, 'Uniformity: The Curse of Modern Life', 24.

[105] Vander Stelt, 'Kuyper's Semi-Mystical Conception', 186, 190.

[106] Chapter 1, 25–30.

[107] Josef Bohatec, 'De Organische Idee in de Gedachtenwereld van Calvijn', *Antirevolutionaire Staatkunde: Orgaan van de Dr. Abraham Kuyperstichting ter bevordering van de studie der Antirevolutionaire Beginselen* 2ᵉ Jaargang (Kok: Kampen, 1926), 32–45, 153–64, 362–77.

an extended reflection on Kuyper's third Stone Lecture.[108] Bohatec begins with the recognition that the organic motif is central to neo-Calvinism and is one of its great merits.[109] Regrettably, he laments, neo-Calvinism's organic contribution has nonetheless garnered a disproportionate lack of scholarly attention.[110]

In attempting to redress this balance, he carefully constructs the argument that Kuyper first incorporated the organic motif via Calvin's theology of church and state. He argues that a theological usage of the organic idea predates Calvin[111] who appropriated organic thinking against a backdrop of philosophical, legal and constitutional debate.[112] The flow of Bohatec's argument is to first examine the organic notion of church and state in the medieval era,[113] following which he explores Calvin's position on the medieval conception of this organic application[114] before finally probing the relationship of church and state in the light of Calvin's organic idea.[115] Bohatec's engagement with Calvin leads to the conclusion that Calvin's organic conception is not without problems[116]; however, he seems to regard the relationship of organic thinking between Calvin and Kuyper as incontestable.

Bohatec's article is of immediate significance: here, one has an official neo-Calvinist publication voicing the claim that its organic concern has come into their thought world directly from Calvin. This corroborates with Mattson's suggestion that Bavinck and Kuyper drew organic thinking from their Reformed heritage, rather than German Idealism. In short, Veenhof's

---

[108] Kuyper, *Lectures on Calvinism*, 8–109.

[109] 'Het is de groote verdienste van Kuyper en de door hem aangegeven richting in de theologie, te hebben aangetoond, dat, naar de opvatting van het Calvinisme, de menschelijke samenleving, evenals al het bestaande in natuur- en geesteswereld, een organische eenheid vormt, een samenstel van ordinantiën, die de souvereine God aan al het geschapene heeft geschonken en die Hij door Zijn steeds werkzamen, almachtigen wil onderhoudt.' Bohatec, 'De Organische Idee in de Gedachtenwereld van Calvijn', 32.

[110] 'Overigens heeft de wetenschap weinig aandacht geschonken aan de organische idee bij Calvijn.' Bohatec, 'De Organische Idee in de Gedachtenwereld van Calvijn', 32.

[111] 'Calvijn is niet de "uitdenker" der organische idee geweest.' Bohatec, 'De Organische Idee in de Gedachtenwereld van Calvijn', 34.

[112] 'Zij was reeds in de Middeleeuwen en in de Oudheid voorwerp van wijsgeerige, juridische en algemeen-staatsrechtelijke studiën. Men moet daarom zijn (Calvijn's) gedachten in hun geschiedkundig verband plaatsen, om ze in hun wezen te begrijpen.' Bohatec, 'De Organische Idee in de Gedachtenwereld van Calvijn,' 34.

[113] Bohatec, 'De Organische Idee in de Gedachtenwereld van Calvijn', 34–45.

[114] Bohatec, 'De Organische Idee in de Gedachtenwereld van Calvijn', 153–64.

[115] Bohatec, 'De Organische Idee in de Gedachtenwereld van Calvijn', 362–77.

[116] 'Daarover, als ook over de geenszins onder-geschikte plaats van de organische idée in het systeem van den Reformator en haar kultuurhistorische beteekenis, kon hier verder niet worden gesproken.' Bohatec, 'De Organische Idee in de Gedachtenwereld van Calvijn', 373.

account (and the reading of Bavinck which has followed) stands or falls in response to Bohatec's article.

Bohatec presents a compelling case. Context adds much weight to his argument. Bohatec was a Calvin scholar of some repute and was well versed in German intellectual history. As a Vienna-based theologian, he wrote with a degree of external perspective on the development of neo-Calvinism. Furthermore, the *Antirevolutionaire Staatkunde* was a neo-Calvinist publication. Its editors included the noted Kuyperians, Anema, Beumer, Colijn, Dambrink, Dooyeweerd, Rutgers, Schuten and Severijn. Writing within four years of Bavinck's death, and six years from Kuyper's, if Bohatec had utterly misrepresented the organicism of neo-Calvinist theology, one would expect to find some scholarly opposition to his article. However, none has yet come to the fore.

Noting that Bohatec's account was approved by an official publication of the Antirevolutionary Party (of which Kuyper was Prime Minister and Bavinck a Member of Parliament), one can only draw two possible conclusions. First, Bohatec's account is accurate; neo-Calvinism did not take its organic metaphor from German Idealism or earlier theological mysticism. The organic idea is a reflection of its Calvinistic heritage. Alternatively, Bohatec has deliberately covered up neo-Calvinism's dependence on Hegel and Schelling. In doing so, he has attempted to pass off its Idealist past as historic Calvinism.

The facts of history suggest that Bohatec was correct. What cannot be denied is that prior to his immersion in Calvin's theology, Kuyper espoused a mystical, non-organic ecclesiology. After serious interaction with Calvin, Kuyper's ecclesiology becomes organic and non-mystical.

Bohatec's claim that Calvin was an 'organic' thinker is generally held to be credible among Calvin scholars.[117] 'Ever since the work of Joseph Bohatec, Calvin scholars have recognized the "passion for order" in the Reformer's thought. Bohatec concentrated on Calvin's "Pathos der Ordnung" in his treatment of law, society, and the state. According to Bohatec, organic thinking was fundamental to Calvin's thought. As a result, his discussions of society, natural law, and the state reflected his desire for unity, harmony, and order as well as his fear of disorder.'[118]

---

[117] This claim is a central theme in various works by Bohatec: see Josef Bohatec, *Calvin und das Recht* (Feudingen: Buchdruck und Verlags-Anstalt, 1934); *Budé und Calvin: Studien zur Gedankenwelt des französischen Frühhumanismus* (Graz: Böhlau, 1950); *Calvins Lehre von Staat und Kirche* (Breslau: Marcus, 1937).

[118] Susan E. Schreiner, *The Theater of His Glory: Nature and the Natural Order in the Thought of John Calvin* (Durham, North Carolina: The Labyrinth Press: 1991), 3.

Indeed, the general thrust of post-Bohatec Calvin studies has been to discover the precise nature of this order in the Reformer's thought. One thus finds scholars such as Ronald Wallace and Lucien Richard arguing that the renewal of the *imago Dei* provides order to Calvin's spirituality,[119] Benjamin Miller claiming that order is central to Calvin's ecclesiology[120] and Susan Schreiner writing that the nature of providence was Calvin's motivation in this 'quest for order'.[121]

Crucially, Bohatec's article does not feature in the analyses of Veenhof or Mattson. However, when placed in conversation with both, it unquestionably favours the latter over the former. With a measure of reserve, Mattson writes of 'the possibility that the source of Neo-Calvinism's organic metaphor is not primarily 19th century German philosophy at all, but rather a fresh appropriation of its own tradition.'[122] Bohatec's account, considered in context, suggests that the neo-Calvinists themselves would speak of this as fact, rather than possibility.

When examining Bavinck's own summary of Calvin's theology and worldview, the following statement – brief and tantalizing as it may be – adds a subtle but significant force to Mattson's argument that Bavinck drew on the Reformed tradition as the source of his organic thought.

Again and again, Calvin's writings include the phrase *coram Deo*, 'in God's presence'. He sets all things, the whole world and in particular humanity, directly in relation to God and placed before his countenance. He examines everything in light of eternity and throws a glimpse of divine glory to the creation. The whole world, in all its length and breadth, is so to be viewed; as an organic and harmonious whole, between God's design and final goal, for which he intended his creation. It is an instrument, an organ, a musical instrument in his hand, and that for the honour of his name. In this world each creation and circle of life takes its place, heaven and earth, plant and animal, human and angel, family, state and society, vocation, science and art. Through the divine will they are all distinguished with wisdom, God has chosen each for its own role. Each has its own nature and law. However, in their diversity they remain

---

[119] Ronald Wallace, *Calvin's Doctrine of the Christian Life* (Edinburgh & London: Oliver and Boyd, 1959); Lucien Richard, *The Spirituality of John Calvin* (Atlanta: John Knox, 1974).
[120] Benjamin Miller, *Calvin's Doctrine of the Church* (Leiden: E.J. Brill, 1970), 190.
[121] Schreiner, *The Theater of His Glory*, 3.
[122] Mattson, *Restored To Our Destiny*, 45.

one, because they all have their origin in the same divine will and all, whether consciously or not, with or against their will, bring to God the glory that is due.[123]

Evidently, Bavinck explicitly linked his own worldview to that which he found in Calvin's writings.

XII. Conclusion

The recent direction of Bavinck studies may be read as an admission that the nature of his thought has not been adequately understood. Something seems to be missing in the presentation of his theology. Noting that this missing factor appears likely to be a conceptual agent of unity, one has begun this investigation by turning to the organic motif. The earlier departure from both the 'two Bavincks' hypothesis and its consequent interpretation of the motif in Veenhof's work creates the space with which to do so. Having made an initial search for an alternative reading of the motif, one free of outmoded presuppositions, the organic idea offers a great deal of promise. It is, according to Bavinck, a reflection on the triniformity of created reality, and works by holding diverse things together.

To understand Bavinck, one must grapple with the specifics of his recurrent organic motif. The loci within which it occurs are simply too important to ignore. Furthermore, this is evidently a live issue in Bavinck studies: the previously accepted account has come under scrutiny and has been found wanting. The 'two Bavincks' foundation upon which it stands has, through the debate between VanDrunen, Kloosterman and Bolt, recently crumbled. The claim that the organic motif belongs to the 'modern'

---

[123] Herman Bavinck, *Johannes Calvijn* (Kampen: J.H. Kok, 1909), 17–18. Dutch original: 'Telkens komt in Calvijns geschrifteen de uitdrukking voor: coram Deo, in de tegenwoordigheid Gods. Hij stelt de gansche wereld, alle dingen, inzonderheid den mensch, rechtstreeks met God in verbinding en plaatst hen voor zijn aangezicht. Hij beziet alles in het licht der eeuwigheid en werpt over alle schepselen den glans van Goddelijke heerlijkheid. De gansche wereld in al haar lengten en breedten komt in te liggen, als een organisch en harmonisch geheel, tusschen het voornemen Gods en het einddoel, dat Hij met zijne schepping beoogt. Zij is een instrument, een orgaan, een speeltuig in de hand van zijn wil voor de eere van zijn naam. In dit wereldgeheel neemt ieder schepsel en elke levenskring zijn eigen plaats in, hemel en aarde, plant en dier, mensch en engel, gezin, staat en maatschappij, beroep, wetenschap en kunst. Zij zijn alle krachtens den met wijsheid en naar verkiezing te werk gaanden wil Gods onderscheiden; zij hebben allen hun eigen natuur en wet. Maar zij zijn toch in hunne verscheidenheid één, want zij hebben alle hun oorsprong in denzelfden Goddelijken wil en zijn alle, bewust of onbewust, met of tegen hun wil, aan de verheerlijking van Gods deugden dienstbaar.'

Bavinck, and is thus merely another symbol of his irreconcilable internal division, has been publicly called into question.

Initially at least, recent critiques of Veenhof's thesis seem to have some mileage. In approaching the motif without the presuppositions of theological bipolarity, the claim that Bavinck's organic motif is best defined from its immediate, rather than historical–etymological, context is an attractive one. This is particularly the case in the light of Bavinck's own emphases in *CW*, Kuyper's concept of organic unity, Bohatec's assertion that neo-Calvinist organicism is an extension of classical Calvinist theology and Bavinck's own description of Calvin's worldview in organic terms.

The working definition of the organic motif thus develops somewhat. Rather than being a direct import from German Idealist philosophy (thus representing Bavinck's own internal division), one moves to see the organic motif in quite different terms.

As will be seen in the following chapters, there is a close relationship between the Trinity and the organic motif in numerous sections of Bavinck's work. In short, one finds that he invokes the organic motif to explain the sense in which the archetypal (Trinitarian) unity of the Godhead acts as the foundation for all consequent ectypal (triniform) unity in the creation. The motif is thus viewed as an agent of conceptual unity, one grounded in Trinitarian foundations and moving towards a triniform goal. The meaning with which Bavinck loads the term begins with a concatenation of unity and diversity (this being rooted in the Trinity, rather than the monism of Idealist thought). Within this, unity is first accounted for, following which it is established that the diverse parts work to a shared ideal. That these parts eternally maintain their pattern of unity-in-diversity (rather than blend into monadic uniformity) is also anti-Idealist. With this in mind, it becomes difficult to sustain that the motif arrived in Bavinck's thought in an unmodified, Idealist sense, and that he therefore used the term in the 'universal sense of the time' (if such a conceptual homogeneity exists).

In reading the organic motif as a Trinitarian concern, the obvious question raised is, of course, whether the Trinity is responsible for the organic motif or *vice versa*. Particularly in Chapter 4, which explores Bavinck's concerns for theocentrism and (in reaction to Scholten's apathy towards the Trinity) using the Trinity as the reference point for all Christian thought, it will be argued that Bavinck intends to place the Trinity first.

The remainder of this book will thus attempt to develop this alternative reading of Bavinck's organic motif in considering the possibility that there is indeed only one Herman Bavinck. In doing so, it will build on the hypothesis that, for Bavinck, this *leitmotif* is the fruit of intense and far-reaching reflection on the created reality in relation to the Trinity. As such, its title, *Trinity and Organism*, attempts to capture the great emphases of Bavinck's dogmatic efforts. Trinity *ad intra* leads to organism *ad extra*.

Chapter 4

The Organic Motif and the Doctrine of God

I. Introduction

Having demonstrated crucial flaws in the formerly normative 'two Bavincks' hermeneutic and its consequent effect on the previously accepted definition of Bavinck's organic motif (wherein various connections are made to identify his core theological identity as irreparably divided, with the organic motif belonging to the 'modern' Bavinck's following of Hegel, Schelling *et al.*) the remaining chapters of this book proceed towards an alternative reading of Bavinck. In the process, one attempts to demonstrate that Bavinck's basic identity and concerns were primarily tied to the thoroughgoing Trinitarianism of historic Reformed orthodoxy.

As it has become increasingly difficult to sustain the claim that the 'modern' Bavinck drew his ever-present organic concerns from Idealist philosophy and Ethical theology, one moves instead to explore the hypothesis that Bavinck's theology of Creator as Trinity necessitates the conceptualization of creation as organism: Trinity *ad intra* leads to organism *ad extra*. The exploration of how Bavinck's view of the Creator affected his view of the created is, in essence, a wider exploration of his tantalizing statement that '[t]he thoughtful person places the doctrine of the trinity in the very centre of the full-orbed life of nature and mankind. . . . The mind of the Christian is not satisfied until every form of existence has been referred to the triune God and until the confession of the trinity has received the place of prominence in our thought and life.'[1]

As such, one attempts to portray Bavinck as a theologian of twofold intent. In context, his first move is to reprioritize the divine triunity (*contra* Scholten's Remonstrant-like view of the Trinity as a matter of secondary importance). Following this, Bavinck's goal in orbing a triniform worldview is to seek out the complex, interconnected web of *vestigia trinitatis*. Beginning

---

[1] Bavinck, *The Doctrine of God*, 329.

at Bavinck's own starting point (the doctrine of God) before progressing to the general and special sense in which the Trinity practices self-disclosure, it will be shown that where Bavinck finds these *vestigia*, his motif of choice is that of the organic.

In pursuing this hypothesis, one consciously departs from Berkouwer's claim that for Bavinck, the organic idea was primarily a pragmatic choice: his assertion is that the motif had no principled foundation in theology; rather it was a coincidentally useful image that Bavinck saw fit to use.[2] Although it cannot be denied that organicist imagery formed a major feature of nineteenth-century European intellectual life and that Bavinck reflects the aesthetics (though as has already been argued, not the substance) of his *milieu*, Berkouwer's assessment charges him with an uncharacteristic passivity of thought. It would have one believe that there was no theological rationale whatsoever behind the motif chosen while Bavinck cautiously treads through what he admits to be intellectual holy ground: God's self-revelation as Three-in-One.

When the radical theocentrism of Bavinck's work is explored (and the close bond between the *vestigia trinitatis* and the organic motif is thus noted), it becomes hard to sustain the aforementioned charge of passive pragmatism.

The numerous layers of unity and diversity within the Godhead provide the foundation upon which Bavinck prioritizes the sin–grace antithesis and which, in turn, supports the synthetic character of the 'grace restores nature' paradigm.

It will be argued that the capacious neo-Calvinist worldview, of which Bavinck was so typical, is rooted in a richly Trinitarian, catholic and Reformed doctrine of God. Indeed, it is the triune, non-sectarian nature of this doctrine of God that lends the neo-Calvinist worldview its coherence and universality.

II. Bavinck, the *Vestigia Trinitatis* and the Organic Motif

In speaking explicitly of the *vestigia trinitatis* in relation to Bavinck's work, one must carefully explain the sense in which that term is invoked. While Bavinck's driving conviction is that nature and history are replete with the hallmarks of triniformity, he does not reflect the Reformers' reticence,

---

[2] Berkouwer, *Zoeken en Vinden*, 62. Gleason supports this reading of the motif: Ron Gleason, 'Herman Bavinck's Doctrine of the Sacraments of the Church: The Sacraments as Means of Grace', (unpublished paper), 3.

which is reflected throughout the later Reformed tradition, to speak in terms of the *vestigia trinitatis*. 'The Reformers tended not only to defend the traditional doctrine of the Trinity as biblical but also to deemphasise the authority of the traditional trinitarian terminology – particularly the more speculative language of the medieval scholastics concerning the character of the trinitarian emanations in the Godhead. The patristic metaphors and various references to *vestigia trinitatais*, whether in the human frame or in the world at large, never became major elements in the doctrinal expositions of the Reformers.'[3]

Most interesting is that while Bavinck consciously locates himself as a son of the Reformation, he does not abstain from the language of the *vestigia*. Rather, he makes careful use of the terminology and, most interestingly, binds it to the organic motif.

> On the other hand, it follows from the doctrine of human creation in the image of God that this image extends to the whole person. While all creatures display *vestiges* of God, only a human being is the *image* of God. . . . Man is the image of God because and insofar as he is truly human, and he is truly and essentially human because, and to the extent that, he is the image of God. Naturally *just as the cosmos is an organism* [italics added] and reveals God's attributes more clearly in some than in other creatures, so also *in man as an organism* [italics added] the image of God comes out more clearly in one part than another, more in the soul than in the body, more in the ethical virtues than in the physical powers.[4]

His explicit willingness to use the language of the *vestigia* is perhaps slightly more evident in the Dutch original: 'Alle schepselen vertoonen vestigia Dei, de mensch is imago Dei.'[5]

The general trend away from discussion of the *vestigia* within the Reformed tradition is explained in the background to the term. In Patristic theology, one finds a growing awareness that the creation is profoundly marked by the specifically triune nature of its Creator. However, the sense in which these triune imprints should be understood was carefully qualified. Augustine, for example, refused to draw a Trinitarian analogy from the shared life of father, mother and child. Instead, he saw a mark of the Trinity in the more abstract

---

[3] Richard Muller, *Post-Reformation Reformed Dogmatics: The Rise and Development of Reformed Orthodoxy, ca. 1520 to ca. 1725, Vol. 4: The Triunity of God* (Grand Rapids: Baker Academic, 2003), 151.
[4] *RD*, 2.555.
[5] Herman Bavinck, *Gereformeerde Dogmatiek* Tweede Deel (Kampen: J.H. Kok, 1928), 516.

interface of the mind's various facets.[6] Augustine's conviction was that cosmic triniformity ought not to be sought out in trite analogies; rather, the existence of the *vestigia* grounded all reality in the pre-existence of its Triune Creator. 'Yet it is not wholly dissimilar; for what does not bear some likeness to God, according to its own kind and measure, seeing that God has made all things exceeding good, precisely because He Himself is the highest good? Insofar, therefore, as anything is, it is good, that is, to the extent it bears some resemblance, though very remote, to the highest good.'[7]

However, by the medieval era the approach to the *vestigia trinitatis* had become markedly speculative and was often used to find vestigial 'proofs' for the Trinity. Carrying on Augustine's Trinitarian concept of the *imago Dei*, whereby the human being bears the divine image in the triad of heart, mind and will,[8] some argued that natural man remained (albeit in a limited sense) capable of a Trinitarian understanding of God.[9]

Studies of post-medieval Europe give numerous examples of this approach to the *vestigia*. In 1620, for example, John Donne remarked in a sermon: 'It is a lovely and religious thing, to finde out *Vestigia Trinitatis*, Impressions of the Trinity, in as many things as we can. . . . Let us therefore, with Saint Bernard, consider *Trinitatem Creatricem*, and *Trinitatem Createm*, a Created and a Creating Trinity; a Trinity, which the Trinity in Heaven, Father, Son and Holy Ghost, hath created in our soules, Reason, Memory and Will.'[10]

The same trend is evident in the poetry of Donne's contemporary John Davies of Hereford.

> So the *Soule's* parted (though in substance one)
> In 't *Vnderstanding, Will* and *Memory*,
> These *Powres* or *Persons* makes one *Trinity*,
> Yet one *substance* indiusible,
> Which perfect *Trinity* in *Vnity*,
> (Both being *Spirituall* and inuisible)
> Doe make the Soule, hir God so right resemble.[11]

---

[6] Augustine, *On the Trinity* (Cambridge : Cambridge University Press, 2002), ed. Gareth B. Matthews, XII.5.5–7.12.

[7] Augustine, *On the Trinity*, 70. On this passage, Klinck comments: 'Mundane analogies, then, are not merely illustrative parallels of the Trinity; they are embodiments of the archetypal trinitarian pattern.' Dennis R. Klinck, '*Vestigia Trinitatis* in Man and his Works in the English Renaissance', *Journal of the History of Ideas*, Vol. 42, No. 1 (January–March 1981), 14.

[8] Augustine, *On the Trinity*, XII, 6.

[9] John P. Dourley, 'The Relationship between Knowledge of God and Knowledge of the Trinity in Bonaventure's *De mysterio trinitatis*', *San Bonaventura Maestro*, ed. A. Pompei, vol. II, 4–45.

[10] George R. Potter and Evelyn M. Simpson, eds., *The Sermons of John Donne*, 10 Volumes (Berkley and Los Angeles, 1953–59), III, 144–5. This should perhaps be '*Trinitatem Creatum*'.

[11] Alexander B. Grosart, ed., *The Complete Works of John Davies of Hereford* (Edinburgh, 1878), 19.

III. The Triad and Unity-In-Diversity

Bavinck's response to both medievalism's focus on triadic patterns and his own tradition's reaction to this trend is carefully measured.

It begins with the admission that threefold patterns are of considerable significance in Scripture. Creation is structured in a threefold manner: heaven, earth and that which is under the earth; three ethnic groups emerge from Noah's three sons; the covenant of grace comes in three dispensations; there were three patriarchs; Christ's public ministry lasted for three years; Christ had three offices; he was crucified on one of three crosses and entombed for three days; he kept close company with three specific disciples; faith, hope and love form the principal Christian virtues and so forth.[12]

He recognizes that outside Scripture, three is also a highly prominent number. The History of Religions School in which Bavinck was educated had noted triad-like patterns in various pagan religions: the Norse gods Odin, Thor and Loki; the three Sephiroth of Kabbalah and so on. He regards these as lesser, however, than the 'logical analogies' in Augustine's theology.[13] In this context, Bavinck reflects the Reformed in his critique of the medieval penchant for triads. 'Medieval theology, working out these ideas in multiple ways, looked for triads everywhere. It found an analogy of the Trinity in the trivium of grammar, dialectic and rhetoric; in the three branches of philosophy: logic, physics and ethics; in the first, second and third persons in grammar; in the active, passive and middle voices; in the singular, dual and plural numbers . . . and so forth.'[14]

Fascinatingly, Bavinck turns this discussion onto Hegel and Schelling, claiming that their triplicity, particularly in relation to Hegel's thesis–antithesis synthesis, stems from this medieval concern. The difficulty with this primarily triad-based approach to the *vestigia*, as Bavinck seems to sense, is ascertaining where the boundaries lie: 'Is every triad to be regarded as an analogue of the Trinity?'[15]

In terms of Bavinck's own Reformed tradition, Calvin, who so regularly draws support for his theology from Augustine, criticizes the Bishop on this point. 'Augustine, beyond all others, speculates with excessive refinement, for the purpose of fabricating a Trinity in man.' In doing so, however, Calvin does not dismiss altogether that the cosmos (and the human being above

---

[12] *RD*, 2.322.
[13] *RD*, 2.323.
[14] *RD*, 2.323–4.
[15] Klinck, '*Vestigia Trinitatis* in Man and his Works in the English Renaissance', 15.

all) bears some Trinitarian imprint. His preference, unsurprisingly, is to say
nothing rather than speculate, making the bare statement: 'I acknowledge,
indeed, that there is something in man which refers to the Father, and the
Son, and the Spirit.'[16]

Calvin's pattern of aversion towards speculation (particularly where the
apparent *vestigia* are used within the framework of natural theology in order
to assert divine triunity), consequent reluctance to use the traditional
vocabulary which had, by this point, become closely associated with this
medieval approach, and more strictly revelation-based approach to cosmic
triniformity, form the tradition in which Bavinck is situated.[17] As will be
seen, Bavinck was not against triads per se. Rather, he was strictly opposed
to speculation and natural theology's use of trinitarian analogies as 'proofs'
for God's triunity. His key development within the idea of *vestigia trinitatis*,
however, lies in the establishment of the non-numerical paradigm of unity-
in-diversity (rather than the medieval triad form) as the norm in terms of
triniform hallmarks.

In doing so, Bavinck carefully frames a doctrine of God somewhere
between those of Calvin and Augustine. Generally speaking, he is bolder
than Calvin in exploring the limits of Trinitarianism: his readiness to call
the human being the 'image of the Trinity' makes this plain.[18] He does,
however, share both Calvin's reluctance to speculate and, to a certain extent,
later Reformed Orthodoxy's rejection of the all-pervasive hunt for 'triads'.
Bavinck echoes this concern, though he is far more reserved in critiquing
Augustine. In typically synthetic fashion, however, Bavinck refuses to deny
the presence of triad patterns in the Trinity's cosmos.

> There is much truth in the belief that creation everywhere displays to us
> vestiges of the Trinity. And because these vestiges are most clearly evident
> in 'humanity', so that 'human beings' may even be called 'the image of
> the Trinity', 'humanity' is driven from within to search out these vestiges.
> The perfection of a creature, the completeness of a system, the harmony
> of beauty – these are finally manifest only in a triad. The higher a thing's
> place in the order of creation, the more it aspires to the triad. One senses
> this effect even in the religious aberrations of humankind. Schelling's

---

[16] John Calvin, *Commentary on Genesis*, Gen. 1:26 (*CTS Genesis*, I), 93.
[17] For a fuller summary of this tradition, see Muller, *Post-Reformation Reformed Dogmatics: The Rise and Development of Reformed Orthodoxy, ca. 1520 to ca. 1725, Vol. 4: The Triunity of God,* 157–65.
[18] *RD*, 2.333.

attempt to interpret mythology along trinitarian lines, for example, is more than a genial fantasy.[19]

Clearly, Bavinck moves to defend Augustine's notion of the *vestigia* in all creatures (and especially in humans)[20] noting that the Bishop 'frankly admits that all these comparisons are but analogies and images, and that in addition to similarity there is also great difference.'[21] As such, Bavinck's work reads as an attempt to redeem, rather than react against, Augustine's position. His conviction is that one should not charge Augustine with the excesses of the medieval period.

However, in noting Bavinck's divergence from the Reformed tradition on this point, one ought not to portray the tradition as utterly univocal on this matter. Calvin's close friend, Pierre Viret (1511–71), made extensive use of patristic metaphors, particularly those of Augustine, and also employed much medieval trinitarian terminology.[22] The settled point across the Reformed tradition seems to be its rejection of the *vestigia* as proofs for the Trinity and the concurrent insistence on the impossibility of finite humans progressing from finite analogies to the infinite. 'Scripture repeatedly tells us that humankind was made in the image of God, not that we have been modelled on Christ, but that he was made [human] in our likeness (Rom. 8:3; Phil. 2:7–8); Heb. 2:14), and that we, having been conformed to the image of Christ, are now again becoming like God (Rom. 8:29; 1 Cor. 15:49; 2 Cor. 3:18; Phil. 3:21; Eph. 4:24; Col. 3:10; 1 John 3:2). It is therefore much better for us to say that the triune being, God, is the archetype of man, while at the same time exercising the greatest caution in the psychological exploration of the trinitarian components of man's being.'[23]

For Bavinck, the three-in-one nature of the Godhead is an utterly unique concept. Although he is sympathetic to the 'higher' analogies of Augustinian logic, his conviction nonetheless remains that triad analogies will always be few in number and should be viewed in strictly analogous terms. The true nature of the three-in-one Godhead cannot be replicated elsewhere. Indeed, even the non-numerical principles of unity-in-diversity are reflected only

---

[19] *RD*, 2.333.

[20] Augustine, *On the Trinity* IV, 10; XV, 2.

[21] *RD*, 2.326.

[22] Pierre Viret, *Exposition familière de l'oraison de notre Seigneur Jésus Christ* (Geneva, 1548), 165. See also Amyraut, *De mysterio trinitatis* (1661), III, 132, 135–49; and Leigh, *Treatise*, II.xvi (126), cited in Muller, *Post-Reformation Reformed Dogmatics: The Rise and Development of Reformed Orthodoxy, ca. 1520 to ca. 1725, Vol. 4: The Triunity of God*, 159.

[23] *RD*, 2.555.

analogously within the cosmos. The divine unity-in-diversity is, in Bavinck's words, 'absolute'.

> The Trinity reveals God to us as the fullness of being, the true life, eternal beauty. In God, too, there is unity in diversity, diversity in unity. Indeed, this order and this harmony is present in him absolutely. In the case of creatures we see only a faint analogy of it. Either the unity or the diversity does not come into its own. Creatures exist in time and space, exist side by side, and do not interpenetrate each other [like the persons in the Trinity]. Among us unity exists only by attraction, by the will and the disposition of the will; it is a moral unity that is fragile and unstable. And where there is a more profound physical unity as, say, between the capacities of a single substance, there is no independence, and the unity swallows up the diversity. But in God both are present: *absolute unity as well as absolute diversity* [italics added]. It is one selfsame being sustained by three hypostases. This results in the most perfect kind of community, a community of the same beings; at the same time it results in the most perfect diversity, a diversity of divine persons.[24]

That said, Bavinck develops a worldview around the notion that the imprints of the Trinity are everywhere. This doctrine is reworked whereby the medieval norm, which was to prioritize a limited number of triadic forms, is inverted: although Bavinck does not entirely dismiss tripartism, he primarily locates the *vestigia* in the non-numerically oriented paradigm of 'unity-in-diversity'.[25] By moving the *vestigia* away from the numerically exclusive triad pattern and instead strongly emphasizing triniformity in the bare presence of united–diversity, Bavinck believes that he has the only true basis upon which to seek the hallmarks of the Trinity in every context.

> There is nothing despicable or sinful in matter. The visible world is as much a beautiful and lush revelation of God as the spiritual. He displays his virtues as much in the former as in the latter. All creatures are embodiments of divine thoughts, and *all of them display the footsteps or vestiges of God*. But all *these vestiges, distributed side by side in the spiritual as well as the material world, are recapitulated in man* and so *organically connected* [italics added]

---

[24] *RD*, 2.331–2.

[25] Bavinck's understanding of the *vestigia* in the *imago Dei*, for example, does not follow Augustine's triad of *memoria, intellectus, voluntas*. Rather, he accentuates 'the very diversity and abundance' of the human being's 'psychic capacities and activities' in which 'we can see features of the image of God'. *RD*, 2.557.

and highly enhanced that they clearly constitute the image and likeness of God. . . . Thus man forms a unity of the material and spiritual world, a mirror of the universe, a connecting link, compendium, the epitome of all of nature, a microcosm and, precisely on that account, also the image and likeness of God, his son and heir, a micro-divine-being (*mikrotheos*).[26]

Rather than ignoring the vastness of the cosmos to find the elusive triad example, a primarily non-numerical concept of the *vestigia* permits one to commandeer and rephrase Kuyper's famous dictum: 'There is not a square inch in the whole domain of our cosmic existence over which the Triune God, who is Sovereign Creator of all, does not cry: "Mine!"'

In this respect, Bavinck's doctrine of God, by virtue of its outstanding emphases on the diversity and oneness of the Godhead, is the foundation for an important development in the Reformed tradition. It represents the neo-Calvinist redemption of the 'marks of the Trinity' concept. In doing so, Bavinck shows that one can be wholly against natural theology *and* wholly for the *vestigia trinitatis*. He moves away from the general post-Reformation aversion to the traditional terminology and, as such, reinvigorates the concept while asking profound questions on the consequences of God's Triunity for the Christian worldview. Whenever the *vestigia trinitatis* is referred to in relation to Bavinck's doctrine of God, it is therefore not used in the medieval sense. Rather, the phrase is qualified to mean that in Bavinck's understanding of Trinity and cosmos, *the Trinity is wholly unlike anything else, but everything else is like the Trinity.* That which is like the Trinity is that which Bavinck consistently describes via the organic motif.

The drive of this chapter is to prove that a Trinitarian, Calvinistic reading of Bavinck's doctrine of God and his pervasive organic motif sheds much light on this theme.

IV. Structural Theology and the Doctrine of God

A new, theocentric reading of Bavinck appears warranted by the theological structure of *Reformed Dogmatics*. Following its setting forth of theology's first principles (Volume One: *Prolegomena*), Bavinck's *Dogmatics* unfolds along an explicitly theocentric pattern. Volume Two, *God and Creation* is overwhelmingly concerned with God the Father. Volume Three, *Sin and Salvation in Christ* emphasizes the redemptive work of God the Son. The

---

[26] *RD*, 2.562.

onus of Volume Four, *Holy Spirit, Church and New Creation*, is God the Spirit, who applies everything accomplished by the Son.

A point of similarity between Bavinck and Karl Barth can be seen in the way that both responded to the dearth of systematic theology in their respective contexts by resurrecting the concept of dogmatics. More so than this, their respective works follow a highly similar triniform metanarrative: the assertion of theological methodology is then expressed in Triune-shaped retelling of redemptive history.

Barth's *Kirchliche Dogmatik* begins with *Prolegomena: Die Lehre vom Worte Gottes* (*CD* 1), before progressing into *Die Lehre von Gott* (*CD* 2) and *Die Lehre von der Schöpfung* (*CD* 3), and *Die Lehre von der Versöhnung* (*CD* 4, which includes Barth's Christology). Barth died before the completion of Volume 5, which appears to have been intended as a tome on redemption under the heading of Pneumatology.[27]

Interestingly, both dogmatic works bear a striking structural similarity to the progression of the Apostles' Creed. In its three sections, the Creed is also triniform, first outlining the Father's role in creation,[28] then describing Christology and salvation[29] and concluding with Pneumatology in relation to ecclesiology and consummation.[30]

In the same vein one finds Calvin's *Institutes*. Parker has argued that Calvin deliberately fashioned the *Institutes* after the Apostles' Creed.[31] Luther's Small Catechism[32] and the Trinity[33] have also been cited as structuring devices. These are, however, by no means settled views.[34] A strong case can also be made to argue that Calvin makes use of a simpler, binary structural theology: God as Creator and God as Redeemer.[35]

Although the *Institutes* do broadly follow the Creed's theology, their genetic match is not exact. In titling his third book, for example, Calvin makes no mention of the Holy Spirit. If one logically follows the Creed, the resurrection should come in Book Four. It is, however, dealt with by Calvin

---

[27] This seems logical from the progression of *Die Offenbarung Gottes in Barth's Prolegomena* §§ 8–18: *Der dreieinige Gott* §§ 8–12, *Die Fleischwerdung des Wortes* §§ 13–15, *Die Ausgießung des Heiligen Geistes* §§ 16–18.

[28] 'I believe in God the Father Almighty, maker of heaven and earth . . . '

[29] 'And in Jesus Christ his Son, our only Lord . . . '

[30] 'I believe in the Holy Ghost . . . '

[31] THL Parker, *Calvin's Doctrine of the Knowledge of God* (Edinburgh: Oliver & Boyd, 1969), 6.

[32] JI Packer, 'Foreword', xi, in *A Theological Guide to Calvin's Institutes*, eds. David Hall and Peter Lillback (Phillipsburg: Presbyterian & Reformed Publishing, 2008).

[33] Philip Butin, *Revelation, Redemption, and Response: Calvin's Trinitarian Understanding of the Divine-Human Relationship* (New York: Oxford University Press, 1995), 19, 124.

[34] For a summary of the various viewpoints, see Charles Partee, *The Theology of John Calvin* (Louisville: Westminster John Knox, 2008), 35–43.

[35] E.A. Dowey, *The Knowledge of God in Calvin's Theology* (Grand Rapids: Eerdmans, 1994), 41–9.

in Book Three. These differences prompt Lane to remark that 'though there are indeed many parallels between the structure of the *Institutes* and that of the Apostles' Creed, if Calvin did intend to base his work upon it, one can only say that he made a bad job of it.'[36] In Parker's defence, however, he has elsewhere stated that Calvin's structural use of the Creed was never that of rigid exposition or fixed replication. Speaking of the 1559 final edition of the *Institutes*, he writes: 'This edition of the *Institutio* is not, however, a direct exposition of the Creed. Only rarely (as Book II, ch. xvi) does it become this. Nor are there chapters devoted specially to its exposition. . . . But even when the Creed is not visible, we should bear it in mind as a character waiting in the wings. What is more, the order of topics in the Creed is not strictly kept. . . . Yet the place of the Creed in the *Institutio* is not purely formal. It determines the understanding and interpretation of the work. We may therefore complete our labelling of the recensions by calling this the "credal" *Institutio*.'[37]

Such a comment is perhaps helpful in appreciating Bavinck's use of structural trinitarianism. Clearly, there is a numerical similarity between the four books in Calvin's *Institutio* and Bavinck's *Dogmatiek*. However, the progression within those volumes is undeniably distinct. Unlike Calvin, whose epistemology is laid out only briefly in the first book of the Institutes,[38] Bavinck begins by dedicating the first volume of Reformed Dogmatics to this subject. That *Reformed Dogmatics* so commences is necessitated by its historical–intellectual context: writing post-Enlightenment, Bavinck is required to justify his epistemological foundations in a way that Calvin never was.[39] Following this, the flow of Bavinck's material is explicitly closer to the Creed than that of Calvin.

Parker's Guide to Calvin makes a subtle but nonetheless important point: in reworking the final edition of the *Institutes* to follow the contours of the Creed more closely (though not strictly), Calvin designed the *Institutes* as a

---

[36] Anthony Lane, *A Reader's Guide to Calvin's Institutes* (Grand Rapids: Baker, 2009), 22.

[37] THL Parker, *Calvin: An Introduction to his Thought* (London: Continuum, 1995), 8.

[38] Calvin, *Institutes* I, 1–8.

[39] It should be noted, however, that Bavinck's sense of obligation to begin Dogmatics with Prolegomena was not universally shared among late nineteenth-century Reformed systematic theologians. The dogmatics of Bavinck's historical contemporary, Samuel Buel, begins with the doctrine of God and contains no prolegomena: Samuel Buel, *A Treatise on Dogmatic Theology*, Vol. 1 (New York: Thomas Whittaker, 1890). Robert Dabney's *Systematic Theology* commences with a brief survey of recent epistemological challenges to theism. It is not, however, a thorough prolegomena *à la* Bavinck: Robert Dabney, *Systematic Theology* (St. Louis: Presbyterian Publishing Company, 1871). Charles Hodge comes closest to Bavinck in terms of prolegomenous breadth and depth: Charles Hodge, *Systematic Theology* (Edinburgh: Thomas Nelson & Sons, 1880), 1–334. None of these works, interestingly, displays Bavinck's structural allegiance to the Apostles' Creed.

profound display of theological catholicity. 'In the description of the shape
of the *Institutio* we have also been given clues to its character. The doctrines
which go to make up the work are no longer a set of *loci communes* selected
and arranged by a private theologian. They now claim for themselves the
reflected authority of the oldest working Creed in Christendom, the Creed
assented to by the Orthodox, the Roman Catholics, the Lutherans, the
Reformed and the Church of England.'[40]

For Bavinck, the same sentiment perhaps carries a more pointed
resonance. In its name, Bavinck has identified his work with a particular
theological tradition. This is theology by a son of the Reformation. In its
nature, however, it lays claim both macro- and microcosmically to a deep
and wide catholicity. This is an exposition of a universal creed written a
millennium before the Reformation. By way of its structural trinitarian
theology, *Reformed Dogmatics* thus reflects the theme of his earlier address to
the Theological Faculty of Kampen, *De Katholiciteit van Christendom en Kerk.*[41]
Indeed, this *tournure d'esprit* was captured in a recent Dutch re-edition of
various shorter articles and speeches by Bavinck: *Gereformeerde Katholiciteit.*[42]
Bavinck was a Reformed catholic.[43] 'Furthermore we must not be blind to
the great faith, true conversion, complete surrender, fervent love of God
and neighbour evident in the life and work of many a Roman Catholic
Christian. The Christian life is too rich to unfold its full glory in only one
form or within the walls of one church.'[44]

Interestingly, the French Reformed theologian Auguste Lecerf criticized
him for exactly this point: 'A canonical discipline: such is the character we
wished to give our work. We have tried to do this until now, even through
H. Bavinck, who, to us, has come closest to the Ideal that we are
contemplating. . . . H. Bavinck, in the introductory section of his Reformed
Dogmatics, that veritable summary of contemporary Calvinism, goes much
further. He gives an outline of the principles of knowledge, both general
and religious, and he formulates the theory of the principles of orthodox

---

[40] THL Parker, *Calvin: An Introduction to His Thought*, 8–9.

[41] Herman Bavinck, *De Katholiciteit van Christendom en Kerk* (Kampen: Zalsman, 1888); available
in English as 'The Catholicity of Christianity and the Church', Calvin *Theological Journal*, 27
(1992):220–51, tr. John Bolt.

[42] Herman Bavinck, *Gereformeerde Katholiciteit (1888–1918)*, ed. Koert van Bekkum (Barnveld:
Nederlands Dagblad, 2008); cf. Tangelder, 'Dr. Herman Bavinck 1854–1921: Theologian of
the Word', 14–51; Bolt, 'Grand Rapids between Kampen and Amsterdam', 267.

[43] On this point, Veenhof's summary of Bavinck's catholicity is most helpful: Veenhof, *Revelatie
en Inspiratie*, 386.

[44] Herman Bavinck, *The Certainty of Faith* (Grand Rapids: Paideia Press, 1980), 37; see also van
den Belt, *Autopistia*, 250–1.

Protestantism. However, he feels no need to show why this Dogmatics must be specifically reformed.'[45]

Ever present in Bavinck's Dogmatics, then, is the reality that Christian orthodoxy predates Geneva and Wittenberg. This much is evident from Bavinck's thorough knowledge and use of, for example, patristic theology. He regularly grounds his positions in the works of Augustine, the Cappadocian Fathers, Tertullian and so on. 'History has its ironies but it cannot be denied: the most ecumenical protestant dogmatic theology in fact appeared in Kampen, the place where theology was practiced in the most isolationist manner.'[46]

This point is supported by Bavinck's own assessment of the dogmatician's goal: 'Accordingly, the task of the dogmatician is not to draw the material for his dogmatics exclusively from the written confession of his own church but to view it in the total context of the unique faith and life of his church, and then again in the context of the history of the whole church of Christ. He therefore stands on the shoulders of previous generations. He knows he is surrounded by a cloud of witnesses and lets his witness merge with the voice of these many waters. Every dogmatics ought to be in full accord with and a part of the doxology sung to God by the church of all ages.'[47]

There is thus the implication that he writes for those outside his own constituency. His authority to do so rests not on the Creed, but rather on that to which Creed refers: God the Father, God the Son and God the Holy Spirit. In the appropriation of all life and redemption history to the Trinity, Bavinck organizes his thoughts in (literally) the most universal terms: the story of God told via the Father's divine creativity, the Son's work of redemption and the Spirit's glory in consummation.

As such, Bavinck reflects his Reformed heritage. Calvin writes: 'To the Father is attributed the beginning of activity, and the foundation and wellspring of all things; to the Son, wisdom, counsel and the ordered

---

[45] Auguste Lecerf, *Introduction à La Dogmatique Réformée* (Paris: Editions « Je Sers », 1931), 9. 'Une discipline canonique: tel est le caractère que nous avons voulu donner à notre travail. Nous avons cherché à le faire jusqu'ici, même par H. Bavinck, qui, à notre sens, s'est rapproché le plus de l'Idéal que nous contemplons. . . . H. Bavinck, dans la partie introductive de sa dogmatique réformée, cette véritable somme du calvinisme contemporain, va bien plus loin. Il donne une esquisse des principes de la connaissance, tant générale que religieuse, et il formule la théorie des principes du protestantisme orthodoxe. Mais il n'éprouve pas le besoin de montrer pourquoi cette dogmatique doit être spécifiquement réformée.'

[46] George Puchinger, cited by George Harinck, 'Herman Bavinck's indrukken van Amerika anno 1892', in *Documentieblad voor de Nederlandsche Kerkgeschiedenis na 1800*, 47 (December 1997), 27. 'Er zit ironie in der gang der historie, maar helt valt niet to ontkennen: de meest oecumenisch protestanste dogmatiek verscheen toch maar in Kampen, waar op de meest isolationistische wijze aan theologie werd gedaan.'

[47] *RD*, 1.86.

disposition of all things; but to the Spirit is assigned the power and efficacy of that activity.'[48]

Calvin's sentiment is continued in the development of Dutch neo-Calvinism. Kuyper writes: 'In every work effected by the Father, Son and Holy Ghost in common, the power *to bring forth* proceeds from the Father; the power *to arrange* from the Son; the power *to perfect* from the Holy Spirit.'[49]

Bavinck closely follows this: 'The Father is the "principle of origination", the Son is the "principle of operation", the Spirit is the "principle of consummation". . . . All "outgoing works" have *one* Author, namely, God; but they are produced by means of the cooperation of the *three* persons; and in the works of creation, redemption, and sanctification, a definite place and order is assigned to each of these three. All things are originated by the Father, are carried out through the Son, and are brought to completion by the Holy Spirit.'[50] Although these ideas are not original to Reformed theology, the functionalism present is consonant with it.

Among the key developments in neo-Calvinist systematic theology lies its reshaping of dogmatics to more explicitly reflect the Creed's triniformity. In doing so, the neo-Calvinists stand within the Reformed tradition, which has historically argued that the Trinity is a fundamental article of the faith, and as such, that it is necessary for salvation.[51] 'The article of the Trinity is not only theoretical, but also practical, since it conduces to gratitude and worship of God – to the end that we may devote our faith and service to the Triune God who has revealed himself to us. And [it conduces] to consolation inasmuch as [by it] we may know that Christ has truly redeemed us and that our salvation has been made secure.'[52]

V. All Theology is the Doctrine of God

The subsuming of dogmatics in its entirety under the doctrines of Father (creation), Son (salvation) and Spirit (consummation) highlights an

---

[48] Calvin, *Institutes*, 1.13.18.

[49] Abraham Kuyper, *The Work of the Holy Spirit*, tr. H. De Vries, (Grand Rapids: Eerdmans, 1941), 19.

[50] Bavinck, *The Doctrine of God*, 317.

[51] By way of a Reformed response to the Remonstrant claim that although the Trinity is a fundamental doctrine, it is of no practical use to the Christian faith, see W. Brakel, *Redelijke Godsdienst* I.iv.35 (D. Donner, 1881); H. Witsius, *Exercitationes*, VI. xxiv (Whitefish, Montana: Kessinger Pub Co, 2009); Calvin, *Institutes*, I.xiii.2.

[52] Turretin, *Inst. theol. elencticae* (1734), III.xxiv.17. Cited in Muller, *Post-Reformation Reformed Dogmatics: The Rise and Development of Reformed Orthodoxy, ca. 1520 to ca. 1725, Vol. 4: The Triunity of God*, 155.

obvious, practical complexity in restating the doctrine of God in both Bavinck and Barth: quite simply, the doctrine of God is no less than the sum total of theology.

As has already been mentioned, Bavinck orders his dogmatics along a triniform contour quite intentionally. Having laid the epistemological foundations in *Prolegomena*, his theology proper begins with twin assertions applicable to all dogmatics. All theology, he proposes, possesses an inherently mysterious quality. Stemming from this, every jot and tittle of theology, from the central loci of its schema to the sub-points of its minutiae, has but one subject: God himself.

In recognizing that the dogmatic venture is, for Bavinck, ultimately and wholly about God, one notes that throughout this process, Bavinck consistently relies on organic terms, concepts and images to speak about the creaturely. Clearly, he has already committed himself to 'referring every form of existence to the triune God' in order that 'the confession of the trinity might receive the place of prominence in thought and life.'[53] When the cosmos is referred to the Trinity, Bavinck consistently seems to confess and exalt the Trinity by speaking of the cosmos (and its contents) via the organic motif. One must therefore carefully examine Bavinck's understanding of the divine: the norms found therein will prove normative in Bavinck's identification of the *vestigia trinitatis*.

VI. Mysterious Dogmatics: Warm or Cold-Blooded

'Mystery is the lifeblood of dogmatics.'[54]

With these words, Bavinck begins his retelling of the doctrine of God. He is quick to qualify the term μυστηριον. Although he rules out a 'scientific' definition (with little explanation), Bavinck explains his position primarily in contradistinction to Roman Catholic notions of divine mystery as esoteric supernatural truths. His main definition of 'mystery' is given at the close of *Prolegomena*.[55]

As was explained earlier, among the major developments in nineteenth-century theology was Leo XIII's reassertion of neo-Thomist theology. Bavinck's doctrine of God ought to be read with this backdrop in mind. In this context, Bavinck charges Catholicism with asserting a form of neo-Gnosticism regarding its dogmatic content. Such a challenge is found

[53] Bavinck, *The Doctrine of God*, 329.
[54] *RD*, 2.29.
[55] *RD*, 1.616–21.

elsewhere in Bavinck's view of Medieval Catholicism, John of Damascus being the outstanding source of influence.[56]

The Roman Catholic concept of mystery, Bavinck claims, relates to the specific aspects of theological content as inherently unknown, unknowable and improvable by reason. His critique of this position sits within his constant nature–grace dialectic. At the core of Thomism, he claims, nature perfects grace. While it has been argued elsewhere that Bavinck's worldview contained significant Thomist elements,[57] Bavinck consistently relates nature to grace via the markedly different paradigm of restoration: grace *restores*, rather than *perfects* (or *elevates*), nature. The significance of this nature–grace rearrangement to Bavinck's thought is such that various works have claimed it is the central feature of his entire theology.[58]

While the relationship of nature and grace takes an obviously central place in his thought, this centrality must be carefully nuanced. Bavinck's worldview, typical of the Dutch neo-Calvinists, is constructed along the lines of creation, fall, redemption and consummation.[59] Noting the triniform glory central to both creation and eschaton within Bavinck's worldview, it is evident that 'grace restores nature' is the central feature between these points. However, one must describe the nature of that centrality with caution, lest it become elevated beyond the Trinity itself. The Triune God is the literal centrepiece of Bavinck's theology: he is the one approached in *Prolegomena* and whose works in creation and providence are the subject of the remainder of *Reformed Dogmatics*. 'The Trinity is the heart of the Reformed vision and "grace restores nature" is subordinate to it.'[60]

In this light, Bristley's helpful summary of Bavinck's contribution to theology first notes his thoroughgoing Trinitarianism before discussing the

---

[56] See Bavinck's discussion of Medieval Christology's mystical departure, under the influence of John of Damascus, from the 'two natures' doctrine of Chalcedon, *RD*, 3.256.

[57] Central to Dooyeweerd's critique of Bavinck is the claim that his *logos*-speculation is inherently neo-Platonic, Thomistic and scholastic: Herman Dooyeweerd, 'Kuyper's Wetenschapsleer', *Philosophia Reformata* 4 (1939):193–232. Hendrikus Berkhof also argues that Bavinck's concept of faith was neo-Thomist: Berkhof, *Two Hundred Years of Theology*, 114.

[58] Veenhof, *Revelatie en Inspiratie*. 345–6; Heideman, *The Relation of Revelation and Reason in E. Brunner and H. Bavinck*, 196.

[59] Albert M. Wolters, *Creation Regained: Biblical Basics for a Reformational Worldview* (Grand Rapids: Eerdmans, 2005), 13–86.

[60] Bolt, 'The Trinity as a unifying theme in Reformed thought: A response to Dr. George Vandervelde', 101. This article reflects a debate between Bolt and Vandervelde concerning the centrality of 'grace restores nature' to the Reformed worldview. Vandervelde argues this to be the case, whereas Bolt's claim is that the Trinity is central (particularly to Bavinck's worldview) and that 'grace restores nature' is a consequence of a thoroughly Trinitarian outlook. See also John Bolt, *Christian and Reformed Today* (Vineland, ON: Paideia Press, 1984) and George Vandervelde, 'A Trinitarian Framework and Reformed Distinctiveness: A Critical Assessment of *Christian and Reformed Today*', *Calvin Theological Journal*, 21 (1986), 95–109.

centrality of 'grace restores nature': 'One of the strengths of Bavinck's theology is his profound understanding of the doctrine of the Trinity. He developed what may be termed a "Trinitarian methodology". For Bavinck, the doctrine of the Trinity was not only the very heart of our faith, but its implications were profound. . . . Another strength is his emphasis on the doctrine of creation. His adage that 'grace restores nature' is a unique insight rooted in the original goodness of creation.'[61]

In recognizing the importance of 'grace restores nature' to Bavinck, it comes as little surprise to find that he expresses strong dissatisfaction with the later theological consequences of neo-Thomism's 'grace elevates nature', two-tiered system: 'In the case of Rome, the mysteries are incomprehensible, primarily because they belong to another, higher, supernatural order, which surpasses the human intellect as such. It therefore has to put a heavy accent on the incomprehensibility of the mysteries, as well as to protect and maintain it.'[62]

In this light, he engages directly with Aquinas (*Summa Theol.*, I, qu. 32, art. 1; *Summa contra Gentiles*, I, 3; IV, 1), noting that within Thomism, the notion of μυστήριον pertains particularly to theology's substantive content.[63] 'It is believable because it is absurd. . . . Certain, because it is impossible.'[64] Bavinck's handling of Thomas must be nuanced. Within Thomas' work, a distinction exists between two types of divine truth. One can be set out with demonstrable proofs, the other, consisting of 'higher' truths, requires acceptance in faith.[65] Having defended natural theology in the first three Books of *Summa Contra Gentiles*, Aquinas moves into Book Four writing: 'In what has preceded we have dealt with divine things according as the natural reason can arrive at the knowledge of divine things through creatures. This way is imperfect, nevertheless, and in keeping with the reason's native capacity. That is why we can say with Job (26:14): "These things are said in part of his ways." We must now deal with those divine things that have been divinely revealed to us to be believed, since they transcend the human intellect.'[66]

[61] Bristley, *Guide to the Writings of Herman Bavinck*, 21–2.
[62] *RD*, 1.621.
[63] See also *Vatican Council I*, session III, 'De fide', chap. 4: 'For by their nature divine mysteries so far surpass the created intellect that, even when transmitted by revelation and received by faith they remain covered with the veil of faith itself, and shrouded in a certain obscurity as long as, in this mortal life, we are exiled from the Lord: for we walk by faith and not by sight!'
[64] Tertullian, *On the Flesh of Christ*, 5; cited in *RD*, 1.620.
[65] Don McGaughey, 'Thomas Aquinas and the Problem of Faith and Reason', *Restoration Quarterly*, 6 no 2 (1962), 67–76.
[66] Thomas Aquinas, *Summa Contra Gentiles* (University of Notre Dame Press, 1991), tr. Vernon J. Bourke, IV.1.

Bavinck's portrayal of μυστηριον is altogether different. Viewed in historical context, *Prolegomena* is for Bavinck, like Barth, an *apologia* for the art of dogmatics. It is the post-Enlightenment reassertion of the possibility and necessity of a distinctly systematic handling of theology as a response to God's self-disclosure. The conclusion of Bavinck's *Prolegomena* is that 'it is the task of the thinking theological mind to gather up and recapitulate all truth in one system.'[67] Indeed, *Prolegomena* is bookended by this conviction.[68]

Although at one level Bavinck's work thus represents a movement towards the demystification of dogma, this is not to say that he has no place for μυστηριον in theology. To the contrary, mystery is nothing less than its 'lifeblood'. Evidently, Bavinck substantially redefines 'mystery' in relation to theology. Grammatico–historically, he first locates μυστηριον within the Greek world of secret religion and politics (Eleusis, Samothrance *et al.*).[69] The New Testament writers, however, gave the word a different meaning. In the Gospels, the Pauline corpus and Revelation, one finds μυστηριον used to describe notions pertaining to the divine kingdom. These notions were either presented in obscure (Matt. 13:11; Mark 4:11; Luke 8:10; Rev. 1:20; 17:5, 7) or hidden ways. It is used to describe Christ's redemption of Jew and Gentile alike (Rom. 16:25; Eph. 1:9; Col. 1:26) and the manner in which this salvation occurs (Rom. 11:25; 1 Cor. 15:51). In its New Testament context, μυστηριον describes that which was previously unknown but has now been revealed. 'The NT term μυστηριον, accordingly, does not denote an intellectually uncomprehended and incomprehensible truth of faith but a matter that was formerly hidden in God, was then made known in the gospel, and is now understood by believers.'[70]

Such an approach is evinced by Bavinck's emphases on theology as 'natural', 'rational' and 'reasonable'.[71] His criticism of Catholicism's

---

[67] *RD*, 1.618.

[68] Compare *RD*, 1.38–46 and 1.618–21.

[69] In context, Bavinck's sources were at the cutting edge of Greco-Roman studies, *RD*, 1.619: E. Hatch, 'The Influence of Greek Ideas and Usages upon the Christian Church', *The Hibbert Lectures, 1888*, trans. A.M. Fairbairn, 7th ed. (London: Williams & Norgate, 1898, 296); Gustav Andrich, *Das antike Mysteriewesen in Seinim Einfluss auf das Christenthum* (Göttingen: Vanderhoeck & Ruprecht, 1894); G. Wobbermin, *Religionsgeschichtliche Studien zur Frage nach der Beeinflussung des Urchristenthum durch das antike Mysterienwesen* (Berlin: E. Ebering, 1896).

[70] *RD*, 1.620; cf. H. Cremer, *Biblico-Theological Lexicon of New Testament Greek*, trans. D.W. Simon and William Urwick (Edinburgh: T & T Clark, 1872), s.v. 'pronoia'. More recent research on Greek mystery religion maintains the general veracity of the works consulted by Bavinck: see R. Gordon Wasson, Carl A. P. Ruck and Albert Hofmann, *The Road to Eleusis: Unveiling the Secret of the Mysteries* (New York: Harcourt Brace Jovanovic, 1978); Francis Walton, 'Athens, Elesius, and the Homeric Hymn to Demeter', *Harvard Theological Review*, 45 no. 2, (1952), 105–14.

[71] *RD*, 1.618.

appropriation of Thomistic principles concerning μυστηριον, then, is that it requires a degree of theological cognitive dissonance not commanded by Scripture.

Various questions therefore arise. If the specific content of theology has been thus demystified, in what sense does μυστηριον remain its very lifeblood? Is Bavinck's concept of theology an arid, scholastic one? Is *Reformed Dogmatics* cold- or warm-blooded?

VII. One-Track Dogmatics: Thinking *Pros Ton Theon*

This question is answered as one perceives the subtle reworking of μυστηριον in Bavinck's system. 'Mystery' is not ejected from his dogmatics. To the contrary, it remains central. It is, however, detached from the substantive content of theology. Bavinck's specific targets are the mystical appropriation of Thomas' notion of 'higher', incomprehensible divine truths to 'the incarnation, the mystical union, the sacraments, etc., and later all the "pure articles" (*articuli puri*) which could not be proven by reason.'[72] Having severed the connection between μυστηριον and dogma, he promptly reattaches it not to the process of theology but to God himself. 'From the very start of its labours, [theology] faces the incomprehensible One. From him it derives its inception, for from him are all things. But also in the remaining loci, when it turns its attention to creatures, it views them only in relation to God as they exist from him and through him and for him. So then, the knowledge of God is the only dogma, the exclusive content, of the entire field of dogmatics.'[73]

The heading of this section is telling: dogmatics begins 'Before the Divine Mystery'. A subtle but drastic change has occurred, as the foremost sense of mystery now belongs to God himself rather than to theology. In short, wherever one finds God, one finds μυστηριον in its archetypal form. Bavinck has thus worked an interesting translocation: although dogmatics itself has been demystified, it has also become the subject of a reinvigorated theocentrism.

His argument is that replacing the Thomistic sense of doctrine as mystical with a more rational theology edifies the believer on two fronts. First, it removes the aforementioned requirement for theological cognitive dissonance. Tertullian's dictum is reversed and dogma becomes acceptable primarily because of its clarity. Second, it reserves μυστηριον for its most

---

[72] *RD*, 1.620.
[73] *RD*, 2.29.

appropriate context: the Godhead. In this twofold movement, doctrine is humbled and God is exalted. As God himself has become the primary μυστηριον, the believer is led to have faith in him rather than, for example, in the incomprehensibly transubstantiated Mass. In that light, Bavinck's doctrine of God is unsurprisingly Protestant: his doctrine of God requires a soteriology centred on *sola fide* and *solo Christo*.

One does well, however, to handle Bavinck's concept of divine mystery carefully.[74] Elsewhere, he wrote extremely critically of 'mystical theosophy' in the works of Böhme.[75] Bavinck's concept of God-as-mystery is defined in relation to his later discussions on divine aseity and self-revelation (whereby all revelation is anthropomorphic, as God is always 'other'). In short, while Bavinck uses the term to protect God's 'otherness', he never uses μυστηριον to dull the sense of God's knowability.

Bavinck's doctrine of God is driven by the desire to situate the believer's sense of truth and awe in God alone. On this basis, theology is continually touched by incomprehensibility through its 'exclusive subject': the Triune God. 'All the doctrines treated in dogmatics – whether they concern the universe, humanity, Christ, and so forth – are but the explication of the one central dogma of the knowledge of God. All things are considered in light of God, subsumed under him, traced back to him as the starting point. Dogmatics is always called upon to ponder and describe God and God alone, whose glory is in creation and re-creation, in nature and grace, in the world and in the church. It is the knowledge of him alone that dogmatics must put on display.'[76]

This citation highlights the aforementioned practical difficulty in sketching Bavinck's doctrine of God. In his system, all theology is the doctrine of God. As has already been noted, 'the imperative task of the dogmatician is to think God's thoughts after him and to trace their unity.'[77] The theologian's vocation, then, is to relate every facet of the creation to its Creator. As a process, theology is the continual reassessment of all else *pros ton theon*.

VIII. God and the Organism

The task of retelling Bavinck's doctrine of God is, therefore, nothing less than a total restatement of his *Dogmatics*. This chapter does not strive at this

---

[74] Indeed, one has already noted that Bavinck's use of the organic has been unhelpfully described as 'semi-mysticism' in Vander Stelt, 'Kuyper's Semi-Mystical Conception', 186, 190.
[75] *RD*, 3.211.
[76] *RD*, 2.29.
[77] *RD*, 1.44.

immense task. Rather, it attempts to recruit the kernel of Bavinck's dogmatic method in order to investigate his organic motif.

At the core of Bavinck's methodology is the principle that an essential coherence exists between Creator and creation. When properly understood, the cosmos will bear the inevitable marks of its triune Maker whose special revelation will also reflect his own being and nature. In the Trinity's cosmos, *vestigia trinitatis* will abound.

As has already been observed, Bavinck utilized the organic motif on numerous levels: dogmatics and ethics 'are related members of a single organism',[78] the cosmos is an 'organism',[79] Christ is the 'organic' centre of revelation,[80] the visible church is an 'organism',[81] Scripture itself is an 'organism'[82] and its inspiration is 'organic'[83] and so forth.

In the world made by God, Bavinck finds it appropriate to label many of the key moments of divine self-revelation via the organic motif. Why is this so? Which aspects of Bavinck's doctrine of God prompt him to so regularly invoke the motif?

Noting the four principles of organic thinking given in *Christelijke Wereldbeschouwing*[84] (the created order is marked by simultaneous unity and diversity; unity precedes diversity; the organism's shared life is orchestrated by a common ideal; this shared life has a common *telos*) one proceeds to explore what, within Bavinck's doctrine of God, shapes this paradigm.

In trying to explicate the precise sense in which Bavinck's doctrine of God so controls his worldview, this chapter takes a particular focus. When examining *Reformed Dogmatics*, one cannot help notice that its content reads like a running battle between Trinitarian and non-Trinitarian theologies of God. Bavinck's constant sparring partners are modalists, pantheists, polytheists, atheists, monists *et al.* Clearly, God's triunity exerts more than a schematic influence on *Reformed Dogmatics*. Micro- and macrocosmically, Bavinck's constant concern is the Trinity.

Ever present in this account of the divine is the theme of unity-in-diversity. Indeed, it structurally and substantively influences Bavinck as he frames a doctrine of God. This chapter, then, proceeds with a two-pronged approach.

---

[78] *RD*, 1.58. 'Dogmatics is the system of the knowledge of God; ethics is that of the service of God. The two disciplines, far from facing each other as two independent entities, together form a single system; they are related members of a single organism.'

[79] 'In virtue of this unity the world can, metaphorically, be called an organism, in which all the parts are connected with each other and influence each other reciprocally.' *RD*, 2.436.

[80] *RD*, 1.383.

[81] *RD*, 4.330.

[82] *RD*, 1.83.

[83] *RD*, 1.431.

[84] *CW*, 50–65.

First, it will explore unity and diversity as central aspects of the divine in Bavinck's theology. Second, it will examine his handling of the christocentric ontological relationship between Creator and creation.

Bavinck's doctrine of God will thus serve as the basis for the two proceeding chapters which probe why he explains the character of this Triune God's general and special self-revelation in organic terms. Only against the backdrop of Bavinck's doctrine of God can one proceed to search for the *vestigia trinitatis* in his wider theology.

IX. Part One: Unity and Diversity in the Godhead

Central to Bavinck's critique of Scholten's theology was that it inadequately conveyed the true character of God's triunity[85] which consequently led to the misappropriation of the cosmos as best described with a mechanical motif.

While Scholten interpreted God in the light of the material principle of determinism (thus regarding the fact of God's triunity as being of relatively little import),[86] his former pupil asserted the opposite. Bavinck infers the nature of providential cosmic order (predestination) from the basic nature of the Trinity. In doing so, Bavinck realigns himself with earlier Reformed orthodoxy. Scholten's reading of causality into the Godhead, for example, is a marked departure from the earlier Reformed tradition. In defining a cause as 'that which gives existence to something else', Witsius argues that the giving of existence has no place within the Trinity.[87]

Due to this, the nature of divine sovereignty in Bavinck's thought stands out as markedly different to that of Scholten. The former speaks of predestination; the latter of predetermination. Indeed, this tension between the two terms is picked up by Bavinck. When discussing Scholten's closed-system materialism,[88] he writes:

In this [nineteenth] century a deeper study of nature, history, and human-ity has demonstrated the untenability of deistic Pelagianism. In its place has come a pantheistic or materialistic, a more ethically or more physi-cally conditioned determinism. Of course, between this determinism and

---

[85] *RD*, 2.43.
[86] Scholten, *De leer der Hervormde Kerk*, 18–20.
[87] Witsius, *Exercitationes*, VII.iv–vii.
[88] Bavinck is principally targeting the following works: Scholten, *Leer der Hervormde Kerk*, espe-cially II, 435–605; Scholten, *De Vrije Wil*, 385 ff.

the doctrine of predestination, despite some surface resemblance, there is a fundamental difference. Neither pantheism nor materialism leaves any room for a counsel of God; they only leave room for an unconscious fate, a blind nature, an irrational will. Still, many philosophers and thinkers have understood and interpreted the ecclesiastical doctrine of predestination in this deterministic sense.[89]

To demonstrate this position, Bavinck also cites the German transcendental realist, Edouard von Hartmann, Schleiermacher and Scholten's mentor, Alexander Schweizer.[90]

Scholten's concept of predetermination contains the implicit denial of the creation's independent nature. History is determined by divine sovereignty working through a vast, unbreakable chain of cause and effect. Bavinck presents a wholly different picture. He frames the exercise of God's sovereignty in explicitly non-coercive terms. The nature of God's sovereign relationship to the cosmos is one which asserts and maintains the real, independent existence of both.[91] 'In the preservation and government of all things, God maintains this distinct existence of his creatures, causes all of them to function in accordance with their own nature, and guarantees to human beings their own personality, rationality and freedom. God never coerces anyone.'[92]

As such, Bavinck's quest to move from Scholten's mechanical, coercive doctrine of providence reflects a deeper departure from Scholten's mechanical, coercive doctrine of God. The concept of God as simultaneously sovereign and non-coercive is rooted, for Bavinck, in the Trinity. One thus builds on the hypothesis that Bavinck arrives at an organic view of the cosmos as a by-product of his renewed Trinitarian view of God.

1. Seeking Divine Norms

In describing the Trinity as Creator-Father, Redeemer-Son and Sanctifier-Spirit, Bavinck builds his doctrine of God on a grand scale. Before this, however, he devotes the first major thrust of *God and Creation* to explorations

---

[89] *RD*, 2.369.

[90] RD, 2.370; cf. Alexander Schweizer, *Die christliche Glaubenslehre nach protestantischen Grundsätzen dargestellt* II, 254 ff.

[91] Bavinck qualifies the sense in which the cosmos has an 'independent' existence: 'The world is not an independent entity on par with, and antithetically related to, God. It is not a second God, but totally God's work, both in its "isness" and its "whatness". From the very beginning it was designed to reveal God.' *RD*, 2.104.

[92] *RD*, 2.104.

of 'Knowing God'[93] and 'The Living, Acting God'.[94] Following this, he progresses to discuss the divine will manifest in creation and providence.[95]

In Parts I and II of *God and Creation* one thus finds Bavinck laying the foundations for his doctrine of God metanarrative. At the heart of these bases lies the outstanding theme of divine unity-in-diversity. Indeed, one is wholly justified in naming this as the centrepiece of *God and Creation: Part II*, which is in turn arguably the most important individual section in Bavinck's entire Dogmatics. In *Part I*, he has established the fact that this mysterious God can be *known*. In *Part III*, he will demonstrate what this God *does* in creation and providence. *Part II*, however, teaches not how to know God or what God does. Rather, it gives Bavinck's answers to the questions who and what *is* God?

In short, Bavinck's most rudimentary characterization of God is as a being of immense diversity and profound unity. This fact exerts a controlling influence on Bavinck's understanding and appropriation of all created reality. It also sets the parameters within which he grasps the overarching scheme of Father as Creator (*RD* 2), Son as Saviour (*RD* 3) and Spirit as Consummator (*RD* 4). To read Bavinck accurately, one must interpret all that follows through the lens of *God and Creation, Part II*.

Bavinck's explanation of divine diversity and unity follows a particular, deliberate order. Interestingly, in *Reformed Dogmatics* he handles divine diversity before divine oneness. Having set out the sense in which God is both utterly incomprehensible[96] and yet intimately knowable,[97] he first explains the vast array of names applicable to God[98] before moving to write of God's manifold attributes.[99]

Most interesting in Bavinck's doctrine of God is that he first handles divine diversity and then, having established that God is non-uniform, explains the sense in which he is united.

2. Divine Diversity of Names and Attributes

Bavinck's discussion of divine diversity begins with an examination of the particular names with which God reveals himself; a subject to which he

---

[93] *RD*, 2.27–94.
[94] *RD*, 2.95–336.
[95] *RD*, 2.337–620.
[96] *RD*, 2.27–52.
[97] *RD*, 2.53–94.
[98] *RD*, 2.95–147.
[99] *RD*, 2.148–255.

attaches enormous importance. Indeed, the section entitled 'The Names of God' in the English translation *Reformed Dogmatics* comprises three major sections in the original *Gereformeerde Dogmatiek* (§§26–8).

This handling of the divine name begins with the bold statement that '[a]ll we can learn about God from his revelation is designated his Name in Scripture.'[100] Etymologically, Bavinck regards 'name' in the Biblical languages (ονομα etc.) as rooted in the concepts of 'sign' and 'distinguishing mark'. A name, in the true sense, is no mere arbitrary tag. For Bavinck, a name is closely bound to the character of its bearer. Interestingly, Bavinck laments the recreation of *name* as a purely aesthetic device in the modern world. 'There is a connection between a name and its bearer, and that connection, so far from being arbitrary, is rooted in that bearer. Even among us [moderns], now that names have for the most part become mere sounds without meaning, that connection is still felt. A name is something personal and very different from a number or a member of a species. It always feels more or less unpleasant when others misspell or garble our name: it stands for our honour, our worth, our person and individuality.'[101]

While this statement no doubt reveals particular aspects of Bavinck's own personality as highly driven towards correctness and accuracy, he is nonetheless cautious to demonstrate that his priorities concerning names are exegetically founded. He cites Adam's mandate to name each animal in accordance with its nature (Gen. 2:19–20) and the numerous examples in Scripture whereby names carry a definite meaning as reflected in their bearers' characters. 'The same is true of God's name. There is an intimate link between God and his name. According to Scripture, this link too is not accidental or arbitrary but forced by God himself. We do not name God; he names himself.'[102]

Bavinck chooses to begin the doctrine of God with God's name, as he finds this to be the most basic factor of both divine self-revelation and humankind's relationship to God.[103] In so commencing, he wastes no time in framing the discussion in terms of divine unity-in-diversity: 'The *one* name of God, which is inclusive of his entire revelation both in nature and in grace, is divisible for us in a great many names. Only in that way do we obtain a full view of the riches of his revelation and the profound meaning of his name.'[104]

---

[100] *RD*, 2.97.
[101] *RD*, 2.97.
[102] *RD*, 2.98.
[103] 'The "divulged" name becomes the name "called upon".' *RD*, 2.99.
[104] *RD*, 2.99.

The knowledge of God thus begins with the many, rather than the one. Divine self-revelation, encapsulated in the name by which God makes himself known, is multifaceted because God is internally diverse.

Prior to the classification of God's names, he introduces the twin factors of accommodation and anthropomorphism. At the outset of his doctrine of God, it becomes clear that Bavinck regards himself as the inheritor of Augustine[105] and Calvin.[106] God speaks into the cosmos using its own terms, concepts and images. In Christ, God not only communicates in human terms; he becomes human. The fascinating factor with Bavinck is the radical degree to which he maintains the principle of accommodation: 'Scripture does not just contain a few scattered anthropomorphisms but is anthropomorphic through and through. From the first page to the last it witnesses to God's coming to, and searching for, humanity.'[107]

A crucial axiom, then, in reading Bavinck is that he regards all revelation as anthropomorphic. Every moment of each act of God's self-revelation accommodates human finitude. Although he writes elsewhere that '[a]s God reveals himself, so is he',[108] there is nonetheless in Bavinck's theology a degree of (non-absolute) distance between God and his self-revelation that one does not find, for example, in Barth, whose conviction is that in revelation, 'God's word is identical with God himself'.[109] This all-pervasive anthropomorphism has an obvious consequence for how one interprets Bavinck on the creation. All that God reveals shows what he is *like*, rather than what he *is*. Wherever Bavinck looks, therefore, he sees accommodating pointers towards God. 'But not all creatures are of equal rank: there is a hierarchy in the realm of creatures. The position and rank that creatures occupy is determined by their kinship with God. All creatures express some aspect of God's being, but of all of them human beings are at the top.'[110]

Thus when he views the relationship of God to the sum total of his general self-revelation in the cosmos, Bavinck's conclusion is that the organic character of the cosmos is, for some reason, analogous to the reality of God's being.

---

[105] *RD*, 2.101–2. Bavinck cites Augustine, *Lectures on the Gospel of John*, tract. 13.5 (on John 3: 22–9).

[106] For a helpful discussion of Calvin on accommodation, see David F. Wright, 'Calvin's "Accommodation" Revisited', *Calvin as Exegete: papers and responses presented at the Ninth Colloquium on Calvin and Calvin Studies* (Grand Rapids: Calvin Studies Society, 1995), 171–90.

[107] *RD*, 2.99–100.

[108] *RD*, 2.111. In context, Bavinck makes this statement while writing against the rigid separation of God's 'ontological existence and his "economic" self-revelation'.

[109] Karl Barth, *Church Dogmatics*, Vol. I, Part 1 (Edinburgh: T & T Clark, 1975), trs. G. W. Bromily et al., 304.

[110] *RD*, 2.103.

Bavinck's classification of God's names begins with two veiled criticisms. The first regards the 'abstract concept of God' in Schelling, Hegel *et al.* This is a criticism Bavinck frequently makes.[111] The doctrine of God ought to be founded on revelation rather than speculation. The second concerns those who 'highlight one attribute of God at the expense of others'. As is seen in the following discussion, Bavinck maintains that each of the divine attributes is identical with the divine essence. Everything Scripture predicates of God, it does so infinitively and perfectly; thus God is love not in part, but in full.

Bavinck relentlessly opposes the identification of God independently of his attributes. Discussion of God via (rather than 'apart from') the categories of his manifold names and attributes is, he notes, a mark of historic Christian orthodoxy. The names of Irenaeus,[112] Augustine,[113] Aquinas[114] and Ursinus[115] are invoked in this regard. In terms of the basic priorities in its doctrine of God, *Reformed* Dogmatics stands in a most catholic tradition.

It is clear that Bavinck finds the historical discussion of the divine names a difficult one. From its very outset, theology has sought the divine attribute that makes God different from his creation. What is the attribute that makes God divine? Into the modern era, theology still struggles to settle on an answer.

Augustine[116] and Aquinas[117] set the early trend followed by the majority of Reformed theologians, whereby God's 'aseity' and 'independence' solve this dilemma.[118] Later, Bavinck himself is highly protective of the divine aseity.[119] Before that, however, he launches a pre-emptive attack on various theologies which departed from this position. Among these figures, one finds some of those from whom Veenhof claims Bavinck inherited the organic motif[120]: Hegel, Schelling, the Groninger School, the Ethical Theologians and Scholten. Interestingly, Bavinck finds major faults with their doctrines of God and charges Hegel with 'logical idealism', Schelling with 'introducing in God a theogonic process', the Groninger and later

---

[111] *RD*, 2.115.
[112] Irenaeus, *Against Heresies*, I, 14; II, 13, 35.
[113] Augustine, *Confessions*; cf. First Vatican Council, *De fide*, ch. 1; Augusburg Confession, art. 1; Gallican Confession, art. 1; Scots Confession, art. 1; Westminster Confession, ch. 2.
[114] Thomas Aquinas, *Summa theol.*, I, qu. 3 ff.
[115] Z. Ursinus, *Tract. theol.*, 46–70.
[116] Augustine, *The Trinity*, V, 2; VII, 5ff; Augustine, *City of God*, XII, 2; Augustine, *On Christian Doctrine*, I, 6.
[117] Aquinas, *Summa theol.*, I, qu. 2, art. 3; I, qu. 3; Thomas Aquinas, *Summa contra Gentiles*, I, 16ff.
[118] *RD*, 2.113–14.
[119] *RD*, 2.151–3.
[120] Veenhof, *Revelatie en Inspiratie*, 268.

Ethical schools with moralism and Scholten with 'speculative intellectualism and monistic determinism'.[121]

Such a fact is significant. Bavinck views God's self-revelation *chez* Hegel and Schelling as inadequately reduced to an esoteric 'name of being'. Conversely, he views the Ethical Theologians as having misappropriated divine self-revelation as merely a 'moral name'. If indeed the most obvious consequence of the doctrine of God in Bavinck's system, the organic motif, has come from *both* the Idealists and the Ethicists, the said motif is among the most inexplicable factors in the history of dogmatic theology. The overwhelming evidence would seem to suggest the contrary. Just as Bavinck resisted reducing the divine name to exclusive categories of either 'being' (Schelling) or 'morality' (the Ethical school), he also resisted cosmologies which corresponded with such theologies. The worldview so aptly described by the organic motif grows out of a wholly other doctrine of God.

In combating Idealism and the Ethical school, Bavinck returns to his earlier veiled criticism: God's attributes should not be played against each other as 'it is the intent of Scripture to let all of God's perfections come equally into their own'.[122] He proceeds to restate Augustine's position on the relationship of God's attributes and essence. In short, each divine attribute is identical to his essence and thus to every other attribute.[123]

As he develops this discussion of the divine names, Bavinck handles various topics, primarily how one may speak of God apophatically and kataphatically; or rather by negation, eminence and causality. However, his response is to prioritize a set of dialectical emphases, whereby God is incomprehensible and knowable, named and nameless; he is 'the Cause beyond all affirmation and denial'.[124]

There is a certain indifference in Bavinck's tone when discussing the various ways in which theologians have divided the divine attributes and names.

> All the above divisions seem to be very different and called by very different names. But materially they are not that far apart. Whether people speak of negative and positive, incommunicable and communicable, quiescent and operative, absolute and relative, metaphysical and

---

[121] *RD*, 2.115.

[122] *RD*, 2.110.

[123] *RD*, 2.126–7; cf. Augustine, *The Trinity*, VI, 4, 6; XV, 5, 8; *Homily* 341, n. 8; *City of God*, XII, 18; *Lectures on the Gospel of John*, tract. 13.

[124] Psuedo-Dionysius, *The Divine Names and Mystical Theology*, ch. 2; cited in *RD*, 2.131.

psychological attributes, of attributes of the substance and subject apart from or in relation to the universe and humankind, actually they consistently refer to the same order in which the attributes are treated. Against all the above arrangements one can lodge virtually the same objections. They all appear to divide God's being in two halves. They all seem to treat first God's absoluteness, then his personality; first God's being as such, then God in relation to his creatures. They all seem to imply that the first group of terms is obtained apart from the creation, and the second from God's creatures, and that, consequently, there is no unity or concord among God's perfections.[125]

Having thus noted this fault, Bavinck goes back to his earlier axioms: first, God's aseity is absolute; and consequently, all divine self-revelation is anthropomorphic. Due to this, Bavinck's starting point is to remind himself that his knowledge of God is true, ectypal and analogical. This does not lead him to cast aside discussion on the categorization of God's names. To the contrary, he notes: 'Since God can be called by many names, we still need to treat them in a certain order.'[126]

He does so by reworking the historical discussion in a fascinating way. Drawing on Irenaeus' earlier emphasis on the proximity of the divine names and attributes, Bavinck creates two categories: first, God's proper names of address; and second, the attributes which pertain to the persons of the Trinity (rather than to the divine being).[127] By way of personal names, he focuses on God as *El, Elohim, El Shaddai, YHWH, YHWH Sabaoth* and *Father*.[128] In terms of attributes, he finds himself bound to speak within the categories of communicable and incommunicable attributes. He recognizes the ultimate paucity of these terms but finds them the best alternative as they guard against both pantheism and Deism.[129] Among God's incommunicable attributes, Bavinck lists independence, immutability, infinity (within which one finds both eternity and omnipresence) and unity. He cites God's intellectual (knowledge, foreknowledge, wisdom and trustworthiness) and moral (goodness, holiness, righteousness) attributes, in addition to his sovereignty, as communicable divine attributes. His constant reticence to unnecessarily separate these categories (and thus allow analogous, ectypal knowledge to overstep its powers) leads him to immediately emphasize the

---

[125] *RD*, 2.133. cf. *RD*, 2.136.
[126] *RD*, 2.135.
[127] *RD*, 2.135.
[128] *RD*, 2.138–47.
[129] *RD*, 2.136.

net effect of both sets of attributes: 'All the attributes of God discussed above are summed up in his perfection.'[130]

The key point in this discussion is that Bavinck has carefully constructed a doctrine of God, and within that, he consistently accents the paradigm of rich internal diversity pertaining to the Godhead.[131] While Bavinck is somewhat undogmatic concerning the various terminologies used to categorize God's names and attributes, his deliberate structuring of the doctrine of God has thus far woven this theme of diversity into its most rudimentary concept of God.

3. Divine Unity of Names and Attributes

Having dealt extensively with the sense in which God is predicated by tremendous internal diversity, Bavinck moves to emphasize that these distinctions exist in perfect unity. In framing the doctrine of God in terms of unity-in-diversity, Bavinck gives a strong indication that the *vestigia trinitatis* will follow suit. In this sense, he departs from the numerically focused 'triad' pattern for the *vestigia* so common to the medieval church and its non-Reformed inheritors. In contrast to their narrow focus on triniformity on the microcosmic level (the *imago Dei* and various threefold analogies), Bavinck sought triniformity macrocosmically: if nature and history are the general revelation of the Trinity, it must, as an 'organism', bear the hallmarks of its divine Creator. Thus, his categories for 'triniformity' deemphasized the previous fixation with 'threeness' and instead focused on the cosmos-wide reality of unity-in-diversity.

In comparison to his vast handling of divine diversity, Bavinck provides a succinct treatment of divine oneness.[132] This brief *exposé* of divine unity takes a twofold direction, first defining the divine oneness as numerically exclusive (thus the three persons are continually one in number) and then as internally qualitative (thus the manifold divine attributes are also in perfect harmony).[133] He uses this excursus to engage with his German contemporary, Julius Wellhausen,[134] whose views were mediated to Bavinck's professor, Scholten,

---

[130] *RD*, 2.249.

[131] It is less clear whether Bavinck intends diversity of names as leading to diversity of characteristics.

[132] Indeed, it receives a mere seven pages: *RD*, 2.170–7.

[133] *RD*, 2.170.

[134] Julius Wellhausen, *Die christliche Religion: Mit Einschluss der israelitisch-judischen Religion*, I, IV, 1, 15, in *Die Kultur der Gegenwart*, ed. Paul Hinnenberg, 24 vols. (Berlin and Leipzig: B.G. Teubner, 1905–23).

by Abraham Kuenen.[135] Despite his Leiden education, which stressed an evolutionary model of Israelite theism (from simple to complex), Bavinck's basic conviction was that Israelite religion did not evolve from polytheism into monotheism. He rather maintains that Scripture, from its outset, posits Trinitarian monotheism. Noteworthy is that in this light Bavinck pairs the history-of-religions approach with the German biologist, Ernst Haeckel, under the banner of an 'inorganic' worldview.[136]

Critiquing non-Trinitarian concepts of the divine unity, Bavinck claims that pantheistic notions of divine oneness are unsatisfactory. Here, Bavinck makes another subtle but profound link between the nature of unity within the Godhead and the cosmos: 'When the confession of the one true God weakens and is denied, and the unity sought in pantheism eventually satisfies neither the intellect nor the heart, the unity of the world and humankind, of religion, morality, and truth can no longer be maintained. Nature and history fall apart in fragments.'[137]

Evidently, Bavinck's position is that if one misunderstands the nature of God's own oneness, a gross misappropriation of unity in every area of created reality (cosmically, socially, spiritually, ethically and epistemologically) will follow. One must read his sentiment regarding 'nature falling apart in fragments' against the backdrop of his 'grace restores nature' *leitmotif*: the key to nature holding together, rather than splintering and losing its oneness, is found in the unity of the one true God. One must thus learn to think about all of these elements (the world, humanity, religion, morality, truth, nature and history) in a profoundly triniform way. The hypothesis thus develops that in order to combat the Balkanization of perceived reality, the neo-Calvinists believed that one must begin with the archetypal unity and diversity of the Godhead.

4. The Holy Trinity

Only having established the concatenous paradigms of divine unity and diversity does Bavinck move on to the section on the Trinity.[138] Following a

---

[135] M.J. Mulder, 'Abraham Kuenen and his successors', *Leiden Oriental Connections 1850–1940* (Brill: Leiden, 1989), ed. Willem Otterspeer, 10.

[136] *RD*, 2.172: 'So, by way of a history-of-religions approach, the theory arises that from very ancient times polytheism rested on a more or less conscious monotheism, somewhat analogously to the way in which, according to Haeckel, the origin of life needs no explanation because it is nothing new, but something in principle inherent already in the inorganic world and in fact in all atoms.'

[137] *RD*, 2.173.

[138] *RD*, 2.256–336.

lengthy exploration of the Scriptural data expressed by the church in Trinitarian language, Bavinck notes the penchant of nineteenth-century philosophy, centred on Schelling's attempt to prove God's triunity via philosophy,[139] for Trinitarian concepts. However, he expresses considerable reservation for this trend: standing foursquare with Aquinas,[140] Calvin[141] and many later Reformed and Lutheran theologians,[142] Bavinck views the Trinity as knowable through revelation, rather than philosophical speculation. God's triunity, it seems, is an utterly unique concept: no adequate analogy or model of the divine triunity exists in the spheres of philosophy or the natural world.

Given his location within the classical Calvinist tradition, Bavinck's position is hardly surprising. However, such an obvious fact raises a question for the basic hypothesis of this work: if no adequate analogy for the Trinity can be found within the creation, can one still maintain that its ubiquitously 'organic' character is rooted in divine triniformity?

The key to understanding Bavinck's relationship of Creator to cosmos lies in his belief that *although God is unlike anything else, all else is nonetheless like him.* This paradigm is intimately related to Bavinck's axiom on revelation being entirely analogous and anthropomorphic. Indeed, it is a necessary consequence of this position. One may shed light on this by way of Bavinck's dissatisfaction with Scholten's handling of God (and the divine triunity) in relation to the world.[143] In short, Scholten interpreted God in the light of the world.[144] The consistent tendency of Bavinck's work is to do the opposite. He reads the cosmos in the light of its Creator, simultaneously guarding the uniqueness of God and the basic fact of general divine self-revelation in the universe.

Bavinck posits the basic pattern of unity-in-diversity in God as the basis for an analogous cosmic unity-in-diversity: 'The Trinity reveals God to us as the fullness of being, the true life, eternal beauty. In God, too, there is unity in diversity, diversity in unity. Indeed, this order and this harmony is present in him absolutely. In the case of creatures we see only a faint analogy of it.'[145]

---

[139] Schelling's attempt to do so was rooted on the concept of 'God' being tripartite: (1) the subject, (2) the object and (3) the identity of the subject-object: F.W.J. Schelling, *Philosophie der Offenbarung*, in *Werke*, II/3 (Stuttgart/Augsburg, J.G. Cotta'scher Verlag, 1856–61), 57 ff.

[140] Thomas Aquinas, *Summa theol.*, I, qu. 32, art. 1.

[141] Calvin, *Institutes*, I.xiii.8; I.xv.4; *Commentary* on Gen. 1:26.

[142] Bavinck cites the works of Hyperius, Zanchi(us), Waleus, van Mastricht, Gerhard, Quenstedt and Hollaz. *RD*, 2.329.

[143] *RD*, 2.43.

[144] Scholten, *De leer der Hervormde Kerk*, 18–20.

[145] *RD*, 2.331.

It is therefore hardly an eisegetical reading of Bavinck to trace the presence of unity-in-diversity within nature and history (as described in the organic motif) to its archetype within the Trinity: Berkouwer's belief that no theological agenda drove Bavinck's use of the motif[146] loses credibility when placed in this light. For Bavinck, cosmic unity-in-diversity, rather than a limited, dubitable repertoire of 'three-in-one' analogies, is the source of all true *vestigia trinitatis*.[147]

5. Concatenation and Synthesis

A careful interplay exists between divine unity and diversity. Bavinck is anxious to found the doctrine of God on a concatenation: if God is the Trinity, the factors of non-uniformity and oneness must exist in uncreated harmony. Each aspect is contingent on the reality of the other. This concatenation is perhaps the outstanding emphasis in his doctrine of God, which has a profound effect on his subsequent worldview, as will be seen in the following chapters on Bavinck's theology of general and special revelation.

> The diversity of attributes, moreover, does not clash with God's simplicity. For that simplicity does not describe God as an abstract and general kind of being; on the contrary, it speaks of him as the absolute fullness of life. It is for this very reason that God reveals himself to finite creatures by many names. The divine essence is so infinitely and profusely rich that no creature can grasp it all at once. Just as a child cannot picture the worth of a coin of great value but only gains some sense of it when it is counted out in a number of smaller coins, so we too cannot possibly form a picture of the infinite fullness of God's essence unless it is displayed to us now in one relationship, then in another, and now from one angle, then from another.[148]

The illustrations selected by Bavinck to demonstrate this point are telling: light has a spectrum of colours; fire can illumine, consume or set aflame; the same grain can be seed, food or fruit. Interestingly, Bavinck is not the author of these illustrations. They are directly taken from, respectively,

---

[146] Berkouwer, *Zoeken en Vinden*, 62.

[147] One must, of course, be careful not to elevate the 'unity-in-diversity' paradigm from becoming a Hegel-style controlling idea that is imposed onto both Creator and creation.

[148] *RD*, 2.127.

Augustine, Moses Maimonides and Basil.[149] The close paradigm between unity and diversity in Creator and creation is evident: God practices self-disclosure macro- and microcosmically in the universe-wide concatenation of oneness and distinction. Indeed, Bavinck explicitly states this parallel: 'In this connection we must remember that God can act in so many different qualities and be called by so many different names, because there is a kinship between him and his creatures. If this kinship did not exist, all the names would be untrue. But now there is in his creatures an analogy to what is present in God himself.'[150]

X. Part Two: The Christocentric, Ontological Relationship Between Creator and Creation[151]

In describing this parallel between unity and diversity as found in both the Godhead and the cosmos, one moves to explore Bavinck's theology of general revelation. However, before this can take place, a conceptual bridge between the doctrines of God and creation must be built: how do the Creator and the creation meet?

This bridge exists in the form of the various ontic categories applied by Bavinck to God, Creation, humanity and the incarnate Christ. Having set out these categories one can begin to grasp the sense in which Bavinck holds Christ as 'the middle of history . . . an organic centre'.[152]

Indeed, one can scarcely underplay the significance of deliberately set ontological boundaries within Bavinck's worldview. While the 'organic' motif is all-pervasive in Bavinck's work, it remains a motif. It is a reflection of deeper, causative factors. In examining the respective ontologies of God and the cosmos, one touches on the profound force which consistently prompts Bavinck's organic language, concepts and imagery.

At the outset, Bavinck creates three rudimentary categories of distinct existence: the divine, the cosmic and the human. How their respective ontologies relate will, according to Bavinck, frame the entirety of one's worldview. 'God, the world and man are the three realities with which all science and all philosophy occupy themselves. The conception which we

---

[149] *RD*, 2.127.
[150] *RD*, 2.127.
[151] An earlier version of this section has been published as James Eglinton, 'To Be or to Become – That Is the Question: Locating the Actualistic in Bavinck's Ontology', *The Kuyper Center Review Volume Two: Revelation and Common Grace*, ed. John Bowlin (Grand Rapids: Eerdmans, 2011), 105–25.
[152] *RD*, 1.383.

form of them, and the relationship in which we place them to one another, determine the character of our view of the world and of life, the content of our religion, science and morality.'[153]

Bavinck's ontology is played out in the nomenclature and categories of 'being' and 'becoming', the former denoting immutability and the latter, mutability. Just as ontic categories were framed in the language of nature, being and hypostasis in the fifth-century, and actualism, essentialism and ontology in current debate, the late nineteenth-century debated within its own semantic field. Thus one finds Bavinck's choice of 'being' and 'becoming' fairly typical *in situ.* Bavinck's vocabulary is shared by Hegel *et al.*, although (as with the shared organicist language) the meaning ascribed to these terms differs radically.[154] Incidentally, it is interesting to note that the four points made in defining the organic motif listed earlier from *CW* were written by Bavinck in a chapter entitled 'Being and Becoming'.[155] Evidently, within this triniform organic worldview there is also a consequent understanding of being and becoming.

In writing against the Hegelian notion that being is in a constant state of becoming, Bavinck strictly applies 'being' to the divine and 'becoming' to the non-divine. How he devises an ontological category for the twofold exercise of the *imago Dei* (in the creation of humanity, followed by the Incarnation) sheds much light on Bavinck's ultimate christocentrism.

In his ascription of 'being' to God, 'becoming' to the universe and 'being *and* becoming' to humanity and the Incarnate Jesus (in whom Creator and created meet), Bavinck evidently finds it most appropriate (by virtue of the breathtaking unity and diversity on show) to describe the Christian worldview as inherently organic in character.

The bulk of information on Bavinck's handling of being and becoming is gleaned by a joint-reading of various passages from Reformed Dogmatics Vol. 2 and *Philosophy of Revelation*.

1. Bavinck and being

Bavinck handles issues of being primarily in Parts 1 and 2 (Knowing God; The Living, Acting God) of Reformed Dogmatics, Vol. 2. At the start of *Knowing God,* he begins a discussion on divine incomprehensibility with the

---

[153] *PR*, 83.
[154] *Contra* Veenhof, *Revelatie en Inspiratie*, 268: 'Kuyper and Bavinck employed the concepts of "organism" and "organic" in the universal sense of the time.'
[155] *CW*, 'Zijn en Worden', 37–68.

following statement: 'But the moment we dare to speak about God the question arises: How can we? We are human and he is the Lord our God. Between him and us there seems to be no such kinship or communion as would enable us to name him truthfully. The distance between God and us is the gulf between the Infinite and the finite, between eternity and time, *between being and becoming*, between the All and the nothing. However little we know of God, even the faintest notion implies that he is a being who is infinitely exalted above every creature.'[156]

In writing this, he sets out the paradigmic relationship between God and the cosmos. This paradigm can be reduced to two elements: (a) the divine being and (b) the absolute distinction that exists between Creator and creation.

While Bavinck goes on to assert the knowability of God, his theology is nonetheless shaped by these gulfs: the divine and the human, the limitless and the limited, the eternal and the temporal, that which is and that which becomes. These are not differing points on the same gradient scale. Bavinck phrases them as polar extremes: the Creator occupies one, the creation another, and a vast gulf stands between them. 'There is nothing intermediate between these two classes of categories: a deep chasm separates God's being from that of all creatures.'[157] It must be noted that Bavinck handles the Creator–creature relationship under two theological categories: ontology and economy. Here he is speaking ontologically. Bavinck affirms that God enters into a relationship with the cosmos in the economy of salvation, but this is a separate issue to their basic ontological relationship.

The two fundamental elements of his ontological paradigm are closely related. Indeed, Bavinck grounds one (the Creator–creation distinction) on the other (the being of God). The creation is ontologically different from God because his state of being is entirely unique.[158] Thus, for Bavinck, God cannot be everything (pantheism) because his being belongs only to himself. Pantheism is an ontological impossibility.

Clearly, ontology is at the heart of Bavinck's theology. The divine being is central to Bavinck's ontological system. How does he define the being of God?

In a discussion of the divine independence, Bavinck explores the development of the terms 'independence' and 'aseity' with regard to God.

---

[156] *RD*, 2.30. Emphasis added.
[157] *RD*, 2.158–9.
[158] 'Moreover, with a view to pantheism, which equates the being of God with that of the universe, it is even supremely important to stress the fact that God has a nature of his own, that he is an independent being, whose essence is distinct from that of the universe.' *RD*, 2.111.

Divine aseity marks out God as absolute being. God's existence does not depend on the cosmos. Indeed, the opposite is true. Furthermore, God's existence does not depend on himself. He is not self-caused, rather he is from everlasting to everlasting. The independence of God's being, for Bavinck, finds its counterpart in the genuine independence of the creature, which stands against both pantheism and the lack of cosmic independence in Scholten's worldview. In this context Bavinck writes: 'But as is evident from the word "aseity", God is exclusively from himself, not in the sense of being self-caused but being from eternity to eternity who he is, being not becoming.'[159]

Such a starting point is fascinating when viewed against the backdrop of Bavinck's Leiden education. There, Scholten's process began with cosmic causality, from which all else (concerning God, the universe and humanity) was to be inferred. Scholten's doctrine of God thus reflected his determinist cosmology. His view of the divine strongly accented the factors necessary to explain a determinist universe (principally identifying God as the original cause and determiner) while allowing the seemingly less 'useful' elements of the doctrine of God (e.g. triunity) to atrophy. Bavinck, however, makes a radical departure from this method. His portrayal of God gives causality a lower place in the hierarchy of truths. One ought not plunder the Godhead for that which humanity deems 'useful', and on this basis ascribe worth to the divine. Rather, Bavinck claims that one must accept God as he is. God, rather than the material principle of absolute causality, is theology's point of origin. To emphasize this, Bavinck draws attention to the fact that God is not self-caused.

His discussion of the divine independence then leads on directly to his handling of divine immutability. In this respect too, Bavinck further outlines the workings of the Creator–creation relationship dynamic. 'If God were not immutable, he would not be God. His name is "being", and this name is "an unalterable name". All that changes ceases to be what it was. But true being belongs to him who does not change. That which changes "was something and will be something but *is* not anything because it is mutable". But God who *is* cannot change, for every change would diminish his being.'[160]

Bavinck's basic conviction is that in his ontological existence (his 'true' being), God cannot change. As such, Bavinck handles being and becoming as separate, mutually exclusive ontological categories. Becoming is not

---

[159] *RD*, 2.152.
[160] *RD*, 2.154.

being because it is in the process of change. Conversely, being is not becoming because it is immutable.[161]

His starting point is that to become is creaturely, but to be is divine.[162] Bavinck primarily frames the divine ontology in non-actualistic terms.

2. Bavinck and becoming

In examining Bavinck's theology of the created, two quotes are of particular significance. 'Becoming is an attribute of creatures, a form of change in space and time. But God is who he is, eternally transcendent over space and time and far exalted above every creature.'[163]

'God alone is the Eternal and Imperishable One. He alone towers above processes of becoming and change. *Things*, by contrast, have a beginning and an end and are subject to change.'[164]

His basic definition of God and God's distinction from the creation finds a parallel form in Bavinck's ontology of createdness.[165] The divine ontology is focused on God's independent, timeless state of being; an ontology quite unlike that of the cosmos. Conversely, the hallmarks of the creation are its dependent, temporal state of becoming, and its ontological difference from the divine being.

A creaturely ontology operates within a framework of creation and eschatology; definite points between which the cosmos is constantly in a process of ceasing-to-be and coming-to-be. The created state of existence is one of continual mutability. His understanding of the created realm as engaged in perpetual becoming can be found in various metanarratives running throughout Bavinck's work.

The overarching theme of creation, fall, redemption and consummation which dominates Reformed Dogmatics marks out the cosmos as continually changing. Having been made without sin, it falls into rebellion against the Creator. The Triune God shows grace to redeem the cosmos. This

---

[161] In this respect, Bavinck regards himself as Augustinian. ('It is instinctual for every rational creature to think that there is an altogether unchangeable and incorruptible God.' Augustine, *The Trinity*, V, 2).

[162] 'The doctrine of God's immutability is highly significant for religion. The difference between the Creator and the creature hinges on *the contrast between being and becoming*. All that is creaturely is in the process of becoming. It is changeable, constantly striving, in search of rest and satisfaction, and finds this rest only in *him who is pure being without becoming*.' *RD*, 2.156.

[163] *RD*, 2.158.

[164] *RD*, 2.417.

[165] The notion of 'creaturely ontology' is here used to explain the technical sense in which Bavinck explains the creation's state of (mutable) existence.

redemption was accomplished in the person of Christ and is now being applied by the Holy Spirit, who is preparing the cosmos for its final consummation. This is the story seen by Bavinck throughout all of revelation, nature and history. Essential to that story is the factor of the creation's inherent mutability.

In Bavinck's critique of the mechanical worldview is the allegation that it denies the possibility of reading cosmic becoming as development. 'In the mechanical worldview, there is no place for development. All differences between things, however great they may be, are ultimately accidental and quantitative. Nothing *becomes*, because there is nothing that *needs* to become, that *must* become. There is no goal or starting point. Development presupposes both. It describes the path from one to the other. . . . There is no development with machines and instruments, it only exists with organic beings.'[166]

As has previously been noted, the idea of grace restoring nature forms a major thread in Bavinck's work. 'Grace does not remain outside our above or beside nature but rather permeates and wholly renews it. And thus nature, reborn by grace, will be brought to its highest revelation.'[167]

That nature can be restored implies that it has undergone a ceasing-to-be (in its fall into sin) and that it is in a process of coming-to-be (in its restoration by grace). Bavinck locates grace as present to restore nature in various places. It is foundational to the working of providence, whereby God is guiding history to a definitive end point of consummation.

The mutable state of the cosmos also lies at the heart of Bavinck's thoroughgoing organic commitments. *Contra* Scholten, Bavinck claims that the cosmos is not a completed, monistic machine driven by a single force of endless cause and effect. Rather, it is unfinished, growing and developing to a point of foreordained eschatological climax. History is the tale of mutability moving into eschatology. The cosmic organism's teleological drive also presupposes its inherent mutability.

He also uses the organic metaphor to describe the economic relationship between God and the cosmos, because their respective ontologies are so utterly different. If one is to maintain the reality of both Creator and

---

[166] *CW*, 58–9. Dutch original: 'In de mechanische wereldbeschouwing is er voor ontwikkeling in eigenlijken zin gene plaats. Alle verschillen tusschen de dingen, hoe groot ook, zijn ten slotte accidenteel en quantitatief. Er *wordt* hier niets, omdat er niets is dat *behoeft* te worden, dat worden *moet*. Er is geen doel en geen uitgangspunt. En ontwikkeling onderstelt juist beide: zij beschrijft den weg, die van het eene naar het andere leidt. . . . Ontwikkeling is er dus niet by machines en instrumenten, maar alleen bij organische wezens.'

[167] Herman Bavinck, 1888 address at the Kampen Theological School (cited in John Bolt, 'Editor's Introduction' in *RD*, 2.18).

created, Bavinck believes, the separate ontic categories of being and
becoming, or immutability and actualism, must be maintained. However,
what Bavinck perceives to be their correct order is of vital importance.
'Philosophy throughout the ages and among all nations and down to the
present day divides itself into two tendencies. With Zeno, "becoming" is
sacrificed to "being", or with Heraclitus, "being" to "becoming". In point of
fact, we can spare neither, for "becoming" presupposes "being". There can
be no question of change if there is no identity and continuity of the
subject.'[168]

In Bavinck's order, being comes first. Its reality is posited in the notion of
becoming. It is the constant factor by which becoming redefines itself.

Bavinck's unwillingness to deviate from this Creator–creature distinction
is striking. Indeed, on this point his closeness to Calvin's *finitum non capax
infinitum* marks out Bavinck's divine ontology as clearly Reformed. This is
neither a Lutheran nor a Roman Catholic account. Rather, Bavinck
formulates a divine ontology in line with the *extra-Calvinisticum*. This points
towards a significant diversion between the early twentieth-century's two
significant movements within the Reformed tradition: neo-Calvinism and
neo-Orthodoxy. In the latter, Barth held election closely to divine ontology.
In the former, Bavinck posits that God's ontology is separate from election.
According to Bavinck, God does not will the ultimate ontic reality, himself,
to be.[169] Thus while God's will proves determinative for all else, his ontology
nonetheless remains separate. McCormack has elsewhere helpfully
described the difference between Barth and Calvin on this point: 'What we
see in the collision between Calvin and Barth, then, is not simply a clash
between two views of the *extent* of election. At the most fundamental level,
it is a clash between a theologian working with what we might call an
"essentialist" ontology and a theologian working with an "actualistic"
ontology.'[170]

Using McCormack's categories, it is clear that Bavinck, like Calvin, is 'a
theologian working with an essentialist ontology'. Bavinck's short work
Johannes Calvijn also makes plain that he saw Calvin as operating within
these ontological parameters: '[Calvin] climbs from the creation to the
Creator, from the temporal to the Eternal, from the visible to the Invisible,

---

[168] *PR*, 97.
[169] *RD*, 2.152.
[170] Bruce McCormack, 'Grace and being: the role of God's gracious election in Karl Barth's
theological ontology', *The Cambridge Companion to Karl Barth* (Cambridge: University Press,
2000), ed. John Webster, 97.

from that which becomes to that which Is, from mutable history to the immutable council of the LORD.'[171]

However, as will be seen, Bavinck's handling of the *imago Dei* is highly distinctive. Bavinck, like Barth, recognizes that the traditional *extra-Calvinisticum* struggles to accommodate the fact that God, in christocentric self-revelation, must somehow enter into 'becoming'. As will be shown, Bavinck's attempt to locate this within the *imago Dei* (generally in humanity and fully in the incarnate Christ) is not without problems. Most unfortunately, Bavinck's constructive theology is particularly hard to engage with on this point. His solution to modern theology's problems with the *extra-Calvinisticum* (as will be seen) centres on the development of an unusual Christological–anthropological *imago Dei* innovation. He brings these concepts together in an uneasy, and potentially unorthodox, manner. Indeed, his solution must be read charitably in order to view its conclusions as falling within the bounds of orthodoxy. Sadly, the lack of clarity with which he writes at this point limits his contribution to this debate. However, one should not be entirely dismissive of his attempted solution. It contains some potential and as such is included in this discussion.

3. The knowability of a 'non-actualistic' God

For Bavinck, the Creator is not the creation, and the creation is not the Creator. This begs the question whether Bavinck's God is any more knowable than the God of Deism? Bavinck writes: 'Deism creates a vast gulf between God and his creatures, cancels out their mutual relatedness, and reduces God to an abstract entity, a pure being, to mere monotonous and uniform existence. It satisfies neither the mind nor the heart and is therefore the death of religion.'[172]

In what sense does Bavinck's system, which also posits 'a vast gulf between God and his creatures', enable a mutual relatedness between Creator and cosmos and prevent the reduction of God to an abstract state of being who exists in dull uniformity?

Bavinck's Trinitarian doctrine of God is conceptualized on ontological and economic levels.[173] When Bavinck speaks of the fundamental ontological

---

[171] Bavinck, *Johannes Calvijn*, 15. Dutch original: 'Hij klimt uit het schepsel tot den Schepper, uit het tijdelijke tot den Eeuwige, uit het zienlijke tot den Onzienlijke, uit het worden tot den Zijnde, uit de wisselende historie tot den onveranderlijken raad des Heeren op.'
[172] *RD*, 2.331.
[173] *RD*, 2.318.

distinction between God and the cosmos, this is not the totality of his doctrines of God or divine knowability. Bavinck is not a Deist precisely because his God is the Trinity whose ontological being is outwardly manifested in revelations and works.[174]

That the ontological essence of the Triune God remains immutable does not, for Bavinck, prevent the outward works of the economic Trinity in the universe. According to Bavinck, true being is the cause of becoming. The two are linked. However, this becoming occurs separately from true being. God's being is the cause of the universe's becoming. Thus difference, even at the starkest ontological level, need not necessitate disunity. A mutable universe, says Bavinck, can still be closely (organically) connected to an immutable God. 'In his being there is no sign of becoming. Conversely, it is God who posits the creature, eternity which posits time, immensity which posits space, being which posits becoming, immutability which posits change.'[175]

How does Bavinck conceptualize the aforementioned 'mutual related-ness' of God to the creation, and particularly between God and human-kind? When examining the application of the Creator–creature distinction in Bavinck's work, one finds two exceptions where being and becoming meet. These exceptions occur in the two instances of God expressing his image in the cosmos: first, in the creation of humanity; and second, in the incarnation of Jesus Christ. These are the only theological loci where Bavinck describes simultaneous being and becoming.

4. Bavinck on being and becoming

In *Philosophy of Revelation*, Bavinck writes:

> Every man lives in his own time, comes into being and passes away, appears and disappears; he seems only a part of the whole, a moment in the process. But every man also bears the ages in his heart; in his spirit-life he stands above and outside of history. He lives in the past and the past lives in him, for, as Nietzsche says, man cannot forget. He also lives in the future and the future lives in him, for he bears hope imperishably in his bosom. Thus he can discover something of the connection between the past, the present, and the future; thus he is at the same time maker and

---

[174] 'The "ontological" Trinity is mirrored in the "economic" Trinity.' *RD*, 2.318.
[175] *RD*, 2.158.

knower of history. He belongs himself to history, yet he stands above it; he is a child of time and yet has part in eternity; he *becomes* and he *is* at the same time; he passes away and yet he abides.[176]

If humanity is created, why does it not comply with the otherwise universal ontological distinction between Creator and creation? Bavinck traces humanity's unique ontology to its creation as the divine image.

Humanity was created, thus it bears the hallmarks of createdness. Mutability is a constant feature of human existence: humans are born and die. However, Bavinck regards humanity, by virtue of its status of divine image bearer, as also exhibiting signs of immutability.

He sees humanity's position as *imago Dei* in distinct senses corporately and individually. The individual human is a psychosomatic union of body and soul. As such, he is the meeting place for the visible and the invisible, the bringing together of heaven and earth. He represents that which is to that which becomes and vice versa.

Bavinck also places a distinct accent on the collective divine image bearing of the human race. The entire triune deity, he claims, is the archetype of humanity. As a race, humans transcend the moment. Individuals come and go but the race continues. Collectively, humanity assigns meaning to the present in relation to an understood past and a hoped for future. Humans, like their Creator, 'bear the ages in [their] hearts'. Knowledge is passed between generations. Indeed, it is the collective property of all humanity.

This notion of humankind's collective possession of knowledge is a common feature in Dutch neo-Calvinism. Kuyper makes use of the concept in his 1908 speech 'Our Instinctive Life': 'All generations labor at enlarging the slowly growing body of science. No one has ever by personal initiative or by dint of extreme effort magically leaped to the level achieved by our present generation. Human knowledge and skill is the common possession of all people collectively, a possession gradually won by the effort of succeeding generations and guided in its development by an invisible power. The result is what we call *progress* in every area of human endeavor, and that result, thus gained, far exceeds the knowledge and skill of animals.'[177] Noting the reference to Ecclesiastes 3, it seems that both Kuyper and Bavinck regard this collective knowledge as relating to the *imago Dei* in that humanity, like its Creator, is capable of amassing knowledge that transcends the immediate.

---

[176] *PR*, 140.
[177] Abraham Kuyper, 'Our Instinctive Life', *Abraham Kuyper: A Centennial Reader*, 258.

Metanarratives are sought throughout cosmic history. Humans become and yet they are. This ontological definition of humanity generates a fascinating set of questions, particularly as one attempts to relate Bavinck's anthropology to Chaledonian Christology. Whether intentionally or otherwise, Bavinck has drawn a parallel between his doctrine of humanity as the *imago Dei* and his theology of Christ as God incarnate. His description of the former portrays the human being as one person in whom two distinct ontological realities are reflected: the divine (that which *is*) and the creaturely (that which *becomes*).

At face value, this carries an echo of the orthodox creedal formula which accounts for the reality of Christ's divinity and humanity: he is fully God and fully man, two natures in one person. Bavinck articulates an anthropology that seems to describe the human via a markedly similar paradigm (two natures in one person), and, it appears, derives that paradigm from humanity's status as *imago Dei*. Several comments stand in reflection upon this.

First, it is interesting that Bavinck here chooses to emphasize man's eternity in the sphere of history and pre-eschaton providence, rather than individual or cosmic eschatology. Even without discussing eschatology, the human collective succeeds in transcending the moment. The human past, just as much as its future, accounts for humanity's eternity. However, as was previously noted, this is not an accent unique to Bavinck.

Second, when one pays close attention to the obvious parallel drawn between the co-presence of mutability and immutability in Christ and humanity (both described by Scripture as the *imago Dei*), various issues arise.

The precise sense in which Bavinck defines human ontology is somewhat unclear. (Indeed, this section in his work is uncharacteristic in its lack of clarity). Whether he regards the human as having two separate ontologies (mutable and immutable) or a dual ontology which combines the two (one ontology in two natures) is hard to discern definitively. This failure to resolve this issue, as will be seen, creates subtle but not insignificant ambiguities in an important area of his thought.

If to be ontologically human (and the *imago Dei*) is to possess two natures (to be and to become, to reflect divinity and createdness), the sense in which Christ became man requires careful attention. A 'three natures in one person' Christology, whereby Christ unites human mutability and immutability to the divine *logos*, is somewhat out of step with catholic Christology. Alternatively, if Bavinck is merely trying to demonstrate that humans are, in some sense, both mutable and eternal, and this is an echo of Jesus as *theanthropos*, his contribution sits more easily within creedal tradition.[178]

Among the various loci of orthodox theology, Christology has perhaps the least room for innovation. For the past two millennia, the church has articulated its theology of the Christ with tremendous technical precision. Creative Christology requires nothing short of the utmost caution and a total submission to the great Christological documents of the early church. This need for reticence and rigorous explanation also stands when the language and paradigms of orthodox Christology are invoked to handle other theological subjects; perhaps none more so than a theological anthropology. Relating one to the other needs more clarity than Bavinck seems to offer within the immediate context of Philosophy of Revelation. Although Bavinck's statements on Christology in Reformed Dogmatics are orthodox and clear, the parallel he draws between Christology and anthropology nonetheless leaves various questions unresolved.

In terms of being-and-becoming in Reformed Dogmatics, Bavinck is aware of the New Testament's use of the verb *egeneto* (from *ginomai*, to become) in relation to the incarnate Son of God. Indeed, among the New Testament's most profound Christological statements is that 'the Word became flesh' (John 1:14). He also highlights the uniqueness of Christ's claim to being: 'before Abraham was, I am' (*ego eimi*, John 8:58).

On the incarnation, Bavinck writes: '[Christ] would not have been like us in all things had he not subjected himself to time and space, to the law of becoming. . . . The incarnation is the unity of being (*ego eimi*, John 8:58) and becoming (*sarks egeneto*, John 1:14).'[179]

On humanity, Reformed Dogmatics also seems to share the humanity as being-and-becoming paradigm seen in Philosophy of Revelation: 'This distinction answered the question what Adam had to become, not what Adam was.'[180]

Clearly, Bavinck is aware of and committed to the Chalcedonian understanding of Christ's natures and person. Indeed, he charges Medieval, Roman Catholic, Lutheran and modern Christologies (principally Kant, Schleiermacher and Ritschl) with straying from Chalcedon's basic

---

[178] It does not seem irresponsible to read Bavinck's thoughts on creation having its presupposition and preparation in the incarnation as easing this tension somewhat, particularly the statement that 'Specifically, the creation of humans in God's image is a supposition and preparation for the incarnation of God.' *RD*, 3.277.

[179] *RD*, 1.380.

[180] *RD*, 2.550; *PR*, 140.

position.[181] For all that the aforementioned section of *Philosophy of Revelation* is slightly ambiguous, it is obvious from *Reformed Dogmatics* that Bavinck believes wholeheartedly in the full reality of Jesus' divinity and humanity. One must therefore assume no intent to contradict or depart from this on his part. The sections 'Divine and Human United' and '"Nature" and "Person"' in *Sin and Salvation in Christ*[182] exert a thoroughly orthodox Christology in this respect.

Chalcedon refrained from defining Christ's person as a confusion or commingling of humanity and divinity. In an ontological exploration of Christ's humanity and divinity, Bavinck attempts to follow suit. Christ, as *theanthropos*, possesses two distinct natures; he is both God and man. The unity of two natures, one immutable and the other mutable, is central to his Christology.

It is unsurprising that Bavinck's Christology itself is of impeccable orthodoxy. The question marks arise not in relation to his Christology, but rather in his apparent invocation of a Christological paradigm to formulate a theological anthropology. Undeniably, Scripture posits a close relationship between Christ and humanity with regard to the *imago Dei* (Genesis 1:26; Colossians 1:15). However, it also makes plain that in addition to becoming an authentic human being, Jesus is also the real second person of the holy Trinity. In short, Jesus is the substance of the divine; something no child of Adam, however much his own eternity analogously reflects the divine, will ever be.

If one may make any criticism of Bavinck, it is simply that he raises a novel development without fully exploring its weighty consequences. Insofar as one reads him as sympathetic towards Chalcedon in attempting to show that whatever humanity ectypally displays (in terms of mutability and eternity) is infinitely surpassed by Christ's archetypal, substantive godness and humanity, Bavinck's incarnational analogy may serve as a useful heuristic tool.

However, one cannot help but read Bavinck on this point and wish he had clarified some of the aforementioned issues. That having been said, one must recognize the particularly awkward conceptual and terminological nature of this debate. Discussion of Christology via ontology is an inherently problematic necessity. As MacQuarrie helpfully notes, '[a]lthough the New Testament itself is almost devoid of philosophical terms, we cannot reflect theologically on its claims for Jesus Christ without getting into ontology.'[183]

---

[181] *RD*, 2.253–74.
[182] *RD*, 3.298–308.
[183] John MacQuarrie, *Jesus Christ in Modern Thought* (London: SCM, 1990), 7.

In order to do so, Bavinck handled debates from different eras (fifth-century Chalcedonian Christological controversy and late nineteenth-century philosophical debates) which discuss a similar remit through distinct, highly contextualized language (nature, person and hypostasis; being and becoming). Furthermore, to relate Bavinck to contemporary debate, one must also incorporate a third terminological subset (ontology, actualism and essentialism). The seeming lack of clarity in Bavinck's own writings on this matter, one suspects, simply reflects the nature of the debate.

It should be remarked, however, that without understanding the vast gulf posited by Bavinck between immutability and mutability, between Creator and cosmos, his Christology remains elusive. Furthermore, in Bavinck's mind, to be human is a wonderful, mysterious privilege. Failure to grasp the otherwise mutual exclusivity of being and becoming renders the reader blind to this fact.

Bavinck's concept of the incarnate Jesus takes on a striking definition when viewed against the backdrop of immutability and mutability. In a broken cosmos, Christ has become fully, ontologically human and, via his unique mediatorship, has become the perfect meeting place of that which was otherwise divided by unfathomable ontic and ethical divides. It does not seem an exaggeration to say that the sense in which Christ stands as the 'organic centre' of all revelation is lost until one grapples with Bavinck's ontological concerns.[184] That Christ somehow holds many diverse things together takes on a breathtaking focus when one observes that in Bavinck's thought, Christ is the perfect meeting place of the otherwise ontologically mutually exclusive: he is the unity of being and becoming. The incarnate Jesus is, for Bavinck, the ultimate ontological impossibility made possible: the *logos* is *ensarkos*.

However, while Bavinck allows the Son of God, in his incarnation, to become, he does not on this basis extend becoming to the Father or the Holy Spirit. The one divine essence remains immutable. As Bavinck maintains the classical immanent and economic Trinitarian categories, he does not apply Christ's being-in-action, a factor he ties to Christ's incarnation and mediatorship, to the Father or the Spirit. In locating being-and-becoming (or, one might say, an ontology of *both* essentialism *and* actualism) in the *imago Dei*, Bavinck attempts to wed a classical Christology to more modern emphases. With some clarification and reworking, such an approach contains potential but, most unfortunately, the lack of clarity with which he explored this concept shrouds it in doubt.

---

[184] *RD*, 1.383.

XI. Conclusion: Bavinck as 'Worldview' Theologian

'God's unity brought about the unity of the world.'[185]

Having recognized the prominent place of unity-in-diversity within Bavinck's doctrine of God and the concurrent unity-in-diversity *vestigia trinitatis* in the organism of the universe, one must query the extent to which Bavinck intentionally orbs these factors together. Clearly, the degree to which he does so will affect the relative force with which one may speak of the organic motif as tied to the *vestigia*.

At this point, it is appropriate to note that while Bavinck's goal in theology was always to be richly catholic in scope, he nonetheless believed that the purest expression of this catholic theology was found in the Reformed tradition. In this Reformed stream, of course, Bavinck rose to prominence within the Dutch neo-Calvinist movement. As such, he ought to be read in light of the neo-Calvinist distinctive of 'worldview'. 'Reformational reflection on worldview has taken distinctive shape as it moved into the twentieth-century, something that can be seen specifically in the work of such Dutch leaders as Abraham Kuyper, Herman Bavinck, Herman Dooyeweerd and D.H.T. Vollenhoven. Their contributions to a more profound and articulate understanding of the biblical worldview have come through theology, philosophy and other academic disciplines, and especially through cultural and social action arising from a deep desire to be obedient to the Scriptures in all areas of life and service.'[186]

What may be termed a broadly neo-Calvinist worldview operates around the anchor points of creation, fall, redemption and consummation. This redemptive–historical hermeneutic provided the neo-Calvinists with a distinctive reading of Scripture and understanding of themselves in the world. Herman Bavinck's nephew, Johan Herman Bavinck, for example, provides an example of neo-Calvinist missiology centred on these points.[187]

Kuyper's Stone Lectures (*Lectures on Calvinism*) assert that Calvinism is nothing less than a 'life system'.[188] 'Calvinists have never thought that the idea of the cosmos lay in God's foreordination as an aggregate of loosely

---

[185] Bavinck, 'Christianity and Natural Science', 99.

[186] Wolters, *Creation Regained*, 1–2.

[187] 'Missions is that activity of the church – in essence it is nothing more than an activity of Christ, exercised through the church – through which the church, in this interim period, in which the end is postponed, calls the peoples of the earth to repentance and to faith in Christ, so that they may be made his disciples and through baptism be incorporated into the fellowship of those who await the coming of the kingdom.' Johan Herman Bavinck, *An Introduction to the Reformed Science of Missions*, tr. David Hugh Freeman (Grand Rapids: Baker, 1960), 62.

[188] Kuyper, *Lectures on Calvinism*, 9–40.

conjoined degrees, but they have always maintained that the whole formed one organic programme of the entire creation and the entire history.'[189]

In this context, Kuyper supports this claim by citing George Bancroft's claim that Calvinism 'has a theory of ontology, of ethics, of social happiness, and of human liberty, all derived from God.'[190] Most interesting is that when Kuyper develops this idea of a worldview drawn from the divine unity, he frequently employs the organic motif.[191]

Indeed, Herman Bavinck's own Stone Lectures (*Philosophy of Revelation*) were essentially an expansion of his earlier work *Christelijke Wereldbeschouwing*. In this book, Bavinck argues that the doctrine of God is the foundation of a coherent worldview:

> The Christian worldview opposes autonomy and anarchy with all its power. It holds that man is not autonomous, but is always and everywhere bound by laws not invented by man, but set forth by God as the rule for life. In religion and morality, in the family, society and the state, everywhere there are ideas, norms which stand above man. *They form a unity among themselves and find their origin and continuation in the Creator and Lawgiver of the universe* [italics added for emphasis]. These norms are the most precious treasures entrusted to mankind, the basis for all societal institutions. . . . These divine ideas and laws are foundations and norms, the goods and treasures, the interconnections and patterns for all creatures. To live in conformity to those norms in mind and heart, in thought and action, this is what it means most basically to become conformed to the image of God's Son. And this is the ideal and goal of man.[192]

The clarity and conviction with which Bavinck asserted not simply the possibility but rather the necessity of theocentrism for a united interpretation of the world stood throughout his career. After its initial release in 1904 and expansion in the Stone Lectures, *Christelijke Wereldbeschouwing* was republished in 1913 and (posthumously) in 1929. What is most apparent in Bavinck's adherence to the neo-Calvinist emphasis on *wereldbeschouwing* is that in his opinion, the divine unity means the idea of *worldview* is both

---

[189] Kuyper, *Lectures on Calvinism*, 115.

[190] George Bancroft, *History of the United States of America* (New York: Appleton, 1890), 405.

[191] For various examples, see Kuyper, *Lectures on Calvinism*, 16, 33, 59, 65, 79–80, 82, 89–96, 113, 115.

[192] *CW*, cited and translated in Gordon J. Spykman, 'Sphere Sovereignty in Calvin and the Calvinist Tradition', *Exploring the Heritage of John Calvin*, ed. David E. Holwerda (Grand Rapids: Baker, 1976), 181–2.

justified and necessitated. The doctrine of God gives reality its basic coherence and thus positions the Christian theist to gather the whole of life together under the doctrine of God.

That this is true of Bavinck has been earlier argued by Harinck.

> It is interesting to note that [Bavinck's] Reformed beliefs did not hamper him in his relationship to the world in which he lived. Many in his environment – particularly those in secessionist circles, but also in modern circles – believed that the first should be subtracted from the second, either from pietistic diffidence toward the world or from the opinion that orthodoxy is equal to small-mindedness and underdevelopment. In relation to our current reflections on the relationship between belief and modernity, Bavinck's spirituality is of great importance. *His starting point was the unity of God* [italics added], which implies a catholic Christian faith – a faith of all times and of all places.[193]

This alternative reading of Bavinck has thus attempted to begin at his own starting point: the doctrine of God. There, one has found an abundance of material which supports the hypothesis that while the language of his organic motif reflects his time, he did not use this language in 'the universal sense of the time'.[194] Rather, one can strongly argue that his paradigmic concerns for the themes of unity-in-diversity and the interconnectedness of distinct elements (ideas which form the kernel of the organic motif) stem from his doctrine of God.

Indeed, if this doctrine of God will translate into general and special revelation, these themes should be evident throughout. The following chapters on the organic motif in those areas will therefore attempt to further construct this reading.

---

[193] Harinck, '"Something that must remain, if the truth is to be sweet and precious to us": The Reformed Spirituality of Herman Bavinck', 260–61.
[194] Contra Veenhof, *Revelatie en Inspiratie*, 268.

Chapter 5

The Organic Motif and General Revelation

I. Introduction

'The whole Trinity is revealed to us in the creation.'[1]

'Now the fact that the world is the theatre of God's self-revelation can hardly be denied.'[2]

Thus far, this book has argued that the basic hermeneutic used in many works on Bavinck (which one has labelled the 'two Bavincks' hypothesis) is demonstrably flawed and, noting the recent developments in Bavinck studies (particularly in the writings of Nelson Kloosterman and John Bolt), a new, united reading of Bavinck's theology has been sought. The particular focus of this work is, of course, Bavinck's frequently employed organic motif. Having noted the particular application of the 'two Bavincks' model to Jan Veenhof's highly influential handling of the motif, a new reading of the organic idea has been proposed: the new hypothesis being that God's triunity is the ultimate source of this pervasive motif.

As the previous chapter demonstrated, the doctrine of God in Bavinck's theology provides an abundance of material in support of this hypothesis. For Bavinck, the Trinity is Godhead in incomparably profound unity-in-diversity. This reality has a direct consequence for the non-divine: 'He, the triune God, shows us in himself the completely perfect system: the origin, type, model and image of all other systems.'[3] However, as was shown earlier, the three-in-one nature of divine triunity exists in utter uniqueness: it cannot be replicated and, according to Bavinck, is revealed analogically in the non-numerically specified pattern of generic unity-in-diversity. If one inserts the classical language of *vestigia trinitatis* into Bavinck's work, the

---

[1] Augustine, *City of God*, 353.
[2] *RD*, 1.56.
[3] Herman Bavinck, *Kennis en Leven* (Kampen: J.H. Kok, 1922), 59. 'Hij, de Drieëenige, toont ons in zich zelven het gansch volkomen systeem: oorsprong, type, model en beeld aller andere systemen.'

hallmarks of the Trinity are not tied to the tenuous 'triads' of medieval theology. Rather, God is glorified in the organic unit that is the time–space continuum. The fundamental argument thus presented is that more often than not, when Bavinck finds triniform cosmic unity-in-diversity, he invokes organic imagery. This chapter (which notes that Bavinck writes in the Reformed tradition, thus maintaining the basic facts of God's self-revelation in general and special categories) explores the character of general divine revelation in relation to the organic motif.

The primary sources in this investigation are Part IV of 'Prolegomena'[4] ('Revelation: *Principium Externum*', §§ 9–10) and *Philosophy of Revelation*. Although the latter work was published a decade later than *RD*, it develops the same themes earlier laid down in *RD*. What will be seen is that Bavinck's life context prompted a lifelong insistence on the validity of divine self-revelation.

II. Bavinck's Doctrine of Revelation in Context

As was briefly touched on in Chapter 1, Bavinck's life took place within a Europe-wide war of ideas. Six years before Bavinck's birth, Johannes Scholten's sparring partner, Cornelis Willem Opzoomer, advised the Dutch Government to remove the theological faculties from its universities.[5] Although this counsel was not immediately followed, it nonetheless sets the backdrop against which Bavinck would emerge.

In the middle of the nineteenth-century, Europe was engulfed in revolution. Although there was no revolution in the Netherlands, the events in neighbouring countries considerably affected Dutch national life. Fearing that his kingdom would be plunged into anti-monarchist violence, the Dutch King William II ordered Johan Rudolph Thorbecke to revise the national constitution. The effect of this revision was the maintenance of William's status and the considerable reduction of his powers. Parliamentary democracy was introduced and suffrage enlarged. Thus while there was no violent revolution in Amsterdam, the revolution's worldview nonetheless gained dominance in the Netherlands and took William II as its *de facto* vassal king.

As the principal framer of the new constitution, Thorbecke significantly influenced it to reflect his liberal political leanings. Interestingly, Thorbecke

---

[4] *RD*, 1.283–322.
[5] Herman Bavinck, 'Theology and Religious Studies: Appendix B', *Essays on Religion, Science and Society*, 281.

was a student of the 'state as organism' theory and as such reflects the broad, 'organic' concerns of the nineteenth-century. 'The structure is guaranteed under the constitution of 1848, whose principal architect, Johan Thorbecke, envisioned the modern state as a complex whole, composed of dynamic but interdependent parts. A student of organic state theory and a sharp critic of the French tradition of centralized government, fundamental to his thinking was the value of the "organic" or "natural" interdependence of the Municipal, Provincial and National layers of government.'[6]

Thorbecke was promoted to Minister of Internal Affairs in 1849, thus becoming, in effect, the first Prime Minister of the Netherlands. Under his government, an attempt was made to reinstate Roman Catholic dioceses, which led to the *Aprilbeweging* protests in 1853. In response, Thorbecke was forced to resign. However, in 1862 he again became Minister of Internal Affairs, which again brought debate on revolutionary values to the forefront of Dutch national life. A central aspect of this conflict was how one ought to relate education to the new constitution's principles. Soon after Thorbecke's return to office, secondary education was brought in line with the constitution. Although Thorbecke died in 1866, the momentum he generated carried on beyond his lifetime. Indeed, Bavinck entered the sphere of higher education just as the secularization of the academy came into full force.

In 1868, Prime Minister Heemskerk argued that due to the new constitution's principles of a separated church and state, the training of ministers belonged in the church seminary, rather than in the university. However, his successor Cornelis Fock stated the following year that theology remained a legitimate academic discipline. By 1874, Prime Minister Geertsema had formally established the Netherlands' first department of religious studies. Shortly after this, Geersema was replaced by Heemserk, who became Prime Minister for a second stint.[7] Heemskerk wasted little time in resuming his earlier drive to abolish the Dutch theological faculties, arguing that they should be closed and replaced by religious studies classes under the authority of literature faculties.

Heemskerk's proposition provoked a variety of responses. While extreme camps formed supporting either the total abolition or a wholehearted support of theology, a middle majority emerged who thought it inappropriate to transform theology into a subgroup of the literary department. A mediating

---

[6] Bernard O'Sullivan and Denis Linehan, 'Regionalism in the Netherlands', in *Regionalism in the European Union*, ed. Peter Wagstaff, (Bristol: Intellect Books, 1999), 88–9.
[7] Jan Heemskerk Abrahamszoon was Prime Minister of the Netherlands for two periods (1874–7 and 1883–8).

position was thus sought which led to the creation of the religious studies department. In 1876, when Bavinck was an undergraduate student at Leiden University, the Higher Education Act was passed. The Act strongly reflected the general lack of agreement between the State and the Netherlands Reformed Church as to the place of theology in the academy and in the church. At the behest of the moderate liberal politician Albertus van Naamen van Eemnes, it was decided that the newly created Religious Studies department was to nonetheless retain its former title: the Faculty of Theology.

Bavinck's later response to this middle way was highly cynical: 'The Chamber had retained the faculty of theology in name but had in effect introduced a department of religious studies. In this way a strange department came into existence in the state universities: a faculty that is *called* theology but is actually a department of religious studies. In this way theology is maimed and robbed of its heart and life. The subjects incorporated in this marvellous department are a motley jumble.'[8]

This view, expressed by Bavinck in 1892, reflects the more immediate response of Barthold Jacob Lintelo baron de Geer van Jutphaas[9] and the later critique of Bavinck's future colleague, Abraham Kuyper.[10]

Bavinck's 'motley jumble' jibe seems founded on his experience of undergraduate and doctoral studies at Leiden. Although the Leiden theological faculty was strongly insistent on its need for metamorphosis into a religious studies department, Bavinck's memories were of an awkward collection of principles and methods: 'The result was a strange mixture of incompatibles lacking all integration and unity of conception. Some of the subjects taught remind one of the old theology programs; others clearly belong to the field of religious studies. This unfortunate development also places the professors who must lecture in these departments in a difficult situation.'[11]

His primary example of such a professor is Johannes Hermanus Gunning. Appointed to a chair at Leiden in 1889, Gunning initially regarded himself as a 'believing' theologian who could also teach the philosophy of religion from an openly Christian perspective.[12] Gunning's

[8] Bavinck, 'Theology and Religious Studies: Appendix B', 283.
[9] Barthold Jacob Lintelo baron de Geer van Jutphaas, *De wet op het hooger onderwijs* (Utrecht: Bijleveld, 1877), 147.
[10] Abraham Kuyper, *Onnauwkeurig?* (Amsterdam: J.A. Wormser, 1889), 9.
[11] Bavinck, 'Theology and Religious Studies', 53.
[12] Johannes Hermanus Gunning, *De wijsbegeerte van den godsdienst uit het beginsel van het geloof der gemeente* (Utrecht: Breijer, 1889), and *Het geloof der gemeente als theologische maatstaf des oordeels in de wijsbegeerte van den godsdienst*, parts I-II (Utrecht: Breijer, 1890).

position soon changed: he no longer believed it possible to participate in the religious studies classes as a 'believing' professor. Gunning's religion classes were taken over by Cornelis Petrus Tiele, while Gunning moved to teach historical theology.

Within this context of uncertainty, one finds the young Herman Bavinck who, remarkably, left his father's conservative seminary at Kampen to pursue 'a more scientific training'[13] at Leiden in 1874. His personal correspondence from this time reveals the concerns of others within his own denomination. Within a few months of the Higher Education Act, his friend Henry Elias Dosker expressed various fears over Bavinck's place within this upheaval: Why was Bavinck studying at Leiden? Would his orthodox faith remain strong in that stronghold of modernism?[14]

His later correspondence with his fellow student Snouck Hurgronje, coupled with the decision to pursue ordination in the Christian Reformed Church, demonstrates a decisive break with the Leiden School.[15]

Viewed in context, one begins to notice Bavinck's lifework taking a distinctive pattern. Between 1881 and 1911 (referred to as the 'period of great activity' in Hendriksen's brief biography of Bavinck[16]) he formulates a reinterpretation of the Reformed faith in response to that of his former teacher Scholten. As he does so, he uses various significant opportunities to lecture and write on a common theme: revelation. The reality of divine self-revelation is, for Bavinck, the crucial factor in resolving the 'theology versus religious studies' conflict into which he was born. *Deux dixit* not only gives theology viability, it makes theology nothing less than 'the queen of the sciences.'[17]

This career-spanning conviction comes to the fore in Bavinck's most significant moments. In 1881, Bavinck entered the pastoral ministry in the Frisian town of Franeker. His stay there was brief; after one year he became a Professor at Kampen. Bavinck's first decade there (in a highly conservative, separatist church seminary) was spent reading widely, reflecting on his experience at Kampen and musing on the 'theology or religious studies' debate. Briefly stated, his conclusion was that theology is necessitated by the reality of divine self-revelation and as such belongs in the scientific university rather than the private ecclesiastical seminary.

---

[13] Bremmer, *Herman Bavinck en zijn Tijdgenoten*, 20.
[14] H. E. Dosker to H. Bavinck, 23 December 1876. H. Bavinck Archives, HDC.
[15] Bavinck to Snouck, November 24, 1880, in *Een Leidse Vriendschap*, eds., de Bruijn en Harinck, 75–6.
[16] William Hendriksen, 'Translator's Preface' in Bavinck, *The Doctrine of God*, 1.
[17] *RD*, 1.54.

This viewpoint formed Bavinck's topic of choice on several key occasions in his career. In 1892, after a decade of study in Kampen and shortly before the release of a first edition of *Gereformeerde Dogmatiek*, Bavinck published a hugely important article: *Godgeleerdheid en godsdienstwetenschap* ('Theology and the Scientific Study of Religion(s)').[18] This short article laid the foundations for much of the material in his *magnum opus, Reformed Dogmatics.* Volume One, *Prolegomena*, is overwhelmingly concerned with the doctrine of revelation. That Bavinck is writing systematic theology in response to the Higher Education Act's denial of revelation is no mere inference: he names the Act twice in the opening sections of Prolegomena[19] and also refers to it during his discussion of general revelation.[20] In this respect, his 1892 article serves as the contextual lead-in to the wider corpus of *Reformed Dogmatics.*

After completing the final edition of *Reformed Dogmatics* in 1901, Bavinck was persuaded by Kuyper to move to the Free University of Amsterdam. His final remark to the students at Kampen was: 'I am a child of the Secession, and I hope to always remain so.'[21] That he did is evident from two major points in his Amsterdam career.

First, Bavinck's 1902 inaugural address at the Free University was entitled *Godsdienst en godgeleerdheid* ('Religion and Theology').[22] Again, one finds him engrossed in this recurrent theme: God's self-revelation means that theology must be done in the academy.

Second, after six years' teaching in Amsterdam, Bavinck was invited to deliver the Stone Lectures at Princeton Theological Seminary. His chosen topic was 'Philosophy of Revelation.' These lectures, published under the same title, were released in English, Dutch and German. After two decades of career-defining publications and orations, the Stone Lectures display an unbroken continuity from his opening salvo in 1892. Bavinck consistently attempted to solve the great debate of his lifetime (whether theology or religious studies was legitimate) by referring to the reality of God's *openbaring.*

Thus, in reading Bavinck, one must not assume that he writes theology in a situation of relative calm. That Bavinck wrote theology at all must be viewed with sensitivity to the context. His was a conviction forged in a

---

[18] Herman Bavinck, 'Godgeleerdheid en godsdienstwetenschap', 197–225. This article has been translated into English and is entitled 'Theology and Religious Studies' in Herman Bavinck, *Essays on Religion, Science and Society*, 49–60.
[19] *RD*, 1.36, 49.
[20] *RD*, 1.306.
[21] Bremmer, *Herman Bavinck en zijn Tijdgenoten*, 192: 'Ik ben een kind der scheiding en dat hoop ik te blijven.'
[22] Bavinck, *Godsdienst en godgeleerdheid* (Wageningen: Vada, 1902).

struggle. The determining influence on this conviction was Bavinck's doctrine of revelation. 'God making God known' gave Bavinck the courage to engage in dogmatic theology. Perhaps one might say that it left him with no other option. In 1934, Barth responded to natural theology's low view of (Christocentric) revelation with a definitive *'Nein!'* In a similar fashion, Bavinck responded to the Higher Education Act's denial of revelation with a career-long *'Nee!'*

This chapter therefore begins with the recognition that Bavinck's commitment to revelation means that theology must be done. It then proceeds to explore the basic character of that revelation in order to discover what this revelation-driven theology resembles. If it is so centred on the Trinity, what shape does it take?

Revelation forms one of the central metanarratives in Bavinck's work. One thus looks to see whether this revelation is somehow 'organic' in character. Clearly, revelation is among Bavinck's *leitmotifs*. Understanding how one relates revelation to the organic motif will therefore add much to this reading of Bavinck's theology.

III. What is Revelation?

In his own context, Bavinck saw that there was no unified opinion on the doctrine of revelation. 'There is an immense confusion prevailing in the efforts to determine the essence and concept of revelation.'[23] This confusion, in his estimation, was caused by the relevant terminology remaining static while its substance was quite radically altered in various directions. 'While this continuation of the old terminology is proof that the concept of revelation represents a value that is also recognized by many persons outside the circle of Christian theology, it nevertheless fosters misunderstanding and confusion. "Revelation" certainly is not a series of sounds without content, not a neutral flag, which can cover all kinds of cargoes, but a word that conveys a specific concept.'[24]

Bavinck identified the post-Reformation fragmentation of the church as central to this confusion on the nature of revelation. 'If Christianity were at one with itself, and there were no other religions, the recognition of its truth would be easier. But it is endlessly divided and torn to pieces. The one church, which was the centre of village and city in the Middle Ages, is

[23] *RD*, 1.295.
[24] *RD*, 1.295.

completely demolished; on every side a number of sects arise around her, each laying claim to be the purest expression of Christian truth, and continually subdividing and multiplying.'[25]

In his immediate context, Bavinck perceived this ecclesiastical cacophony as followed by inchoate definitions in the works of modern philosophy and theology. A succinct summary of Bavinck's own understanding of revelation is found in *Our Reasonable Faith*.[26] Here Bavinck elucidates his idea of revelation as the self-disclosure of God. Whether this self-revelation occurs in general or special form, he claims it always has three characteristics.

First, 'it always comes from *God himself* acting in his freedom.'[27] Revelation is always a sovereign, divine act. Second, 'every revelation which proceeds from God is *self*-revelation. God is the origin and He is also the content of His revelation.'[28] Third, 'the revelation which proceeds from God, and which has God as its content, also has God as its purpose. This revelation is of him and through him, and it is to him also. . . . Revelation, therefore, cannot have its final purpose in man; in part it passes him by and soars on beyond him.'[29] This brings Bavinck's doctrine of revelation firmly into alignment with his broader worldview that all things begin and end with the glory of the Triune God. As such it would be hardly surprising if the basic character of the Trinity's self-revelation were developed along the lines of unity, diversity, relationship, linkage and interconnectivity. One would expect, therefore, that revelation would have an inherently organic character.

One has thus far acknowledged that as Bavinck's career progresses, his understanding of revelation remains substantially the same. It might be said that his various publications and lectures are, in essence, expansions of an unwavering central proposition: revelation is the unveiling of the divine. This reality is the foundation of all religion, philosophy, nature, history, human experience, culture and future hope. Everything is somehow linked to God via revelation. 'This is already clear: if we are to know God he must reveal himself. . . . This study does not concern itself with the knowledge of "humanness", which can be obtained by scientific research, by anatomy, physiology, and psychology, but deals with human origin and destiny, with our relation to God, our misery due to sin, our need for redemption, our

---

[25] *PR*, 203. Cf. Avery Dulles, *Modes of Revelation* (New York: Orbis Books, 2002), 6–8.
[26] Bavinck, *Our Reasonable Faith*, 34–6.
[27] Bavinck, *Our Reasonable Faith*, 34.
[28] Bavinck, *Our Reasonable Faith*, 35.
[29] Bavinck, *Our Reasonable Faith*, 36.
[30] *RD*, 1.287.

memories of paradise, and hopes for the future. All these things exist in a domain that is not accessible to science but can be uncovered for human beings only by revelation.'[30]

For such a seemingly important theme, Bavinck writes relatively little dedicated material on general revelation in *Reformed Dogmatics*.[31] Covering a mere twenty pages, he handles the topic in five sections ('Natural and Supernatural' Revelation, All Revelation is Supernatural, General Revelation is Insufficient, General Revelation and the Universality of Religion, and General Revelation and Christian Discipleship).[32] Following this, he returns to the theme in a chapter on the relationship between general and special revelation.[33]

One notes Berkouwer's critique of the trends concerning general revelation in Bavinck's era: overemphasis on general revelation led to a non-christocentric general religion.[34] Is Bavinck merely a reactive theologian who underemphasizes general revelation, intentionally or otherwise, to this end? A more nuanced reading of Bavinck would perhaps be to suggest that he carefully sets out the principles of divine revelation (in terms of its broad and narrow uses) and crafts his material appropriately.

IV. Bavinck's *'Nee!'* to Natural Revelation

As one begins to explore Bavinck's handling of revelation, it is worth noting the conceptual battleground in which he locates himself. Having argued that revelation is essential to all religion,[35] he proceeds to describe the considerable growth of deistic rationalism in the eighteenth-century.[36] Interestingly, this brush with deism prompted a resurgence in support of revelation as an epistemological source in both philosophy and theology. However, Bavinck chooses to define his position by proximity to the earlier Reformed distinction between revelation in general and special categories.

In terms of historical theology, Bavinck traces the Patristic development of 'natural' and 'supernatural' categories of revelation via the works of

---

[31] One notes, however, that Bavinck's work, *Our Reasonable Faith*, contains helpful summaries of his positions on both general and special revelation. See 'General Revelation' (32–43), 'The Value of General Revelation' (44–60), 'The Manner of Special Revelation' (61–72), 'The Content of Special Revelation' (73–94).

[32] *RD*, 1.302–22.

[33] *RD*, 1.353–85.

[34] Gerrit Berkouwer, *General Revelation* (Grand Rapids: Eerdmans, 1955), 13.

[35] *RD*, 1.284–7.

[36] *RD*, 1.2.

Irenaeus,[37] Tertullian,[38] Augustine[39] and John of Damascus.[40] He then critiques this movement as becoming inherently dualistic, particularly in the development of medieval Roman Catholic theology. To account for its hamartiological and anthropological distinctives, the Reformation radically redefined the two categories of revelation. 'The Reformers indeed assumed a revelation of God in nature. But the human mind was so darkened by sin that human beings could not rightly know and understand this revelation either. Needed, therefore, were two things: (1) that God again included in special revelation those things which in themselves are knowable from nature; and (2) that human beings, in order to again perceive God in nature, first had to be illumined by the Spirit of God.'[41]

The ground for Bavinck's firm *nee!* to natural revelation is the belief that all revelation is inherently supernatural. In support of this, he makes the interesting exegetical point that Scripture uses the same terminology (*apokaluptein*, *phanerouv* and so forth) to describe what might be titled 'natural' and 'supernatural' events (Job 12:22; 33:16; 36:10; Rom. 1:18, 19).[42] Interestingly, Scholten's definition of αποκαλυτρειν and φανερουν was somewhat different: in *De Leer der Hervormde Kerk*, he claims that the words refer, respectively, to subjective (internal) and objective (external) illumination.[43] Bavinck finds this definition to be exegetically weak[44] and as such, he feels himself justified in rejecting both Scholten's position and the pre-Reformation distinction between natural and supernatural revelation.

V. General Revelation as Narrow And Broad

A Christological focus is crucial to Bavinck's view of general revelation as inherently narrow in usefulness. 'General revelation, therefore, is insufficient for human beings as sinners; it knows nothing of grace and forgiveness'.[45]

---

[37] Irenaeus, *Apology*, II, 8, 10, 13.
[38] Tertullian, *Apology*, II, 18.
[39] Augustine, *Confessions*, V, p. 5; VIII, 26.
[40] John of Damascus, *Exposition of the Orthodox Faith*, I, ch. 1, V.
[41] *RD*, 1.304.
[42] *RD*, 1.307.
[43] Scholten, *De Leer der Hervormde Kerk*, 163 ff. Also see Johannes Scholten, *Dogmaticus Christianae*, 2nd ed., (Lyons: P. Engels, 1858), I, 26.
[44] *RD*, 1.325.
[45] *RD*, 1.313.

Indeed, he then claims that '[g]eneral revelation can at best communicate certain truths but conveys no facts, no history, and therefore changes nothing in existence.'[46] As such, general revelation cannot lead one to Christ as the 'organic centre' of all nature and history.

Although Bavinck's dedicated focus on general revelation in Reformed Dogmatics is relatively brief, and his first major emphasis on its narrow, limited use, his concept of general revelation is at the same time extremely broad.

> That work of God outward began with the creation. The creation is the first revelation of God, the beginning and foundation of all subsequent revelation. The biblical concept of revelation is rooted in that of creation. . . . In creating the world by his word and making it come alive by his Spirit, God already delineated the basic contours of all subsequent revelation. . . . All that is and happens is, in a real sense, a work of God and to the devout a revelation of his attributes and perfections. That is how Scripture looks at nature and history. Creating, sustaining, and governing together form one single mighty ongoing revelation of God.[47]

Thus, while Bavinck writes relatively little on the theory of general revelation, his application of that theory is virtually ever-present. In short, one must always read all of his work on nature and history under the heading of divine self-disclosure. Central to his conception of general revelation is that divine transcendence inhabits all of God's works: 'If God's dwelling lies somewhere far away, outside the world, and his transcendence is to be understood in the sense that he has withdrawn from creation and now stands outside of the actuality of this world, then we lose him and are unable to maintain communication with him. His existence cannot become truly real to us unless we are permitted to conceive of him as not only above the world, but in his very self in the world, and thus as indwelling in all his works.'[48]

For Bavinck, God cannot practice self-disclosure at a distance. God must either 'inhabit' his revelation (which is, in turn, comprised of all nature and history) or he must refrain from self-disclosure altogether.[49]

---

[46] *RD*, 1.313.
[47] *RD*, 1.307.
[48] *PR*, 21.
[49] This concept of God 'inhabiting' his works should, of course, be read with due regard to Bavinck's overwhelming opposition to pantheism.

VI. General Revelation as Creation (Nature) and Providence (History)

As will be seen in Chapter 6, Bavinck takes a non-static view of special revelation. By virtue of its *organic* inspiration, Scripture is 'God *breathed*' and also 'God *breathing*'.[50] When one notes his similarly non-static definition of general revelation, the parallel between the respective natures of general and special revelation becomes apparent. In both, he writes of revelation as both an act and a work: special revelation *was* and *is* inspired; general revelation both *was* (in the act of creation) and *is* (in the work of providence) revelatory.[51]

Bavinck does not limit general revelation to the topic of creation. The God who shows himself in the act of creation continues to practice self-revelation in the providential sustaining of that creation.[52] The general revelation of the Trinity cannot be captured in an aorist-style act of creation. Rather, it continues throughout the work of providence.

In attempting to read Bavinck in context, one takes note of the Leiden brand of theism against which he writes. As has been seen, Bavinck reworked the doctrine of God along Trinitarian lines: Bavinck's God exercises sovereignty without coercion in relation to his non-arbitrary attributes.

His overwhelmingly pro-revelation, pro-supernaturalist sympathies flesh out the departure from the anti-revelation, anti-supernatural Leiden theology mentioned by Bavinck in his private correspondence.[53] Indeed, it is hard to read the statement 'Those who wish to banish the supernatural from religion, hence from their prayers, from their communion with God, are killing religion itself'[54] as anything but a clear attack on Scholten's brand of Christianity. In *De Vrije Wil*, Scholten handles prayer and supernaturalism with reference to the debate between the Reformed and

---

[50] *RD*, 1.440: 'Similarly Scripture is a living and active word, a "discerner" of the thoughts and intentions of the heart. It not only *was* inspired but is still "God-breathed" and "God-breathing". Just as there is much that precedes the act of inspiration (all the activity of the Holy Spirit in nature, history, revelation, regeneration), so there is much that follows it as well. Inspiration is not an isolated event. The Holy Spirit does not, after the act of inspiration, withdraw from Holy Scripture and abandon it to its fate but sustains and animates it and in many ways brings its content to humanity, to its heart and conscience.'

[51] N.H. Gootjes notes that Bavinck's concepts of general and special revelation are linked by a distinctive parallelism, though he does not explain the parallel: N.H. Gootjes, 'General Revelation in its Relation to Special Revelation', *Westminster Theological Journal*, 51 (1989), 367, footnote 27.

[52] Berkouwer, *General Revelation*, 292.

[53] Bavinck to Snouck, 24 November 1880, in *Een Leidse Vriendschap,* eds., de Bruijn en Harinck, 75–6.

[54] *RD*, 1.308.

the Remonstrants. Caricaturing these camps as representing, respectively, determinism and indeterminism,[55] Scholten claims that the Reformed practice of prayer is marked by a pious resignation that God's will shall be done. The only purpose of prayer is to bring the Christian volition into submission before the predetermined divine plan.

He labels the Christian who prays to God with requests for supernatural providence as nothing less than an *egoïstische bidder*: a selfish supplicant.[56] This concept of providence (as the general revelation of the divine) is consistent with Scholten's doctrine of God: arbitrary, rigid, predetermined and predetermining. It is out of step, however, with the doctrines of God and providence found in Calvin and Bavinck.

VII. Calvin, Scholten and Bavinck on God and Providence

At this point, one must momentarily restate the central thrust of this thesis. In the third chapter, Bohatec's claim that the Dutch neo-Calvinists inherited their distinctive 'organic' paradigm from Calvin was noted, as was Bavinck's own claim that Calvin had an essentially organic worldview.[57] It nonetheless seems beyond doubt that Bavinck and Kuyper must, at some level, reflect their own era's penchant for organic imagery. While this work is sceptical of Veenhof's 'two Bavincks' and belief in a 'universal sense of the time'[58] concerning organic motifs, it does recognize that a broad, cross-disciplinary movement away from eighteenth-century mechanism took place between the mid nineteenth and early twentieth centuries.[59] Aside from the 'two Bavincks' foundation, one's main critique of Veenhof's thesis is that he does not pay sufficient attention to the uniquely Reformed, Trinitarian forces which shape Bavinck's organicism. Thus, although it is accepted that Bavinck writes with an aesthetic typical of the late nineteenth-century, one must nonetheless explore Bohatec's belief that the substance of neo-Calvinism's organic expression is nonetheless inherently rooted in Calvin's own theology.

---

[55] 'De Gereformeerden verweten aan de Remonstranten, dat door hun indeterminisme het gebed doelloos werd, in zover het gebed van de overtuiging uitgaat, dat God op het willen der menschen invloed uitoefent.' Scholten, *De Vrije Wil*, 257.

[56] Scholten, *De Vrije Wil*, 261.

[57] Bohatec, 'De Organische Idee in de Gedachtenwereld van Calvijn', 153–64; 362–77; Bavinck, *Johannes Calvijn*, 18.

[58] Veenhof, *Revelatie en Inspiratie*, 268.

[59] See, for example, N.O. Lossky, *The World as an Organic Whole* (Oxford: University Press, 1928), tr. Natalie Duddington; John Bascom, *Aesthetics, or, the Science of Beauty* (Boston: Crosy & Nichols, 1862).

One has already traced the development of Bavinck's organic motif within the larger context of a reaction against the central emphases of his former teacher, Scholten. Where the latter was mechanical in relation to God (and thus monistic rather than Trinitarian) and the cosmos (thus taking a rigidly determinist interpretation of providence), Bavinck sought a starting point in a non-mechanical, Triune God, which led to a Trinitarian rereading of providence as non-coercive. His choice of organic imagery ought to be read within this movement.

When seeking an earlier equivalent of the debate between Scholten and Bavinck on organicism and mechanism, Calvin's debate with the Libertines, a debate ostensibly about providence (as the 'history' element of general revelation) but primarily concerned with the nature of God, provides a useful historical precedent.

While historical context means Calvin is far less likely to be stylistically 'organic', the kernel of Bohatec's and Bavinck's claims is that the substance expressed in neo-Calvinism's organic motif is nevertheless present in Calvin's theology. If this is so, one would expect this to be evident in Calvin's own handling of God in relation to providence. Clearly, as Calvin wrote before the advent of Newtonian physics, he never responded to determinism in its mechanical, post-Enlightenment form. However, he did engage with a philosophical form of determinism that, while based on a non-scientific, pre-Enlightenment rationale, requires a similar response in relation to the doctrines of God and providence.

His doctrine of providence develops over the course of his writing career. In the 1536 *Institutes*, providence makes only a few, sporadic appearances. Over the following two decades, various polemical debates (involving the Libertines, the Stoics, the Epicureans and the astrologers) caused Calvin to massively expand his handling of this doctrine. It is in his conflict with the Libertines, however, that one finds Calvin responding to a deterministic concept of providence (and thus, a deterministic view of general revelation).[60] 'The treatise against the Libertines contains Calvin's strongest rebuttal of determinism and his most vigorous defence of secondary causality.'[61]

Some confusion surrounds Calvin's opposition to the 'Libertines' as the epithet is later used of a group led by Ami Perrin who opposed the proximity

---

[60] John Calvin, *Contre la Secte Phantastique et Furieuse des Libertines qui se Nomment Spirituelz*, *Joannis Calvini Opera Quae Supersunt Omnia*, Vol. VII; *Corpus Reformatorum* Vol. XXXV (Brunswick: CA. Schwetschke et Filium, 1868); 145–248.

[61] Schreiner, *The Theater of His Glory*, 18.

drawn by Calvin between ecclesiastical and civil discipline.[62] However, it seems evident from the content of the tract that it is not directed against Perrin and his followers. Rather, Calvin writes to Margaret of Angoulême, the Queen of Lower Navarre, concerning her support of another group also called Libertines. His dispute with the second group of Libertines concerns theological, rather than civil, matters: in short, he charges them with both antinomianism and (pantheistic) determinism.[63] These charges stem from their belief in a single Spirit inhabiting all creatures which causes all things.[64]

The relevance of this sixteenth-century dispute to a study of Bavinck's organic motif is that it demonstrates Calvin's critique of determinism (in what can justly be viewed as the approximate pre-scientific equivalent of Scholten's position) and explains his alternative. What will be seen is that Calvin's response to Stoic determinism is essentially carried over by Bavinck in response to scientific determinism. This, in turn, strongly supports the hypothesis that his organic motif is a continuation of historic Reformed orthodoxy associated with its views on the natures of God and revelation.

A popular stereotype of Calvin interprets the content of his 'predestination' by antithesis of his opposition to 'free will'. However, this caricature seems inadequate when one considers his firm rejection of Stoic determinism in the *Institutes*.[65] In this tract, he charges Libertine determinism with various faults.

First, it renders God the author of sin; second, it destroys the human conscience; and third, it makes moral judgement pointless and meaningless.[66] At the core of these *trois conséquences exécrables* is that Stoic determinism sits inconsistently with the twofold knowledge of God and self: the two are 'joined by many bonds.'[67] One immediately observes a striking similarity between Bavinck and Calvin: both are concerned to adequately explain bonds, connections and the uniting of the diverse. In Bavinck's writings, this connectional aspect is crucial to the organic motif.

Determinism, in its earlier Stoic form for Calvin, and in its later scientific form for Bavinck, does not adequately convey the realities of God, mankind or their relationship. The Libertines' determinism, Calvin believes,

---

[62] Johnathan Zophy, *A Short History of Renaissance and Reformation Europe: Dances Over Fire and Water* (New York: Prentice Hall, 2003), 226.

[63] It seems that these Libertines were the subject of his attack in *Institutes* I.ix.

[64] Calvin, *Contre la Secte des Libertines*, Ch. XIII.

[65] Calvin, Inst. I.xvi.8 and *Defensis Sanae et Orthodoxae Doctrinae de Servitute et Liberatione Humanii Arbitrii Adversus Calumnias Alberti Pighii Compensis, Johannis Calvini Opera Quae Supersunt Omnia*, Voi. VI, *Corpus Reformatorum*, Voi. XXXIV (Brunsvigae: C. A. Schwatschke et Filium, 1867), 257.

[66] Calvin, *Contre la Secte des Libertines*, Ch. XIII, 186.

[67] Calvin, *Institutes*, I.i.1.

rests on God possessing an arbitrary sense of omnipotence. 'Calvin's alternative to the arbitrary omnipotence of the divine Spirit of the Libertines is not "chance" or "fortune" or a radical indeterminism. The alternative is rather the constant care of God's fatherly hand, or providence.'[68]

Chapter 14 of this tract is perhaps the most important source of information on Calvin's response to determinism. Here, he distinguishes predestination from predetermination in three ways.

Initially, Calvin writes of 'the order of nature'.[69] God's sovereignty over the creation is not exercised via distant processes of causality. Rather, the Creator is constantly, intimately involved with the creation. In this respect, God's freedom is seen in his fatherly care; he graciously sustains each part of the creation, thus allowing it to be true to its own nature.[70]

A striking similarity exists between Calvin and Bavinck on the nature of God in relation to divine providence in the cosmos. The former writes: 'This universal operation does not at all hinder each creature, whether in heaven or on earth, from having or retaining its own quality and nature, or from following its own inclination.'[71]

It is evident that for both theologians, God's gracious providence sustains and restores, rather than subverts, nature.

The latter then states: 'In the preservation and government of all things, God maintains this distinct existence of his creatures, causes all of them to function in accordance with their own nature, and guarantees to human beings their own personality, rationality and freedom. God never coerces anyone.'[72]

Following this, Calvin writes on acts of 'special' providence. If he is consistently opposed to both determinism and chance, how does Calvin deal with the specific outworking of the divine will? The crucial difference between Calvin and the Libertines on this point concerns the authentic reality of human existence. Libertine radical determinism, like Calvin, was strongly opposed to 'free will'. However, the Libertines, Calvin alleges, made humans no more capable of true volition than stones. Calvin's

---

[68] Allen Verhey, 'Introduction' in John Calvin, 'Treatise Against the Libertines', *Calvin Theological Journal*, 15 no 2 N 1980, trs. Robert G Wilkie and Allen Verhey, 200.

[69] Furthermore, while the sense in which Calvin regarded the universe as ordered has been the subject of much debate among Calvin scholars (see pp. 88–9), the importance of nature as distinctly 'ordered' is evident in the works of both men. Indeed, for Bavinck, the orderliness of nature is a central feature in his definition of the organic motif: although created reality is a unity full of diversity, that diversity is not cacophonous or chaotic. Rather, the diverse parts operate by a common ideal. Cf. *CW*, 50–65.

[70] Calvin, *Contre la Secte des Libertines*, Ch. XIV, 187.

[71] Calvin, *Contre la Secte des Libertines*, Ch. XIV, 187.

[72] *RD*, 2.104.

response is to affirm the simultaneous reality of human existence and volition and the sovereign, divine will. Humans make authentic choices consistently with their natures; God works in and through these actions. God constantly allows the cosmos to exist in freedom, but he remains in no way constrained by that freedom.

While Calvin, typically of his linguistic context, does not express his doctrine of providence in organic terms, he nonetheless frames this doctrine to exclude a mechanical exercise of God's will whereby the independent existence of the creature is devalued. Bavinck appears to inherit Calvin's doctrine of providence in this sense, which is expressed contextually via the 'organic' motif.

Finally, Calvin handles the Pneumatological aspect of providence. In short, regenerating grace does not remove human freedom. Despite the believer acting consistently with his fallen nature and choosing sin, the Holy Spirit nonetheless works towards his salvation. As the *imago Dei*, God's freedom is the font of his own.

Verhey's concluding comment on Calvin against the Libertines is that

> Calvin's position in this treatise rejects determinism but refuses the in-determinist option. It is a subtle alternative that hinges, it seems to me, on a certain view of the freedom of both God and man, a view I have attempted to describe above. It must be observed that in any reconstruction of someone's thought, some construction occurs as well. It must also be observed that questions remain, notably, the question of predestination. But the commonplace that Calvin is a determinist has been challenged and a clue to Calvin's position on divine sovereignty and human responsibility has been discovered: *God's freedom or power of sovereignty does not deny, disregard or destroy human freedom or human responsibility. It creates it, preserves it and brings it to fruition. They are not contradictions which must be resolved in a paradox but are, like the knowledge of God and of ourselves, 'joined by many bonds'.*[73]

In different historical contexts, Bavinck and Calvin wrestled with determinism. Both saw fit to deny determinism (in its differing pre- and post-Enlightenment forms) on the grounds of it failing to convey God's own character and his relationship to the creation. Both responded to determinism by restating the doctrine of God, whose own divine norms preclude a mechanical connection between Creator and cosmos. This

---

[73] Allen Verhey, 'Introduction', 205. Italics added for emphasis.

doctrine of God, interestingly, also rules out indeterminism: God's Triunity prohibits both determinism and indeterminism.

Despite Scholten's caricature of Calvin as a determinist,[74] Calvin's understanding of predestination is quite distinct from predetermination. Their difference is evident in the doctrine of providence, the character of which is grounded in the divine nature. Like Bavinck, Calvin draws a close association between 'universal providence' (encompassing nature and history) and general revelation.[75] Both theologians favour the image of God's 'fatherly hand', rather than an arbitrary omnicausality, guiding the path of providence.[76] Indeed, the differing natures of predetermination and predestination are suggested in their very names. In the Calvin–Bavinck sense, predestination's focus is inherently teleological: it places the onus on an eternally established *destiny*. Predetermination, particularly in Scholten's anti-supernaturalist sense, is emphatically non-teleological. Its constant focus is the immediate action of cause-and-effect. Its focus is on the moment rather than the *telos*.

In *Christelijke Wereldbeschouwing*, Bavinck makes a clear connection between teleology and the organic motif: 'The organic worldview is therefore thoroughly teleological, not in the rationalist sense where the human mind is considered the benchmark and goal of all things, but in the higher sense which Scripture calls us to know. . . . This teleology is not by causality and is in conflict with mechanical philosophy.'[77]

In the Calvin–Bavinck worldview, the fixed points are as follows: (a) Divine sovereignty is established. (b) In this sovereignty, God has foreordained the *telos* of church and cosmos. (c) The work by which God brings church and cosmos towards the *eschaton* (providence) is wholly consistent with (i) the intra-Trinitarian relationship and (ii) the reality and nature of the cosmos.

The 'fatherly hand' of God thus works in non-mechanical providence: he shepherds the cosmos to its foreordained eternal destiny. This

---

[74] 'De Gereformeerden verweten aan de Remonstranten, dat door hun indeterminisme het gebed doelloos werd, in zover het gebed van de overtuiging uitgaat, dat God op het willen der menschen invloed uitoefent.' Scholten, *De Vrije Wil*, 257.

[75] Calvin, *Contre la Secte Phantastique et Furieuse des Libertines*, 187.

[76] Compare Bavinck's statement that 'it is God's fatherly hand from which they receive all things' (*RD*, 1.321) with the numerous references to God's 'hand' in Calvin's *Contre la Secte Phantastique et Furieuse des Libertines* (186, 187, 190).

[77] 'De organische wereldbeschouwing is daarom ten slotte ook door en door teleologisch, niet in den platten zin van het rationalisme, dat den verstandsmensch als maatstaf en doel van alle dingen beschouwd, maar in dien verheven zin, welken de Schrift ons kennen doet. . . . De teleologie is niet met de causale, maar wel met de mechanische beschouwing in strijd'. *CW*, 65.

non-determinist definition of providence allows Bavinck to consistently maintain that grace sustains and perfects, rather than subverts, nature: in the predestining work of providence, 'God never coerces anyone.'[78] A key element to Calvin's critique of the Libertines is that once nature is given the absolute power to predetermine, it becomes deified.[79] 'In a statement reminiscent of his polemics against Stoicism, Calvin argued that nature was not a goddess who ruled over all things, for this governance must be reserved only to the will of God.'[80] One may perhaps make the same criticism of Scholten, whose idolization of determinism came at the cost of God's triunity.

Transposed into the sixteenth-century, it would seem that Scholten would be more comfortable among the Libertines than among the Calvinists. In terms of the doctrines of God and providence (viewed as God's general self-revelation), Bavinck's claim (*contra* Scholten) to the title *Reformed* Dogmatics is a strong one.

VIII. The Disappearance and Reappearance of the Organic Motif

Bavinck sees such a mechanical approach to revelation in relation to providence as inherently lifeless. Does he propose a living alternative? To answer this question, one must focus on his concept of general revelation as simultaneously broad and narrow. Although Bavinck's summary of general revelation as a theory is brief, the application of this idea is, quite literally, as broad as the universe. 'Precisely as Christians, by faith, they see the revelation of God in nature much better and more clearly than before. The carnal person does not understand God's speech in nature and history. *He or she searches the entire universe without finding God.* But Christians, equipped with the spectacles of Scripture, see God in everything and everything in God. . . . As a result of this general revelation, they feel at home in the world; it is God's fatherly hand from which they receive all things also in the context of nature.'[81]

Noting the obvious Calvin reference,[82] Bavinck believes that special revelation is required to properly understand its general counterpart.

---

[78] *RD*, 2.104.
[79] Calvin, *Contre la secte phantastique et furieuse des Libertins*, 186.
[80] Schreiner, *The Theater of His Glory*, 18.
[81] *RD*, 1.321. Emphasis added.
[82] Cf. Calvin, *Institutes*, I.vi.1.

General revelation has a highly limited use until read through Scripture, wherein it takes on a much wider usefulness. As such, the cosmos bears few obvious triniform hallmarks when viewed without the correct revelational spectacles. However, when one re-reads the world through the looking glass of Scripture, nature and history together become the general theatre of Triune glory. 'In the light of Scripture, both creation and providence also exhibit traces of God's threefold existence. But these traces can only be seen by the eye of faith and are significantly distinguished from the clear portrayal that lies before us in Scripture.'[83]

An interesting factor in this discussion is the point at which Bavinck begins to frequently describe general revelation (as nature and history) via the organic motif. In *Reformed Dogmatics*, the initial chapter on general revelation contains very few uses of the motif. The only clear reference to the 'organic' occurs in a critique of natural science's practice of inferring 'the organic from the inorganic'.[84] Here Bavinck is hardly using the motif to further his own argument. In constructing a theory of general revelation, the organic motif initially seems to make a sharp disappearance. However, as one tries to understand Bavinck on this point, his Reformed principle of reading general revelation through the lens of Scripture must be borne in mind.

Indeed, it is while Bavinck builds a case for the inability of general revelation to adequately reveal God to sinners that his 'organic' descriptors become muted. This should not, however, be taken to prove that the true character of general revelation is anything other than wholly organic. In fact, it supports the argument that general revelation is truly 'organic' in character.

This becomes apparent, however, only when Bavinck goes on to read nature and history through Scripture. It is at this point that the organic imagery makes a dramatic return. By faith, Bavinck now 'searches the entire universe' and finds God everywhere. The cosmos is now seen 'in its organic interconnectedness'.[85]

His worldview now works 'to discover the harmony that holds all things together and unites them and that is the consequence of the creative thought of God. Not identity or uniformity but unity in diversity is what it aims at.'[86]

The result of this line of thought is an understanding of general revelation where, '[i]n the organic world a force is at work that does not arise

[83] *RD*, 1.342.
[84] *RD*, 1.316.
[85] *RD*, 1.346.
[86] *RD*, 1.368.

from the inorganic'.[87] The hypothesis thus develops that when general revelation is rightly read, it gives ever-present pointers to the Holy Trinity. As such it should hardly be surprising that when Bavinck describes general revelation in its limited use, he refrains from the organic motif. Unless aided by Scripture, general revelation's most strikingly triniform features will go unnoticed. In fact, it stands to reason that had Bavinck described general revelation in its narrow sense using the organic motif, the 'Trinity *ad intra*, organism *ad extra*' hypothesis would be considerably weakened. However, the motif's disappearance prior to and reappearance after Bavinck's reading of the Trinity's general revelation through its special revelation strongly supports the claim that the motif is essentially Trinitarian.

When one reads general revelation well, hallmarks of its divine Creator will appear throughout. One would therefore expect Bavinck's most ubiquitous theocentric metaphors to hint at this. In this light, the organism is his metaphor of choice.

IX. The Organic Character of General Revelation

Clearly, Bavinck regards the organic motif as appropriate in relation to general revelation. At a rudimentary level, the cosmos, with its vast display of unity-in-diversity, seems a likely subject for organic imagery. Such a claim is, one notes, commonplace among the broadly 'organicist' concerns of the nineteenth-century.

However, Bavinck attempts to ground his distinctive appropriation of the organic motif to general revelation on theological grounds. In short, he finds general revelation's role as a linking concept crucial to its very nature, thus yielding it suitable for organic conceptualization.

In an extended discussion at the close of his chapter on general revelation, he describes the application of general revelation to Christian discipleship.[88] Again, one must read this discussion against the backdrop of Scholten's mechanical, anti-supernatural account of Christian piety. It is here that Bavinck deploys the aforementioned 'Scriptural spectacles' analogy,[89] explaining the need to reread general revelation through special revelation. In doing so, the Christian sees God as ever-present. 'The whole Trinity is revealed to us in the creation.'[90]

---

[87] *RD*, 1.346.
[88] *RD*, 1.320–2.
[89] *RD*, 1.321.
[90] Augustine, *City of God*, 353.

Bavinck makes an intriguing statement that such a grasp of Scripturally viewed general revelation creates a new experience of life in the cosmos. 'As a result of this general revelation, they feel at home in the world; it is God's fatherly hand from which they receive all things also in the context of nature.'[91] The same notion is found in Calvin's theology of general revelation: it provides the Christian with a new basis for existence in the cosmos.

> Calvin believed that this creation is to function as the arena of Christian activity and contemplation. For Calvin, the need for salvation does not leave believers analysing their own condition; justification by faith and predestination release their energies and direct them outward to the world. The certitude of salvation experienced through union with Christ allows Christians to combat the devil as well as to look at the book of nature surrounding them in creation. Christians are to be active in the ordering of society, the upbuilding of the church, the combating of demons, and the study of nature, not because this world can offer salvation or fulfilment but because these activities express the glory of God within his created order.[92]

Like Calvin,[93] Bavinck closely allies the loci of general revelation and providence. To this pairing, both men also add the factor of common grace. 'In general revelation, moreover, Christians have a firm foundation on which they can meet all non-Christians . . . in general revelation they have a point of contact with all those who bear the name "human".'[94]

The universality of general revelation thus renders it a linking concept across all humanity. Although 'only the eye of faith sees God in his creation', general revelation nonetheless grants the human race a rudimentary form of unity in diversity. This section of Bavinck's work is replete with illusions to Calvin. Bavinck's statement that 'there comes divine speech to every human. No one escapes the power of general revelation'[95] bears a striking similarity to Calvin's famous dictum that '[t]o prevent anyone from taking refuge in the pretence of ignorance, God himself has implanted in all men a certain understanding of his divine majesty. Ever renewing its memory, he repeatedly sheds fresh drops.'[96]

---

[91] *RD*, 1.321.
[92] Schreiner, *The Theater of His Glory*, 122.
[93] Calvin, *Contre la Secte Phantastique et Furieuse des Libertines*, 187.
[94] *RD*, 1.321.
[95] *RD*, 1.321.
[96] Calvin, *Institutes*, I.iii.1.

The crescendo of Bavinck's idea of general revelation as a unifying power comes at the conclusion of Chapter 10:

> Finally, the rich significance of general revelation comes out in the fact that it keeps nature and grace, creation and re-creation, the world of reality and the world of values, inseparably connected. Without general revelation, special revelation loses its connectedness with the whole cosmic existence and life. The link that unites the kingdom of nature and the kingdom of heaven then disappears. . . . In a word, grace is then opposed to nature. In that case it is consistent, along with the ethical moderns, to assume a radical break between the power of the good and the power of nature. Ethos and φυσις are then totally separated. In that scenario we at bottom face a revival of Parsism or Manicheanism. By contrast, general revelation maintains the unity of nature and grace, of the world and the kingdom of God, of the natural order and the moral order, of creation and re-creation, of φυσις and ethos, of virtue and happiness, of holiness and blessedness, and *in all these things the unity of the divine being.* It is one and the same God who in general revelation does not leave himself without a witness to anyone and who in special revelation makes himself known as a God of grace. Hence general and special revelation interact with each other.[97]

Although it can only be detected through the lens of special revelation, the unity of the three-in-one Godhead is revealed throughout nature and history. However, it is not (as was previously noted) made known in the triads of medieval scholasticism. Rather, Bavinck finds general revelation (as nature and history, or creation and providence) to be replete with the Trinity insofar as it can analogically convey the nature of the divine: this leads Bavinck to abandon the search for triad forms in favour of a macro- and microcosmic emphasis on the paradigm of unity-in-diversity. The universe, in a limited way, reveals the Trinity because it is not a monad.

In addition to this, general revelation (as a theological concept) forms the bond between the 'organically related' concepts of nature and grace. This statement demonstrates the overwhelming importance of general revelation to Bavinck's worldview. As has been well argued elsewhere, the (organic) relationship of grace to nature is perhaps *the* central theme in Bavinck's work. Within that, one must emphasize that general revelation is the factor which prevents grace from being opposed to nature. To further

[97] *RD*, 1.322.

qualify this, it should be stated that the aspect of general revelation which does so is its reflection of the *unity of the divine being*. The Godhead's own paradigm of unity-in-diversity restoratively connects grace and nature.

Bavinck's conception of general revelation as inherently triniform is shared by his neo-Calvinist contemporary, Abraham Kuyper. Both men were of the opinion that a common *raison d'être* is found across created reality: the glory of the Triune God. Kuyper writes that God has 'impressed a religious expression' on the cosmos. This is so for 'the whole of unconscious nature'.[98]

A century before the neo-Calvinist movement, highly similar thoughts also became apparent in the writings of the American Calvinist Jonathan Edwards. Like Bavinck, Edwards frames the doctrine of God in terms of unity-in-diversity: God's essence is expressed in a complex interweaving of holiness, beauty and love.[99] What is apparent in Bavinck, Kuyper and Edwards is that God's triunity has a profound effect on general revelation. The common background to their writings is Calvin's concept of the cosmos as the 'theatre of God's glory'.[100]

In Chapter 6, the explicitly organic nature of special revelation will be examined. The following quotation thus seems an apt segue: 'But as a disclosure of the greatness of God's heart, special revelation far surpasses general revelation, which makes known to us the power of his mind. General revelation leads to special, special revelation points back to general. The one calls for the other, and without it remains imperfect and unintelligible. Together they proclaim the manifold wisdom which God has displayed in creation and redemption.'[101]

---

[98] Kuyper, *Lectures on Calvinism*, 45.

[99] ''Tis in God's infinite love to Himself that His holiness consists. As all creature holiness is to be resolved into love, as the Scripture teaches us, so doth the holiness of God Himself consist in infinite love to Himself. God's holiness is the infinite beauty and excellence of His nature, and God's excellency consists in His love to himself as we have observed.' Jonathan Edwards, 'An Essay on the Trinity', *Treatise on Grace and Other Posthumously Published Writings*, ed. Paul Helm (Cambridge and London: James Clarke, 1971), 110.

[100] Kuyper, *The Work of the Holy Spirit*, 514–15. For a helpful comparison of Kuyper and Edwards in this respect, see John Bolt, 'Trinitarian beauty and the Order of Common Grace', *A Free Church, A Holy Nation: Abraham Kuyper's American Public Theology* (Grand Rapids: Eerdmans, 2001), 212–23.

[101] Bavinck, *Philosophy of Revelation*, 28.

Chapter 6

The Organic Motif and Scripture

As has been said he places himself foursquare on the doctrine of inspiration. But he is unafraid of all critical attacks on the Scriptures. These are to be expected "because the writings of prophets and apostles originated in, not outside, the sphere of history. . . . In entering into a human, the Holy Spirit entered into his style and language and intellectual equipment." Hence the diversity but also the organic oneness of the Scriptures. Striking in Bavinck's theology is the comparison between the incarnation of the Logos in the flesh and that of the Holy Spirit in the word.[1]

I. Introduction

In the light of Scripture, both creation and providence also exhibit traces of God's threefold existence. But these traces can be seen only by the eye of faith and are significantly distinguished from the clear portrayal that lies before us in Scripture. In the works of nature it is at most only the Father as Creator who speaks to us by the Word (Logos) and the Spirit. But in the works of grace, God comes to us as Father in the entirely unique sense of the Son, and as Father he consequently also reveals himself to us by that Son, more precisely by the Son who became incarnate in Christ and by the Spirit acquired by that Christ. Hence in the subject of revelation, both that connection and the difference between general and special revelation clearly emerges.[2]

The direction of this book has, thus far, been first to challenge the general principle by which Bavinck is often interpreted (that of irreconcilable dualism), before critiquing the application of this principle to Veenhof's handling of the organic motif in Bavinck's theology. As an alternative to Veenhof's 'two Bavincks' understanding of the motif, the following has

---

[1] Dosker, 'Herman Bavinck', 23.
[2] *RD*, 1.342.

been proposed: Bavinck's doctrine of God, in addition to outlining the particular three-in-one nature of the Trinity, also lays great emphasis on the non-numerically oriented paradigm of divine unity-in-diversity. The idea that all revelation is analogous and anthropomorphic leads Bavinck away from the idea that the *vestigia trinitatis* will be found solely in a limited number of 'triad' patterns. Rather, his focus on the general principle of unity-in-diversity brings the entirety of nature and history, as a creation-wide organic unit, within the remit of reflected triniformity.

As the organic idea is Bavinck's motif of choice when describing such cosmic unity-in-diversity, the hypothesis that a theology of Trinity *ad intra* leads to a cosmology of organism *ad extra* is thus advanced. In the previous chapter, the pattern of Bavinck's use of the motif in relation to general revelation (whereby the motif is rarely used while Bavinck explains the limitations of general revelation until it is read through the lens of Scripture, following which he makes numerous references to the motif) noted that where the Trinity is revealed with greater clarity, Bavinck writes in increasingly organic terms. However, the previous chapter ended with Bavinck's acknowledgement that '[g]eneral revelation leads to special, special revelation points back to general. The one calls for the other, and without it remains imperfect and unintelligible. Together they proclaim the manifold wisdom which God has displayed in creation and redemption.'[3]

As such, discussion of general revelation in Bavinck's theology must be followed by a similar focus on his use of the organic motif within the theology of special revelation.

II. The 'Two Bavincks' Hypothesis and Scripture

It must be noted at the outset of this chapter that the 'two Bavincks' hypothesis has profoundly directed much debate on the doctrine of Scripture in Bavinck's theology. Just as the hypothesis is used to read irreconcilable dualism into various other areas of his thought, it has been the bedrock of claims that Bavinck's theology of Scripture is unworkable and, ultimately, impossible to follow holistically. Those who read him through the 'two Bavincks' lens invariably find abundant material for caricature in his doctrine of Scripture.

As was seen in a previous chapter, Henk Vroom writes that 'a time bomb lay under Bavinck's view of Scripture. He combines two opposing lines: that

---

[3] *PR*, 28.

of absolute authority and the broad, unshakeable certainty of faith on the one hand and openness in the search for the true meaning of texts and their correct application in modern life on the other. For this reason later generations could choose which of Bavinck's lines they wished to follow. Among Bavinck's students some followed one line of thinking, and others followed another.'[4]

Yarnell, writing on the same topic, claims that '[t]he contradictions in Bavinck with regard to the priority of Scripture and reason form an almost schizophrenic picture.'[5] The work of Rogers and McKim on Bavinck's doctrine of Scripture also explicitly rests on the 'two Bavincks' hypothesis. In *The Authority and Inspiration of the Bible*, they claim the support of the more 'progressive' Bavinck.[6] At the same time, the *Gereformeerde Kerken in Nederland* Synodical Study on Scripture '*God met ons*' similarly portrayed the 'two Bavincks' on Scripture.[7]

The inherent claim is that Bavinck's doctrine of Scripture presents such disconnected mutual exclusivities that the reader is left with a dualistic choice: to follow one of the two Bavincks in insisting either upon the firm authority of Scripture or the need to seek out its meaning and application in the modern world. To use Yarnell's most unfortunate choice of adjective, it is difficult and undesirable to follow a schizophrenic.

However, as this book has thus far attempted to read Bavinck through a different hermeneutical lens – particularly with regard to the organic motif – it is logical to continue this process into the realm of God's special revelation. At the most rudimentary level, the claim thus far has been that within Bavinck's worldview, all of life (in its unity and diversity) is centred on the unity of God. At the outset, then, one asserts that Bavinck's idea of God as characterized by superlative internal coherence lends a degree of coherence to Bavinck's own theological self-understanding. In short, this work considers the possibility that in appropriating Bavinck's work, one should accent his striving for unity, rather than his alleged struggle with division. In fact, its conviction is that one should always choose to emphasize the march towards unity simply because Bavinck, post-Leiden, did not find himself in an all-engrossing theological identity crisis.

---

[4] Vroom, 'Scripture Read and Interpreted: The Development of the Doctrine of Scripture and Hermeneutics in Gereformeerde Theology in the Netherlands', 363.

[5] Yarnell, *The Formation of Christian Doctrine*, 51.

[6] Rogers and McKim, *The Authority and Inspiration of the Bible: An Historical Approach* (San Francisco: Harper & Row, 1979).

[7] Gereformeerde Kerken in Nederland, Generale Syonde, *God met ons: over de aard van het Schrift-gezag* (1979). English version: *God with Us: On the Nature of the Authority of Scripture*, trans. Secretariat of the Reformed Ecumenical Synod (Grand Rapids: Reformed Ecumenical Synod, 1982).

In arguing this, the nature of God's self-revelation and the consequent organic motif are of considerable importance. With that in mind, one must progress to discuss the Triune God's special revelation and Bavinck's use of the motif in that context.

As such this chapter does not attempt a complete review of the debates concerning Bavinck on Scripture. It suffices to simply note that the now discredited 'two Bavincks' hypothesis, in encouraging one to pit Bavinck against himself, has most likely played some part in the current state of affairs. When Bavinck is approached without this agenda, however, it remains to be seen whether the unifying nature of the organic motif lends a degree of coherence to his doctrine of Scripture that has, until this point, largely gone unnoticed. Thus this chapter narrows its remit to the 'organic' nature of Biblical inspiration in Bavinck's theology.

III. Scripture as Organic

'Scripture is an organic principle, the seed, the root, out of which the plant of dogmatics grows. Mechanical use of Scripture is therefore entirely blocked off. Dogmatics is not a scroll of texts or a collection of dicta probantia. On the contrary, it is the truth of Scripture itself taken up in and elaborated independently by the intellectually and scholarly formed consciousness of the believer and confessed and maintained as his own conviction also in the field of science.'[8]

Writing on Bavinck's concept of organic inspiration, Berkouwer offers the following sage advice:

> It is clear . . . that the use of the term 'organic' by itself, that is, by means of an organ or an instrument, throws little light on the discussion. The idea of organ even receives a place in what is usually called 'mechanical' inspiration. The idea of human 'mediation', of man's own activity and cooperation, is intuitively linked today with the word 'organic' in contrast to a monergistic inspiration. Every aspect of the organic was certainly not meant to apply by analogy to inspiration, as the term functions in biology, for example. . . . For that reason, it is misleading to disqualify the term 'organic inspiration' by linking it to all sorts of nineteenth-century views concerning organisms.[9]

[8] Herman Bavinck, 'Confessie en Dogmatiek', *Theologische Studiën* 9 (1891), 258–75, 267.
[9] Gerrit Berkouwer, *Holy Scripture* (Grand Rapids: Eerdmans, 1975), 154; tr. Jack B. Rogers; Dutch original: *De Heilige Schrift* (Kampen: J.H. Kok, 1966–7).

Evidently, Berkouwer's concern is that one reads Bavinck on this point in the full recognition that he does not use the word 'organic' in 'the universal sense of the time'.[10] What is perhaps slightly unusual is Berkouwer's ambiguity in describing whether Bavinck's use of the motif regarding Scripture is distinct from its wider use in his theology. 'True, the word is often used in a wider connection, as when Bavinck deals with an "organic" worldview or with an "organic" interdependence of the human race, and when Kuyper places the "inspired organism" of Scripture over against any atomism. However, the real intention in the doctrine of Scripture is the interest in the peculiar and conscious functionality of man in the revelation of God.'[11]

Noting that the basic wider use of the motif in Bavinck's worldview is to unite the diverse, using it to bring together the roles of God and human beings in the writing of Scripture hardly seems to mark this out as an incongruent application of the motif.

IV. An Initial Distinction

At the outset, it is worth noting a distinction in Bavinck's application of the motif to the theology of Scripture. On a grand scale, he portrays Scripture as a single *organism*, one which epitomizes the large-scale unified diversity of authors, genres, original and subsequent audiences, theological sub-plots and languages. Indeed, this organism holds together the diverse self-revelation of God as Creator-Father, Redeemer-Son and Sanctifier-Spirit. As such, Bavinck reads Scripture presupposing its overall unity. Together its astonishingly diverse components function as a single, living organism.

> The Scriptures may not be conceived atomistically as if God would have inspired every word and every letter in isolation from each other, each with its own meaning, with its own divine content. *Inspiration must be conceived organically, so that also the smallest part finds its place and meaning, even if it is much further removed from the centre than other parts.* There is one Spirit through which the entire Scriptures have come through the minds of the writers. Certainly there is variety in the way in which the same life is

---

[10] *Contra* Veenhof, *Revelatie en Inspiratie*, 268. Cf. W. Maurer, 'Das Prinzip des Organischen in der evangelischen Kirchengeschichtsschreibung des 19. Jahrhunderts', *Kerygma und Dogma* (1962), 265.

[11] Berkouwer, *Holy Scripture*, 154.

immanent and active in the various parts of the body. There is a diversity
of gifts, also in the Scripture, but it is the same Spirit.[12]

However, there is also a second sense in which he applies the motif to the
theology of Scripture. Rather than using it to combat 'atomistic' hermeneutics, he invokes the motif to unite Scripture's divine and human authorship.
In this sense, the motif is applied in the term '*organic* inspiration'.

Noting that the organic motif applies to special revelation both micro-
and macrocosmically, it seems surprising and disappointing that discussion
on this area of his work has been so consistently marked by disunity. Perhaps
more than any other area of Bavinck's work, discussion of his doctrine of
Scripture makes plain the limitations of the 'two Bavincks' model. An
underemphasis on and outright misunderstanding of the ever-present
organic motif precedes the cacophony that constitutes much recent debate
concerning Bavinck on Scripture.

In addition to this, one notes that the direction of debate concerning
Bavinck on Scripture has been shaped by the desire to draw Bavinck's
position into more recent theological conflict, as opposed to placing the
primary onus on his own context. By attempting to define Bavinck against
the Old Princeton theologian, B.B. Warfield, Rogers and McKim set this
trend in motion. A study of the more recent texts prompted by Rogers
and McKim establishes this point.[13] The issue of whether McGowan or
Gaffin is correct on Bavinck's proximity of Warfield on Scripture is, at the
present time, of secondary importance. The primary point is that the
norm has been to study Bavinck's doctrine of Scripture against the
sideshow of Old Princeton, rather than against the backdrop of his Leiden
education.

Indeed, it is only when the development of 'organic inspiration' is viewed
in the light of the doctrine of Scripture in Dutch theology before and after
the work of his professors, Scholten and Kuenen, that his need to invoke
the motif is understood.[14]

---

[12] *RD*, 1.409. Italics added for emphasis. A highly similar application of the motif is found in
Bavinck's application of it to the unity-preceding-diversity of the visible church: 'In the first
place, therefore, the ingathering of the elect must not be conceived individualistically and
atomistically. . . . The church is an organism, not an aggregate; the whole, in its case, precedes the parts.' *RD*, 3.524.

[13] See McGowan, *The Divine Spiration of Scripture: Challenging Evangelical Perspectives*; Gaffin,
God's Word in Servant-Form: Abraham Kuyper and Herman Bavinck on the Doctrine of Scripture.

[14] Indeed, it is not unknown to see Bavinck's concept of organic inspiration handled with no
reference to either contemporary or historic developments. See Donald Bloesch, *Holy Scripture: Revelation, Inspiration and Interpretation* (Downers Grove: InterVarsity, 1994), 122.

V. Studying Scripture at Leiden: Scholten and Kuenen

As has been noted earlier in this thesis, post-Enlightenment theology existed in a somewhat of a timelag in the Netherlands.[15] Just as it took the writings of Kant, Hegel, Fichte, Schelling and Schleiermacher a considerable time to gain influence among Dutch intellectuals, the rapidly developing field of critical Biblical studies initially gained very little ground in the Netherlands. This was to change primarily through Johannes Scholten and Abraham Kuenen, Bavinck's professors at Leiden. In commenting on the rise of Kuenen in particular, De Vries has claimed: 'It seemed at the time that Holland, of all countries, was one of the least likely to produce a scholar of his stature. Little of the advance that had taken place in France and Germany had found acceptance in the Netherlands, which, like England, was in the grip of an anticritical traditionalism. For several centuries past, Holland had been renowned as a foremost seat of learning . . . but now for some time biblical scholarship had been in a state of doldrums.'[16]

Before Scholten and Kuenen, Dutch theology was, generally speaking, uninterested in the questions posed of the Biblical text by modern theology.[17] In the period from 1850 to 1860, however, this situation changed dramatically. With the development of Scholten's Leiden school grew the insistence that the Biblical text should be studied with complete critical freedom. Scholten's own theological development was crucial to the doctrine of Scripture espoused by the Leiden theologians.

In his *Leer der Hervormde Kerk*, Scholten argues that Scripture is the 'formal principle' of the Reformed faith.[18] His doctrine of Scripture distinguishes the 'Word of God' from the Bible itself: for Scholten, the former contains, though is not itself, the latter. Human reason forms the basis by which one may judge what, within the Bible, is the *waarheid*.[19]

Vanderlaan's cynical critique of Scholten's approach to Scripture in this light is that '[h]ere we find the real Scholten. This rational argument, from nature and man to God, is the heart of his system. It is, indeed, "reason and

---

[15] Chapter 1, 10.

[16] De Vries, 'The Hexateuchal Criticism of Abraham Kuenen', 32.

[17] J. Nat, *De studie van de Oostersche talen in Nederland in de 18e en 19e eeuw* (Purmerend, 1929); H. Oort, 'Kuenen als godgeleerde', *De Gids* (1893), 524–7; M. Beek, 'Abraham Kuenen', *Vox Theologica*, 7 (1935–6), 150.

[18] Scholten, *De leer der Hervormde Kerk*, i., 59. 'De Heilige Schrift de eenige kenbron en toetssteen der Christelijke waarheid.'

[19] Scholten, *De leer der Hervormde Kerk*, i., 114.

conscience" which furnish his theology, and Scripture is only a confirmation, an expression of it.'[20]

This criticism seems to have mileage, bearing in mind Scholten's methodology of 'reflection [on God and Scripture] grounded on observation [of the natural world]' ('*bespiegeling gegrond op waarneming*')[21] which led to his Remonstrant-like judgement of the Trinity as an unnecessary and unprofitable doctrine. Although Scholten was primarily a systematic theologian, he also published in the field of New Testament studies. In 1855, he published the key early work espousing German higher critical convictions in the Netherlands.[22] His support of the German higher critical approach to the text was popularized by Conrad Busken Huet's *Brieven over de Bijbel* (1858). In 1864, Scholten's *Het Evangelie naar Johannes* outlined his rejection of the supernatural in the life of Christ.[23]

In tandem with this, Abraham Kuenen popularized the same approach to the Old Testament. Having completed his doctorate in 1851, he was employed alongside Scholten the following year and worked with him until Scholten's death in 1881. Kuenen's significance to Old Testament studies is all the more interesting given that he was originally employed to teach the New Testament. By 1885, he was teaching both Old and New Testament studies. However, his obvious interest in the Old Testament, coupled with a growing body of publications, persuaded the Dutch government to create a chair of Old Testament Criticism for Kuenen in 1871. His influence grew further in the aftermath of the Higher Education Act of 1876. As a result of this Act, the incumbent Leiden Old Testament professor, A. Rutgers, was deemed unsuitable to carry on in the new *de facto* Religious Studies department. Rutgers was removed from his position and Kuenen was promoted.[24] Like Scholten, Kuenen firmly rejected the notion that the Bible contains supernatural revelation. Rather, it affirms what one can rationally deduce from observation alone.[25]

Kuenen's personal influence in the Netherlands was enormous. 'Interpreted narrowly, Kuenen's school consisted of his own pupils and

---

[20] Vanderlaan, *Protestant Modernism in Holland*, 33.

[21] Scholten, *De leer der Hervormde Kerk*, i, lxi.

[22] Johannes Scholten, *Kritische inleiding tot de Schriften des Nieuwen Testaments* (Leiden 1855).

[23] Interestingly, the year before, Scholten published a book objecting to Renan's *Vie de Jésus* on the grounds that Jesus is the embodiment of humanity's religious ideal: Johannes Scholten, *Het Leven van Jezus door Ernest Renant. Toespraak bij de opening der akademische lessen* (Leiden, 1863).

[24] M.J. Mulder, 'Abraham Kuenen', *Abraham Kuenen (1828–91)*, eds. P.B. Dirksen and A. van der Kooij (Leiden: Brill, 1993), 3.

[25] Abraham Kuenen, 'Hugo de Groot als uitlegger van het Oude Verbond', *Verslagen en mededeelingen der Koninklijke Akademie van Wetenschappen, Afdeeling Letterkunde* (1883), 48.

colleagues at Leiden, together with other close supporters. . . . Eight of Kuenen's pupils wrote doctoral dissertations in the field of OT, and in all of them his critical methods were followed. In a wider definition, Kuenen's school comprised also the Amsterdam humanists on the left, and the Utrecht and Groningen moderates on the right, since they all scrupulously employed his scientific principles – if not always his theological presuppositions – and they accepted his documentary hypothesis in its leading points.'[26]

That he was a man of considerable personal charisma is beyond doubt. The young Bavinck was particularly taken with Kuenen, as Henry Elias Dosker notes. Indeed, this personal fondness for Kuenen, alongside his disagreement with Kuenen's approach to Scripture, caused Bavinck no shortage of difficulty at this time. 'He had many a bitter struggle at Leiden. Keuenen especially, with his "heart of gold", was his idol among his professors. I remember his letters of that period, his description of serious doubts and questionings and battles; but all these struggles only tested and purified his faith.'[27]

The large number of biographies, and their often hagiographical character, further emphasize Kuenen's personal gravitas.[28]

VI. Bavinck's Response to Leiden and Groningen on Scripture

Some awareness of the immediate backdrop to Bavinck's own formulations on Scripture, especially concerning his use of the organic motif at this point, is necessary to paint a coherent picture. Although Bavinck's origins lay in the pietistic movement which showed little interest in the questions directed at the Biblical text by the likes of Scholten and Kuenen, he did not dismiss his professors out of hand.

---

[26] De Vries, 'The Hexateuchal Criticism of Abraham Kuenen', 54.

[27] Dosker, 'Herman Bavinck', 15. Bavinck's 'heart of gold' assessment is typified by Kuenen's response to the 'Grafian hypothesis' controversy. In this example, one of Kuenen's ideas (that the Levitical law and connected sections of the Pentateuch were not written until after the kingdom of Judah had fallen, and that the Pentateuch was not accepted as authoritative until Ezra's reformations) was publicized by K.H. Graf who was given the critical acclaim, despite the model belonging to Kuenen. With a remarkable lack of hubris, Kuenen refrained from commenting on this until four years after Graf's death, when, in passing, he noted his role in the hypothesis in a journal article: see W. van der Vlugt, *Levensbericht van Abraham Kuenen* (Leiden, 1893), 114.

[28] Philip Wicksteed's biography of Kuenen is perhaps the most obsequious: Philip Wicksteed, 'Abraham Kuenen', *The Jewish Quarterly Review*, Vol. 4, No. 4 (July 1982), 571–605.

As was noted in Chapter 2, Bavinck was influenced by Scholten and Kuenen while a student. However, his letters with Snouck Hurgronje make plain that once he left Leiden, he distanced himself from their modernism.

Having left Leiden, many things in the modern theology and world-view look different to me than when I was so strongly under the influence of Scholten and Kuenen. I learned much in Leiden, but I have unlearned much too. The latter could partly have had negative effects on me; I am starting to recognise them more and more. The time in which the convictions of our youth were thrown into crucible of critique is now over. What matters at this moment is to be faithful to the convictions we now have and to defend them with the weapons that are at our disposal.[29]

Interestingly, when reflecting on his departure from their theology, Bavinck draws a caveat regarding the doctrine of Scripture.

Their contemplations on Scripture aside, Kuenen and Scholten have not had much influence on me, if by that you mean losing my faith and taking on theirs. But they have indeed had (and it could be no other way) an influence on the power and manner with which I embrace those truths. That naïve and childlike faith, with its unlimited trust in the truth as it has been instilled, you see, has been lost; and that is a great deal; in that way their influence has been great and strong. Now I know that I can never regain that. That said, I find it good and am thankful for losing it. In that innocence there was much that was untrue and had to be purified. But still, there is that naïve (and I know no better word) something, that is good, that is a consolation; something that must remain if the truth is to stay sweet and precious to us.[30]

[29] Bavinck to Snouck, 24 November 1880, in *Een Leidse Vriendschap,* eds., de Bruijn and Harinck, 75–6.
[30] *Een Leidse Vriendschap,* eds., de Bruijn and Harinck, 81. Dutch original: 'Kuenen en Scholten hebben op mij (behalve in de Schriftbeschouwing) niet veel invloed gehad, als ge daaronder verstaat het verliezen van geloofswaarheden en het aannemen van andere, van de hunne. Maar zij hebben wel (hoe kon het anders) invloed gehad op de kracht en de wijze, waarmee ik die waarheden omhels. Het naïve van het kinderlijk geloof, van het onbegrensd vertrouwen op de mij ingeprente waarheid, zie, dat ben ik kwijt een dat is veel, heel veel; zoo is die invloed groot en sterk geweest. En nu weet ik wel, dat ik dat nooit terugkrijg. Zelfs vind ik het goed en ben ik er waarlijk en oprecht dankbaar voor, dat ik heb verloren heb. Er was ook in dat naïve veel, wat onwaar was en gereinigdmoest worden. Maar toch, er is in dat naïve (ik week geen beter woord) iets, dat goed is, dat wel doet; iets dat blijven moet, zal de waarheid ons ooit zoet en dierbaar wezen.'

Although Bavinck inverted Scholten's *modus operandi* of '*bespiegeling gegrond op waarneming*', whereby it became 'reflection on the cosmos based on observation of God as self-revealing Trinity', he was nonetheless marked from Leiden onwards by their insistence on asking profound questions concerning the humanness of the Biblical text. However much he missed the childlike faith in approaching the text from his pre-Leiden days, this 'innocence' was now gone forever. Interestingly, Bavinck did not view this loss of hermeneutical 'innocence' as a bad thing. Rather, he viewed it as useful.[31] Indeed, he critiqued pre-modern theology for its failure to take Scripture's authentic human authorship seriously.[32] In formulating this critique, he generalizes that until the modern era, limited efforts were made to do so. However, the weakness of these attempts resulted in a concept of inspiration which leaned towards mechanism. 'The Reformed confessions almost all have an article on Scripture and clearly express its divine authority; and all the Reformed theologians without exception take the same position. Occasionally one can discern a feeble attempt at developing a more organic view of Scripture.'[33]

Thus Bavinck recognizes that in the early Reformed tradition, there existed an underdeveloped notion that Scripture did not simply 'fall from heaven'. However, the general attempt to account for Scripture's humanness, over time, became mechanical: Scripture's human authors became vehicles commandeered by the Holy Spirit.[34] Accordingly, Bavinck saw the rise of modern theology's emphasis on the humanness of Scripture as a necessary response to pre-modern theology's inadequate handling of the topic.

In addition to this historic background, Bavinck has a secondary reason to pursue a new investigation on the human authorship of Scripture: he must pursue a degree of symmetry between his concepts of general and special revelation. General revelation, he has earlier written, takes place within the twofold paradigm of nature and history. As the divine practices general self-disclosure, he bonds together a continuum of both time and

---

[31] 'It is noteworthy that the secessionist Bavinck, even in his critical assessment of his student days, spoke of Leiden as *useful*. He did not forget modern theology and its critical questions for orthodoxy (as far as he was concerned particularly regarding contemplations on Scripture), but it never satisfied him.' Harinck, '"Something that must remain, if the truth is to be sweet and precious to us": The Reformed Spirituality of Herman Bavinck', 252.

[32] *RD*, 1.381. 'The earlier theology almost completely allowed revelation to coincide with divine inspiration, the gift of Scripture. It only incidentally referred to revelation and conceived of it much too narrowly. As a result Scripture came to stand in complete detachment and isolation and made it seem as it had suddenly dropped out of heaven.'

[33] *RD*, 1.415.

[34] *RD*, 1.415.

space.[35] Having attempted to confront the historical aspect of general revelation directly, Bavinck must now do the same with the occurrence-in-history aspect of special revelation.

> Scripture clearly teaches that this revelation bears a historical character and unfolds its content only gradually over the course of many centuries. Modern theology sees and recognises this fact much more keenly than earlier theology. The 'history of revelation' is a discipline of only recent date and deserves to be pursued seriously. It shows us that special revelation is akin to general revelation in nature and history, and especially to general revelation as it is expressed in the religions of the world, yet is essentially different from them and inspired and guided by an idea of its own. . . . The incarnation of God is the central fact in special revelation, the fact that sheds light upon its whole domain.[36]

However, one should not interpret Bavinck's willingness to ask hard questions of Scripture's human authorship as an agreement with the wider worldview of Scholten and Kuenen. Although he wrote that modern theology has 'rightly made a distinction between divine revelation and Scripture', Bavinck also argued that it quickly 'fell into the opposite extreme'.[37] Although Scripture and revelation should be distinguished, Bavinck never envisaged that they should be detached. His response to this detachment was to critique the two dominant theological stables of his day: the Leiden (Scholten and Kuenen) and the Groningen schools (the *Heusdiaans*).

In responding to the Groninger theologians, Bavinck invokes various slogans typical of their *tournure d'esprit*: 'Not the letter but the Spirit', 'not Scripture but the person of Christ', both of which are references to the Heusdiaan slogans *'Niet de leer, maar het leven . . . Niet de leer, maar de Heer!'*[38] The problem with the Groninger school's choice of revelation over Scripture, according to Bavinck, is that without Scripture, one knows virtually nothing concerning Jesus. 'With the fall of Holy Scripture, therefore, all of revelation falls as well, as does the person of Christ.'[39] As such, Bavinck

---

[35] 'Bavinck agrees with Augustine's concept of the creation of the world together with time, and not in time. Where there is nothing, neither is there time and space.' Chris Gousmett, 'Bavinck and Kuyper on Creation and Miracle', *Anakainosis*, Vol. 7, No. 1–2 (September/December 1984), 6.

[36] *RD*, 1.343–4.

[37] *RD*, 1.381.

[38] *RD*, 1.381. English: 'Not the doctrine, but the life. . . . Not the doctrine but the Lord!'

[39] *RD*, 1.382.

believed it was impossible to guard one's concern for *het leven* or *de Heer* while placing them in opposition to *de leer*.

Bavinck's opposition to this life–doctrine dichotomy is rooted in his perception of Calvin's relationship between the two: 'For [Calvin], God was not merely a God who was far away; he was also nearby. He felt God's presence. He walked in the light of his countenance. He directed his whole soul and body to God as an offering and was consumed by his obedience. For him, doctrine and life were one.[40] He wanted the Christian life to be so. The word had to act in him, doctrine had to live, faith had to become action.'[41]

To the Leiden school, which claimed a high view of *de leer* (indeed, it wanted to study Scripture with a hitherto unparalleled scientific credibility) but which divorced it from *de Heer* and denied the reality of the supernatural, Bavinck offered a parallel critique.

Both schools are one-sided, the one that fails to do justice to revelation for the sake of Scripture as well as the one that fails to do justice to Scripture for the sake of revelation. In the former, divine revelation, in the latter, divine inspiration does not come into its own. In the one, people have Scripture without scriptures; in the other, scriptures without Scripture. In the former [Groninger and pre-modern theology] there is a neglect of history; in the other [the Leiden school] contempt for the Word. The former lapses into orthodox intellectualism; the latter is in danger of Anabaptistic spiritualism. The right view is one in which Scripture is neither equated with revelation nor detached from it and placed outside of it.[42]

Thus, the background to Bavinck's own doctrine of Scripture is a tale of problems left unresolved. First, general pre-modern theology had failed to adequately account for the text's humanness (which was carried over into Bavinck's pietistic background). Second, among the Groningers, their devaluing of the written word in favour of an experiential Christ-encounter

---

[40] This stands in interesting contrast to the emphasis of the *Heusdiaan* theologians in Bavinck's nineteenth-century Netherlands, whose motifs were 'not doctrine, but the Lord' (*niet de leer maar de Heer*) and 'not doctrine, but life' (*niet de leer, maar het leven*). James Hutton Mackay, *Religious Thought in Holland during the Nineteenth Century* (London: Hodder & Stoughton, 1911), 50–7.

[41] Bavinck, *Johannes Calvijn*, 18. Dutch original: 'Voor hem was God niet alleen een God van verre, maar ook van nabij. Hij gevoelde zijne tegenwoordigheid. Hij wandelde in het licht van zijn aanschijn. Hij wijdde zijn gansche ziel en lichaam Gode ten brandoffer, en verteerde het in zijne gehoorzaamheid. Leer en leven waren bij hem één. En zoo wilde hij, dat de Christen leven zou. Het woord moest in hem daad, de leer leven, het geloof werk worden.'

[42] *RD*, 1.382.

had also failed to respect the text as written in history. Third, the Leiden school, in its radical rejection of the supernatural, and its reassessment of the text simply as a record of human observation, had sought to remedy the faults of pre-modern theology. However, in so doing, Scholten and Kuenen had ignored the divine authorship of the text and, as such, had fundamentally misunderstood the nature of Scripture as divine and human.

In short, this is a picture of unnecessary antitheses, dualisms and oppositions. The core problem is the sense in which Scripture can be both human and divine. The tendency perceived by Bavinck is to always choose one or the other. In context, it seems evident that Bavinck sought some kind of synthetic model whereby one might affirm that Scripture is the product of both divine and human authors.

However, an immediate problem arises: insofar as the concept of inspiration is approached without an initial paradigm of unity-in-diversity, it becomes very difficult to maintain this dual nature. As has already been seen, Bavinck's worldview is founded on such a principle, which emanates from the unity of the Godhead: Trinity *ad intra* leads to organism *ad extra*. A theology of inspiration which guards simultaneous human and divine authorship can be nothing less than *organic* in character.

Evidently, Bavinck did not write a doctrine of Scripture primarily to distinguish himself from (or identify himself with) the Old Princeton theologians.[43] Rather, if one may commandeer Vroom's imagery, Bavinck's concern for an organic handling of inspiration was prompted by the time bomb that lay ticking in the doctrine of Scripture until that point. Unless the principle of unity-in-diversity could be drawn into the debate, its essential character risked becoming forever lost.

VII. The Organic Inspiration of Scripture

The immediately preceding context of Bavinck's handling of organic inspiration is as follows. In typical fashion, he portrays monism and theism in a bifurcated manner. The former exists in two forms: pantheism and materialism. Both are essentially monistic in their urge to reduce all forces, materials and laws to a single force, material and law. Christian theism, conversely, celebrates the diverse nature of the universe. In this context,

---

[43] The same phenomenon occurs with regard to Kuyper's doctrine of Scripture: see Harriet A. Harris, 'A Diamond in the Dark: Kuyper's Doctrine of Scripture', *Religion, Pluralism and Public Life: Abraham Kuyper's Legacy for the Twenty-First Century* (Grand Rapids: Eerdmans, 2000), ed. Luis E. Lugo.

Bavinck describes the cosmos as an 'organic world' and states that '[s]upernatural revelation is entirely compatible with such a worldview. In it, after all, nature does not for a moment exist independently of God but lives and moves in him. Every force that asserts itself in it originates from him and works according to the law he has put in it. God does not stand outside of nature and is not excluded from it by a hedge of laws but is present in it and sustains it by the word of his power. He works from within and can generate new forces, which in nature and operation are distinct from the existing ones.'[44]

From this, he moves on to defend the possibility of the miraculous as an essential component in the Christian theistic worldview. 'Nature, i.e., the cosmos, furthermore, is still far too frequently conceived as a ready-made machine that is now driven by a single force and always moves under the governance of a single law.'[45] The cosmos, Bavinck alleges, is far from being a finished product. Instead, it is essentially teleological in character, and as such is engaged in a process of constant becoming; it moves providentially towards a foreordained eschatological climax. 'Scripture teaches us, however, that revelation serves the end of re-creating the creation, which was corrupted by sin, into a kingdom of God. Here revelation assumes a completely proportionate and teleological place in the world plan God made and realised in the course of the ages.'[46]

The presence of the miraculous is essential within an organic worldview. Conversely, the absence of the miraculous is essential to a mechanical worldview. In this light, Bavinck writes vigorously against the anti-supernaturalism of Scholten and Kuenen:

> But those who deny 'miracle', i.e., those who deny not just one or another specific miracle but the possibility of miracles, box God in and bind him to nature. In principle they assert that God does not have an adequate existence of his own, one that is distinct from the world. Consequently they also have to deny – as being miraculous – creation, divine providence, answers to prayer, direct fellowship between God and human beings. Moreover, they lose all grounds for believing in a future victory of the kingdom of God, in a teleology operative in world history, and therefore end in pantheistic or materialistic naturalism.[47]

---

[44] *RD*, 1.370.
[45] *RD*, 1.372.
[46] *RD*, 1.372.
[47] *RD*, 1.375.

Indeed, his comment on 'answers to prayer' should be read against the backdrop of Scholten's teaching on prayer in *The Free Will*.[18] Bavinck moves from this to discuss incarnation, language and the Bible. His handling of this section is crucial in properly understanding his theology of inspiration. Two points stand out as fundamentally important in understanding and interpreting what will follow: his parallel between Scripture and Christ; and the ongoing, holistic organic nature of inspiration. These are the foundations upon which he builds, and the yardsticks by which his following statements must be measured.

Regarding the aforementioned parallel, perhaps his most important expression here is that '[s]cripture is the servant form of revelation'. Noting that 'the bearer of the ideal goods of humankind is language', he acknowledges that God accommodates this fact. 'To be able fully to enter the life of humankind and for it fully to become its possession, revelation assumes the form and fashion of Scripture.'[49] The key movement in this section is the parallel drawn between two branches of miraculous, special revelation: the incarnation of Scripture and the incarnation of Christ.

VIII. Divine and Human Counterbalances

Having framed a doctrine of Scriptural inspiration against the chaos of the 'orthodox' and 'modernist' groups in his day, it will come as no surprise that Bavinck's theology of inspiration cannot be pigeonholed into liberal or fundamentalist camps. He belongs in neither. Bavinck is not a mechanical Biblicist who ignores or grudgingly concedes the humanness of Scripture. Neither is he a modernist who holds onto a high view of Scripture for purely sentimental reasons. Rather, his concerns for Trinity *ad intra* leading to organism *ad extra* prompt him to insist on both the divinity and humanity of Scripture. Central to this study is the observation that between these notions, Bavinck creates a concatenation; to neglect either will misrepresent his position considerably. 'In writing about faith and the power of Scripture, Bavinck did not fit in with the terminology and the spirituality of modern theology – not even with that of his own Reformed theology.'[50]

As such, the 'two Bavincks' hypothesis and its effects on debate over his doctrine of Scripture stand out as particularly unhelpful. To restate the

---

[18] Scholten, *De Vrije Wil*, 259–60.
[49] *RD*, 1.380.
[50] Harinck, '"Something that must remain, if the truth is to be sweet and precious to us": The Reformed Spirituality of Herman Bavinck', 260.

crux of Chapter 2, because Bavinck's approach to theology is catholic in spirit and synthetic in nature, if one approaches him looking to find symptoms of division, it is more than possible to portray him eisegetically as riddled with division. In this context, it is easy to employ the language of internal time bombs and schizophrenia. However, in the light of the recent developments mentioned in Chapter 2,[51] the general consensus has become that there are insufficient grounds to speak of 'two Bavincks'. It no longer suffices to read Bavinck on Scripture as though the 'two Bavincks' hypothesis had not been discredited. Such a new approach appears to be validated by the connection drawn by Bavinck between the unity of the Godhead and the unity of the Scriptures: 'All the Scriptures preach the unity of God, that is the unity of the God of nature and the God of mercy.'[52]

Particularly when one remembers that the divine–human nature of Scripture is envisaged Christocentrically by Bavinck, the claim that his doctrine of Scripture is irredeemably divided becomes strained. Revelation, he writes, has an ongoing nature which divides into two epochs, which meet in the Incarnation of Christ. 'In Christ, in the middle of history, God created an organic centre; from this centre, in an ever widening sphere, God drew the circles within which the light of revelation shines.'[53] In Bavinck's grand story, there is a Christocentric meta-narrative, whereby he is the organic centre of all revelation. Pre-Incarnation, revelation points to him. Post-Incarnation, it points from him. In writing of Christ as the 'organic centre' of all revelation, Bavinck is making an important assertion regarding Christ-centred organic thinking: there is an intimate, organic connection between the person of Christ (as fully divine and human) and the nature of inspiration.

As inspiration has a permanent link to Christ himself (in that it emanates from him, in organic terms), Bavinck develops the idea that inspiration should not be conceived of solely as an act of divine validation when the text was first written. Rather, he proposes that, by virtue of the text's organic connection to Christ, it has a permanent quality of inspiration.

---

[51] Bolt, 'The Van Drunen/Kloosterman Debate on "Natural Law" and "Two Kingdoms" in the Theology of Herman Bavinck', 12; Kloosterman, 'A Response to "The Kingdom of God is Twofold": Natural Law and the Two Kingdoms in the Thought of Herman Bavinck by David VanDrunen', 175.

[52] Herman Bavinck, *Modernisme en orthodoxie: Rede gehouden bij de overdracht van het rectoraat aan de Vrije Universiteit op 20 oktober 1911* (Kampen, 1911), 37. Dutch original: 'Heel de Schrift predikt de eenheid Gods, dat is die eenheid van de God der natuur en van den God der genade.' Commenting on this passage, Harinck writes: 'God is one, and as a result, Christianity is Catholic.' Harinck, '"Something that must remain, if the truth is to be sweet and precious to us": The Reformed Spirituality of Herman Bavinck', 259.

[53] *RD*, 1.383.

Holy Scripture is not an arid story or ancient chronicle but the ever-living, eternally youthful Word, which God, now and always, issues to his people. It is the eternally ongoing speech of God to us. . . . Divine inspiration, accordingly, is a permanent attribute of Holy Scripture. It was not only 'God-breathed' at the time it was written; it is 'God-breathing'. It was divinely inspired, not merely while it was written, God breathing through the writers; but also, whilst it is being read, God breathing through the Scripture, and the Scripture breathing Him [He being their very breath]. Having come forth from revelation, it is kept alive by divine inspiration and made efficacious.[54]

In charting the rise of critical Protestantism, Bavinck discusses various views on inspiration and revelation, from which he distinguishes his own position. First, he holds inspiration to be more than the mere preservation of the writer from error. Second, he dismisses the notion that inspiration is the arousal of religious affections in the writers of Scripture. 'All of revelation in Scripture is one continuous proof, however, that God not only speaks to human beings metaphorically, by nature and history, facts and events, but also repeatedly comes down to them to convey his thoughts in human words and language. Divine inspiration is above all God speaking to us by the mouth of prophets and apostles, so that their word is the word of God.'[55]

In that sense, a dynamic understanding of inspiration is inadequate, as it 'confuses inspiration with regeneration and puts Scripture on par with devotional literature'.[56]

IX. Mechanical Inspiration

Immediately before his defence of organic inspiration, Bavinck presents the alternative: mechanical inspiration. He recognizes that two opposing worldviews will take a mechanical view of inspiration.

First, the Leiden-style mechanical theist will gravitate strongly to the notion that inspiration occurs mechanically in that the author is inspired non-supernaturally, as the process of cause and effect lead him to write in response to natural (external and internal) factors. 'Some writers use this term when they reject all special guidance of the Holy Spirit in the writings of biblical

---

[54] *RD*, 1.384–5.
[55] *RD*, 1.429.
[56] *RD*, 1.389.

books.'[57] This kind of mechanical revelation, Bavinck writes, ultimately leads to a consistently mechanical worldview in which all revelation is rejected. 'According to them, any kind of miracle, all prophecy, all supernatural influence of God in the world and in human beings is contrary to the nature of things. So no revelation can exist other than that which comes to human beings in the ordinary course of nature and is historically as well as psychologically mediated. The inspiration that the biblical authors enjoyed is then on a par with, or least only different in degree from, the heroic, poetic or religious inspiration that other people experienced as well.'[58]

Second, one may view inspiration mechanically from the opposite worldview: that God dictated Scripture to the human authors, and thus their humanity made no contribution at all to the writing of Scripture. 'This detaches the Bible writers from their personality, as it were, and lifts them out of the history of their time. In the end it allows them to function only as mindless, inanimate instruments in the hand of the Holy Spirit.'[59]

Noting the problems that come with mechanical inspiration, and that such an approach (albeit for differing reasons) was common to both 'orthodox' and 'modern' trends, Bavinck proposes organic inspiration as a better solution. His conviction is that the absence of a 'unity-in-diversity' paradigm, as exemplified in the triniform organic motif, will always lead to those who gravitate to either extreme. Conversely, Bavinck believes that organic thinking is the only thing which will formulate a doctrine of inspiration in which Scripture is simultaneously divine and human. Indeed, his argument endorses a specifically organic view of inspiration as strengthening, rather than weakening, the doctrine of Scripture.

X. The Servant Form of Scripture

Bavinck has already laid the foundation for his understanding of organic inspiration by writing that 'Scripture is the servant form of revelation. Indeed, the central fact of revelation, i.e., the incarnation, leads to Scripture'.[60] This assertion rests on an intimate parallel between the incarnation of the Word (who 'does not merely become a human but a servant, flesh'[61]) and the incarnation of the word in Scripture. This parallel is also found in Kuyper's

---

[57] *RD*, 1.430.
[58] *RD*, 1.430.
[59] *RD*, 1.431.
[60] *RD*, 1.380.
[61] *RD*, 1.380.

doctrine of Scripture.[62] 'In Christ and the Holy Scripture we have to do with related mysteries. In the case of Christ there is a union between divine and human factors. The same is true of Scripture; here, too, there is a primary author and a secondary author. To maintain properly the relationship between these two factors is the great work of dogmatics. . . . Everything depends here on the right insight that the Word has become flesh in Christ and is stereotyped in Scripture.'[63]

The obvious rationale is that in its construal of Jesus as simultaneously fully human and fully divine, Chalcedon has already set a precedent by which later theologians may account for the divine and human authorship of Scripture. Post-Bavinck, this basic argument has been employed by different theologians in various ways. Barth used the incarnation–inspiration analogy to defend the 'writtenness' of Scripture. 'There is no point in ignoring the writtenness of Holy Writ for the sake of its holiness, its humanity for the sake of its divinity.'[64] This attitude towards the inscripturation of Scripture formed the basis for Barth's exegetical method.[65]

Vatican II used the same analogy to explain the sense in which human language can facilitate the divine word. 'God's words, expressed through human language, have taken on the likeness of human speech, just as the Word of the eternal Father, when he assumed the flesh of human weakness, took on the likeness of human beings.'[66]

Käsemann has used the analogy to defend the subjection of Scripture to higher critical methods, arguing that anything else would be Docetism.[67]

Interestingly, Warfield was critical of the analogy, writing that '[i]t has been customary among a certain school of writers to speak of the Scriptures, because thus "inspired", as a Divine-human book, and to appeal to the analogy of our Lord's Divine-human personality to explain their peculiar qualities as such. . . . Between such diverse things there can exist only a *remote analogy*; and, in point of fact, the analogy in the present instance amounts to no more than that in both cases Divine and human factors are involved, though very differently'.[68]

---

[62] Kuyper, *Sacred Theology*, 180.

[63] Abraham Kuyper, *Locus de Sacra Scriptura, creation, creaturis*, Vol. 2 (Grand Rapids: J.B. Hulst, n.d.), 1.59, 63, 72. Cited in Gaffin, *God's Word in Servant Form: Abraham Kuyper and Herman Bavinck on the Doctrine of Scripture*, 22.

[64] Karl Barth, *Church Dogmatics* I/2 (Edinburgh: T & T Clark, 1956), 463.

[65] Barth, *Church Dogmatics* I/2, 469.

[66] *Dei Verbum* § 13.

[67] Ernst Käsemann, 'Vom Theologischen Recht historisch-kritisch Exegese', *Zeitschrift für Theologie und Kirche* 64/3, (1967), 259–81.

[68] Benjamin Breckenridge Warfield, *The Inspiration and Authority of the Bible* (Phillipsburg, New Jersey: P&R, 1948), 162.

He goes on to state the obvious difference between the incarnation of the Son and the inspiration of the Scriptures. 'There is no hypostatic union between the Divine and the human in Scripture; we cannot parallel the "inscripturation" of the Holy Spirit and the incarnation of the Son of God. The Scriptures are merely the product of Divine and human forces working together to produce a product in the production of which human forces work under the initiation and prevalent direction of the Divine.'[69]

However, one suspects that Bavinck might defend himself on this point by falling back on his insistence on the analogous nature of all revelation and, due to this, the humility that ought to characterize the dogmatician's endeavour. Accordingly, one may offer a twofold accent on Bavinck's likely response. First, for Bavinck there are only *remote* analogies. The nature of the analogous is that it is likeness rather than replication. Second, however, is the insistence that there are remote *analogies*. It is possible to speak of the unrepeatable and incomprehensible via analogies. Indeed, this is the only way by which one may speak of them.

What is important to note, at this point, is that Bavinck saw unity-in-diversity as the only solution to mechanical inspiration and its associated problems. In pursuing this line of thought, he was not inventing something wholly new. His frustration with the pre-modern Reformed tradition was not that it had no theology of organic inspiration. Rather, he was critical that it made only a 'feeble attempt at developing a more organic' doctrine of Scripture.[70] One can observe that the *Réveil* movement, which served as a forerunner to the birth of neo-Calvinism, gave Bavinck some sense of the incarnation–inscripturation parallel as potentially receptive to the organic motif. Isaac Da Costa, the poetic voice of the *Réveil* and disciple of Groen van Prinsterer, wrote that '[t]he written Word has a divine and human nature, as does the personal Word of God'.[71]

That the *Réveil* theologians influenced Bavinck on this point has been noted by van den Belt.[72] Particularly when reading Da Costa's strong

---

[69] Warfield, *The Inspiration and Authority of the Bible*, 162.

[70] *RD*, 1.415. Cf. Maurice Eugene Osterhaven, *The faith of the Church: a Reformed perspective on its historical development* (Grand Rapids: Eerdmans, 1982), 64. 'We should note here Luther's and Calvin's accent on the organic nature of Scripture and on God's intention in giving it to the church. As an organism, these Reformers held, Scripture presents a unified message concerning God's grace made manifest in Jesus Christ and the Christian's call to live unto him. That is the Bible's single theme, and everything drawn from Scripture must be related to that theme.'

[71] Isaac Da Costa, 'Het Woord en de Schrift Van God', *Opstellen van godgeleerden en geschiedkundigen inhoud*, (Amsterdam, 1862), 5.

[72] van den Belt, *Autopistia: The Self-Convincing Authority of Scripture in Reformed Theology*, 279.

simultaneous defences of Scripture's Spirit-inspired infallibility and the authentic humanity of its authors, it becomes clear that Bavinck's own recent tradition provided a basis upon which to develop a theology of organic inspiration.[73] A strong case can be made that in developing this analogy, Bavinck was recovering and developing that which already existed within his own tradition.

Van Keulen has compared Bavinck and Kuyper's theologies of organic inspiration, particularly as regards their use of Christology, concluding that Bavinck is more consistently organic than Kuyper: 'On the basis of this analogy [between Incarnation and Inscripturation] a difference between their theologies of inspiration can also be designated. Bavinck stressed that the divine and the human elements are not separate, nor can they supplant one another. He seeks the right balance: everything is divine and everything is human. Kuyper speaks in his Encyclopaedie of a divine and a human "factor" in the characters. This gives the impression that the divine and the human are not only distinguishable, but also separate.'[74]

In trying to reconcile the use of the incarnation–inscripturation parallel in Bavinck and Kuyper with Chalcedon's earlier relation between Christ's divine and human natures, it is worth noting that in both Chalcedonian Christology and the later analogy employed by the neo-Calvinists, the two 'natures' are real, but are not finally equal. In both, the priority and initiative are attributed to the divine nature. In Chalcedonian Christology, Christ, in his pre-hypostatic union as the Word, was enfleshed. Similarly, Bavinck and Kuyper regard God as the primary author of Scripture. The contours of Chalcedon permit them to give priority to the divine nature while maintaining a high view of its human counterpart.[75]

Perhaps Bavinck's key statement in this organic relationship is that 'the word of revelation similarly assumes the imperfect and inadequate form of Scripture'.[76] When one reads of Scripture as 'imperfect and inadequate' (particularly in a context of modernism), what Bavinck means by this must be probed; to misunderstand this statement will considerably skew one's

---

[73] Isaac Da Costa, *Opstellen van godgeleerden en geschiedkundigen inhoud* Tweede Deel (Amsterdam: H. Höveker, 1861), 8–10.

[74] 'Aan de hand van deze analogie kan tevens een verschil tussen hun schriftbeschouwing worden aangewezen. Bavinck benadrukt dat het goddelijke en het menselijke in de schrift niet te scheiden zijn, evenmin mogen zij elkaar verdringen. Zo zoekt hij naar de juiste balans: alles is goddelijk en alles is menselijk. Kuyper spreekt in zijn Encyclopaedie over een godelijke en een menselijke "factor" in de schrift. Dit wekt de indruk dat het goddelijke en het menselijke niet alleen te onderscheiden, maar ook te scheiden zijn.' Dirk Van Keulen, *Bijbel en dogmatiek*, (Kampen: Kok, 2003), 163–4.

[75] On this point, see Gaffin, *God's Word in Servant-Form*, 22.

[76] *RD*, 1.380.

wider picture of Bavinck's doctrine of inspiration. What will be seen is that Bavinck views Scripture in those terms as a feature of its incarnate character, rather than as a factor attributed to its human form. Particularly when Bavinck's view of Scripture is read consistently with his high, orthodox Christology, it becomes apparent that while Bavinck used terminology typical to his modernist context, his theology was different from that of Scholten and Kuenen.

As Bavinck begins to describe the aforementioned incarnational parallel, the organic motif facilitates its development. 'In view of all this, the theory of organic inspiration alone does justice to Scripture. In the doctrine of Scripture, it is the working out and application of the central fact of revelation: the incarnation of the Word. The Word has become flesh, and the word has become Scripture; these two facts do not only run parallel but are most intimately connected.'[77]

He then goes on to describe that organic connection in the following terms. 'Christ became flesh, a servant, without form or comeliness, the most despised of human beings; he descended to the nethermost parts of the earth and became obedient even to the death of the cross. So also the word, the revelation of God, entered the world of creatureliness, the life and history of humanity, in all the human forms of dream and vision, of investigation and reflection, right down into that which is humanly weak and despised and ignoble. The word became Scripture and as Scripture subjected itself to the fate of all Scripture.'[78]

It thus becomes apparent that when Bavinck writes of Scripture as imperfect and inadequate, he is following the contours of a Christology within which Christ entered a state of humiliation and limitation at the Incarnation. This follows on from his earlier statement that Scripture 'is the product of God's incarnation in Christ and in a sense its continuation, the way by which Christ makes his home in the church'.[79]

This relationship is central in deciphering Bavinck's doctrine of inspiration. Gaffin acknowledges its importance: 'This passage is noteworthy because it proves to be the base for much of Bavinck's subsequent development of the doctrine of Scripture.'[80] He notes that the central controlling feature of Bavinck's thought here is the close internal connection between incarnation and inscripturation, and by virtue of this, Scripture's servant form.

---

[77] *RD*, 1.434.
[78] *RD*, 1.435.
[79] *RD*, 1.380–1.
[80] Gaffin, *God's Word in Servant-Form*, 56.

Failure to grasp this has been at the core of various misrepresentations of Bavinck's organic understanding of inspiration. In Rogers and McKim, one finds the claim that the organic inspiration of Scripture is used by Bavinck to defend Scripture's salvific (divine) message from its errant (human) form.[81] However, this analysis seems to misunderstand that the motif is concerned to combat mechanical theories of inspiration precisely by *uniting* the divine and human authorship of the Bible. Their handling of Bavinck also ignores his own insistence on plenary inspiration: 'In the thoughts are included the words, and in the words, the vowels.'[82]

Bavinck himself notes that when one starts thinking organically, the kind of arguments typified by Rogers and McKim tend to disappear:

> But if divine inspiration is understood more organically, i.e., more his-torically and psychologically, the importance of these questions vanishes. The activity of the Holy Spirit in the writing process, after all, consisted in the fact that, having prepared the human consciousness of the authors in various ways (by birth, upbringing, natural gifts, research, memory, reflection, experience of life, revelation, etc.), he now, in and through the writing process itself, made those thoughts and words, that language and style, rise to the surface of that consciousness, which could best inter-pret the divine ideas for persons of all sorts of rank and class, from every nation and age.[83]

---

[81] Rogers and McKim, *Authority*, 399. Arguments that Bavinck was not an inerrantist have been made recently in Andrew McGowan, *The Divine Spiration of Scripture*. McGowan's claim is that "[a]spects of Scripture which the inerrantists "explain away", pose no problem for Bavinck. He goes so far as to say that "the guidance of the Holy Spirit promised to the church does not exclude the possibility of human error". Such a claim could never be made by an iner-rantist', (158). McGowan takes this half-sentence from a much earlier section of *RD* where Bavinck is defining 'dogma'. In context, Bavinck attempts to distinguish dogma from rev-elation, but does not discuss Scripture. In writing of the relationship between dogma and creedal statements, he notes that 'the confession of the church supplies us with an excel-lent – though not infallible – means to find our way amid many and varied errors to the truth laid down in God's word' (*RD*, 1.31). It should thus be noted that Bavinck draws a strong contrast between the 'not infallible' confession of the church and 'the truth laid down' in Scripture. Following this, he critiques the Roman Catholic tendency towards claims of dogmatic perfection via papal infallibility. In that context, he notes that Protestant theology has a much surer footing regarding the development of dogmatics. The full sentence (from which McGowan cites only part) is: 'On the basis of Protestant assumptions, however, this is much more the case, for here the Holy Spirit promised to the church does not exclude the possibility of human error' (*RD* 1.32). Whether Bavinck was an inerrantist or not, there is clearly abundant scope for any Protestant theologian to maintain inerrantist views on Scrip-ture and errantist views on the church's confession.

[82] *RD*, 1.438.

[83] *RD*, 1.438.

XI. The Organic Nature of Inspiration

Returning to the hypothesis being explored in this book, that a theology of Trinity *ad intra* leads to a cosmology of organism *ad extra*, one notes that Bavinck grounds the possibility of incarnation (simultaneous divinity and humanity) on the sense in which the cosmos is both united to and separate from its creator and preserver. 'God confers on the world a being of its own, which though not independent, is distinct from his.'[84] For Bavinck, this is the basis upon which one may believe in both incarnation and inscripturation. 'In the preservation and government of all things, God maintains this distinct existence of his creatures, causes all of them to function in accordance with their own nature, and guarantees to human beings their own personality, rationality and freedom. God never coerces anyone.'[85]

Bavinck's emphasis on God's organic co-operation, rather than coercion, stands out strongly when one remembers Scholten's absolute mechanical determinism. In terms of this organic divine–human co-operation in relation to Scripture, the underlying thought is that without the organic motif (as facilitator of unity-in-diversity), one cannot conceive of a divine–human union in inscripturation. Within a mechanical theistic framework, God can dictate or deliver Scripture, and that through a human agent, but it is not through a process of unity-in-diversity. Rather, it happens through coercion: the mechanical interaction of God and man. At the core, his conviction is that mechanical inspiration is inconsistent within a Trinitarian worldview. Instead, he claims it to be appropriate only within non-trinitarian religions. Organic inspiration is, for Bavinck, the most authentic Christian expression of inspiration. 'Just as every human thought and action is the fruit of the action of God in whom we live and have our being, and is at the same time the fruit of the activity of human beings, so also Scripture is totally the product of the Spirit of God, who speaks through the prophets and apostles, and at the same time totally the product of the activity of the authors. "Everything is divine and everything is human".'[86]

This is what has been elsewhere described as a *concursus divinus*.[87] The fact that Bavinck posits a rigid concatenation between the human and

---

[84] *RD*, 1.432.
[85] *RD*, 1.432.
[86] *RD*, 1.435.
[87] Rein Fernhout, *Canonical Texts: Bearers of Absolute Authority* (Amsterdam: Editions Rodopi, 1994), 193. 'Bavinck also views the relation between the two authors in terms of the *concursus* doctrine, which indeed he does not state in so many words here, but in other places shows his adherence to it.'

divine authors would seem to suggest that Henk Vroom's assessment of organic inspiration ('This doctrine can be elaborated in different ways; it is possible for the contribution of the biblical authors to be personal to a greater or lesser degree')[88] is not strictly accurate.

How can God inspire without coercion? Bavinck anticipates this question in discussing the relationship of organic inspiration to pneumatology. 'The so-called "impulsion to write" yields a tangible proof of the Spirit-led organic activity of the prophets and apostles, for in only a few texts is there any indication of a direct command to write; and these texts by no means cover the entire content of Scripture.'[89]

This is then developed into the assertion that organic, Spirit-impelled inspiration preserves the full humanity of the Scriptural authors. 'We observe that the prophets and apostles, as they proceed to write, completely remain themselves. They retain their powers of reflection and deliberation, their emotional states and freedom of the will. Research (Luke 1.1), reflection, and memory (John 14.26), the use of sources, and all the ordinary means that an author employs in the process of writing a book are used. So far from being spurned or excluded by divine inspiration, these means are incorporated into it and made to serve the goal that God has in mind.'[90]

Bavinck's position is that within a triniform, 'organic' universe, the physical and metaphysical can come together. This has happened in the Incarnation of the Word, and can also be seen in the inscripturation of the word. 'In view of all this, the theory of organic inspiration alone does justice to Scripture. In the doctrine of Scripture, it is the working out and application of the central fact of revelation: the incarnation of the Word. The Word has become flesh, and the word has become Scripture; these two facts do not only run parallel but are most intimately connected.'[91]

XII. The Ongoing Nature of Inspiration

The second major aspect in Bavinck's doctrine of organic inspiration is its ongoing nature. He firmly rejects the notion that the inspiration of Scripture was limited to the moments within which it was written. Rather, he regards

---

[88] Henk Vroom, *No Other Gods: Christian belief in dialogue with Buddhism, Hinduism and Islam* (Grand Rapids: Eerdmans, 1996), 122.
[89] *RD*, 1.435.
[90] *RD*, 1.433.
[91] *RD*, 1.434.

inspiration as a continuous activity of the Holy Spirit. 'Similarly Scripture is a living and active word, a "discerner" of the thoughts and intentions of the heart. It not only was inspired but is still "God-breathed" and "God-breathing". Just as there is much that precedes the act of inspiration (all the activity of the Holy Spirit in nature, history, revelation, regeneration), so there is much that follows it as well. Inspiration is not an isolated event. The Holy Spirit does not, after the act of inspiration, withdraw from Holy Scripture and abandon it to its fate but sustains and animates it and in many ways brings its content to humanity, to its heart and conscience.'[92]

The continuous nature of revelation rests on two already established foundations: the essentially historical nature of revelation[93] and the placing of Christ as the organic centre of all revelation.[94] These points, in turn, highlight the redemptive, salvific, redemptive goal of divine revelation. This redemptive revelation continues throughout all of history, building up through the 'dispensation of the Son' into the 'dispensation of the Spirit'. Within this dispensation, the Spirit is continually inspiring Scripture in order for it to accomplish its redemptive purpose. 'Divine inspiration, accordingly, is a permanent attribute of Holy Scripture. It was not only "God-breathed" at the time it was written; it is "God-breathing".'[95] In this context, Bavinck quotes Bengel: 'It was divinely inspired, not merely while it was written, God breathing through the writers; but also, whilst it is being read, God breathing through the Scripture, and the Scripture breathing Him [He being their very breath].'[96]

Within his Trinitarian framework, Bavinck has a carefully developed doctrine of the Holy Spirit's ongoing illuminative role in organic inspiration. The Father prepares the circumstances, and through the application of the Word, the Holy Spirit assumes a redemptive, illuminating role.

XIII. Conclusion

What seems apparent is that when Bavinck's doctrine of Scripture is approached without the division-seeking presuppositions of the 'two Bavincks' hypothesis, the application of the organic motif renders this area of his thought considerably less fractured than the 'two Bavincks' advocates

---

[92] *RD*, 1.440.
[93] *RD*, 1.379.
[94] *RD*, 1.383.
[95] *RD*, 1.385.
[96] *RD*, 1.385.

would make out. This is not to say that there are no tensions in his thought. Indeed, as Harinck notes, Bavinck's attempt to be both orthodox and modern with regard to Scripture meant that he did not fit in – either with the modern theologians or in his own *gereformeerde* context.[97] In that sense, Vroom's observation that future generations of Bavinck students failed to replicate his position no doubt contains a grain of truth. However, the question lingers as to why this was so. When one probes the workings of Bavinck's system, where all subsequent unity develops from the sublime unity of the Godhead, it certainly seems that replication of his doctrine is not impossible. Having noted that arguing for organic inspiration meant Bavinck did not 'fit in' to either modern or orthodox camps, it is most likely the case that the Bavinck students to whom Vroom refers were not primarily *Bavinck* students. Rather, one suspects that they were students of either 'orthodoxy' or 'modernity' who failed to depart from their own presuppositions and thus felt the need to 'choose which strain of Bavinck's thought to follow'. Evidently, few were willing to embrace the whole doctrine and cease to 'fit in' to their theological and ecclesiastical backgrounds.

Had Bavinck simply tried to fit in to either side of this debate, he would not have been able to pose the hard questions asked, for example, in 'Herman Bavinck on Scripture and Science'.[98] One is left appreciative of Bavinck's efforts not to take sides in this debate, but rather to explore the sense in which Scripture is both human and divine. Without an organic model of thinking, it seems unlikely that he would have pushed as far in this direction.

---

[97] Harinck, '"Something that must remain, if the truth is to be sweet and precious to us": The Reformed Spirituality of Herman Bavinck', 260.

[98] Herman Bavinck, 'Herman Bavinck on Scripture and Science', *Calvin Theological Journal*, 27 No. 1 (April 1992), tr. Al Wolters, 91–5.

Chapter 7

The Organic Motif and Ecclesiology

I. Introduction

The final chapter focuses on the application of the organic motif on Bavinck's theology of the church. It will explore the motif's role in a unique ecclesiological development in the neo-Calvinist movement, whereby the visible church was defined as both institution and organism. Following this, the consequences of an organic church in terms of how the church should pursue a degree of triniformity will be probed.

At the outset, one writes consciously in the immediate aftermath of what Otto Dibelius called *Das Jarhundert der Kirche*.[1] The twentieth-century, within which ecclesiology formed such a prominent topic of debate, has now drawn to a close. At the beginning of the twenty-first century, this discussion shows no sign of abatement.[2] As Western society has slid into a set of decidedly post-Christian cultural norms, the church must carefully consider its own nature and calling. For the church in the modern-day secular West, much can perhaps be gained from Bavinck's creative application of trinitarian thought to the doctrine of the church.

II. Trinitarian Ecclesiology within Bavinck's Structural Theology

In Chapter 4, it was observed that Bavinck's *Reformed Dogmatics* is carefully arranged to follow the trinitarian progression of the Apostles' Creed. This observation led to the conclusion that for Bavinck, there is a real sense in which all theology is the doctrine of God.[3]

---

[1] Otto Dibelius, *Das Jarhundert der Kirche* (Berlin: Furche-Verlag, 1926).
[2] Gerard Mannion, *Ecclesiology and Postmodernity: Questions for the Church in our Time* (Collegeville: Minnesota, 2007).
[3] *RD*, 2.29.

This is evident by the sense in which each locus of dogmatics is handled in relation to the members of the Godhead. *Prolegomena* accounts for creation in relation to the doctrine of God the Father; and *Sin and Salvation in Christ* brings hamartiology and soteriology under the purview of Christology. Now, one arrives at ecclesiology, which is dealt with in Volume Four: *Holy Spirit, Church and New Creation*. Within the structural theology of *RD*, the concept of 'church' is read under the heading of Pneumatology.

Although within this scheme, redemption is planned by the Father and accomplished by the Son, it is applied by the Spirit. In this sense, Bavinck's ecclesiology binds the church to the Holy Spirit. Indeed, it is the unique creation of the Spirit who calls it into existence. Bavinck's framing of ecclesiology-within-Pneumatology is no mere structural convenience. This much is evident in his explanation of each aspect of the church's identity and vocation in relation to the Holy Spirit. Within Bavinck's triniform structural theology, the church is (both literally and metaphorically) inconceivable without the Holy Spirit.

The *ecclesia*, he insists, is a new community fashioned by the Holy Spirit. As such, its essence is spiritual.[4] Its government is also spiritual. The Spirit's work means the church has an utterly unique composition as an ordered, living organism.[5] Furthermore, the church's power is inherently related to the Holy Spirit. Its mission is not world domination through violence, political clout or slick marketing. Rather, the church has, through the Holy Spirit, an unparalleled spiritual power in which to communicate Christ's gospel.[6] Through the church's possession of the means of grace, the Spirit uses the church to redeem the world.[7]

As the church ponders its ongoing existence in the post-Christian West, Bavinck's Trinitarian ecclesiology provides a timely reminder: the *ecclesia* is the Triune God's church. Desired by the Father, paid for by the Son and gathered by the Holy Spirit, the church is a unique possession treasured by the entire Godhead.

The overt connection between the Trinity and the church in Bavinck's system makes it hardly surprising that he employs the organic motif extensively in this area.

---

[4] *RD*, 4.273–352.
[5] *RD*, 4.326–88.
[6] *RD*, 4.389–440.
[7] *RD*, 4.441–588.

III. Ecclesiological Debate in the Netherlands

In discussing Bavinck's doctrine of Scripture, however, one must first describe Kuyper's handling of the topic which forms the backdrop to Bavinck's own ecclesiology.

The first dedicated nineteenth-century work on ecclesiology in the Netherlands was written by N.C. Kist at Leiden in 1828. Like Kuyper, who would later publish a key work on ecclesiology in the thought of Calvin and Łaski, Kist's work was penned in an academic competition. In 1828, the *Teylers Godgeleerd Genootschap* (Teyler's Theological Society) organized this essay competition which was won by Kist's piece. His treatise on ecclesiology was published in 1830 and rereleased in expanded form in 1835.[8]

The importance of ecclesiological thinking came to the fore between these publications. In 1834, the Secession (*Afscheiding*) was accompanied by the emancipation of the Roman Catholic section of the Netherlands. The wholesale revision of the Dutch Constitution in 1848 further affected debate on the nature of the church. With the new Constitution came a revision of the *Algemeen Reglement* (General Regulations) which had previously governed the church's relationship to the Dutch State. By 1851, the two had been formally separated. This was a period of considerable literary output on ecclesiological matters.

Johan Thorbecke, the framer of the new Constitution, sought to create a new secular welfare state. This movement drew considerable criticism from the Reformed Church, which saw care for the poor as one of its central roles in national life. The Groningen school became involved in the debate. In 1856, its Divinity Faculty organized an academic competition on ecclesiology, posing the following question: 'Had the church been an aim or a means for Jesus, or both?'[9]

The Groninger publication *Waarheid in liefde* was given a new subtitle in 1857: 'Dedicated in particular to building up the Evangelical Catholic church of the future.'[10]

---

[8] Vree and Zwaan, *Abraham Kuyper's Commentatio (1860), The Young Kuyper about Calvin, a Lasco, and the Church, I: Introduction, Annotations, Bibliography and Indices*, 15.

[9] This competition was won by E.R. Borgesius (Groningen) and J. Knappert (Leiden).

[10] *Waarheid in liefde, een godgeleerd tijdschrift, voor beschaafde christenen* (1845 ff.: J. Zoon, 1837–72). Between 1857 and 1861, its subtitle was: *Nieuwe reeks, bijzonder gewijd aan de opbouwing der evangelisch-katholieke kerk der toekomst*.

In 1859, the Groningen theological faculty staged another essay competition. The topic on this occasion was the ecclesiology of John Calvin and Jan Łaski. It has been speculated that the Groningers chose a Calvin-related topic in order to combat the influence of the professedly 'pro-Calvin' Scholten in Leiden.[11] Hofstede de Groot's writings on Scholten from this period would certainly add weight to such a suggestion.[12] The fervently nationalistic Heusdiaans, of course, were keen to include Jan Łaski in the study due to his proximity to the Dutchman Erasmus and his role in the Dutch churches in Emden and London. Indeed, Hofstede de Groot had been raised in Emden, in the shadow of Łaski's influence.[13] Furthermore, the anniversary of Łaski's death was soon to occur. By this point, the Groningers had publicly rejected almost all of Calvin's theology[14] and no doubt hoped that exposure to the quasi-Dutch Łaski would demonstrate a better approach to the church. In April 1859, the competition was announced. It specified a comparison of the ecclesiologies of both Calvin and Łaski with specific reference to their respective personal life contexts. Such an emphasis on the nationality of a particular theologian was typical of the Groningen approach. 'The Groningen theologians themselves had always done so, whereby they, following in the footsteps of their master Ph. W. van Heusde, had laid particular emphasis on the influence of someone's nationality on his thoughts and behavior.'[15]

There is also another layer of complexity in the rivalry between Leiden and Groningen on this point. In Leiden, Scholten and Rauwenhoff typified the optimistic, evolutionary spirit of the nineteenth-century: humanity was predetermined to develop into moral perfection through the State. Within this scheme, the church was largely superfluous. Rauwenhoff once quipped that, '[w]hat actually lay in the beautiful dream of the Kingdom of God on earth can be fulfilled in and through the State'.[16] This dramatically low view of the church sets the scene within which various Leiden-influenced

---

[11] Vree and Zwaan, *Abraham Kuyper's Commentatio (1860), The Young Kuyper about Calvin, a Lasco, and the Church, I: Introduction, Annotations, Bibliography and Indices*, 17.

[12] Petrus Hofstede de Groot, *Beantwoording van J.H. Scholten, hoogleeraar te Leiden* (Groningen: A.L. Scholtens, 1859), 137. At this time, Hofstede de Groot held a *privatissimum* in Groningen on Scholten's handling of the Reformed tradition.

[13] J.B.F. Heerspink, *Dr P. Hofstede de Groot's leven en werken*, (Groningen: P. Noordhoff, 1898), 3–11.

[14] Vree, 'P. Hofstede de Groot en de armenverzorging door vrouwen. Een hoofdstuk uit de geschiedenis van de Groninger inwendige zending', 218.

[15] Vree and Zwaan, *Abraham Kuyper's Commentatio (1860), The Young Kuyper about Calvin, a Lasco, and the Church, I: Introduction, Annotations, Bibliography and Indices*, 18.

[16] L.W.E. Rauwenhoff, cited in John Halsey Wood, 'Church, Sacrament and Civil Society: Abraham Kuyper's Early Baptismal Theology, 1859–74', in *Journal of Reformed Theology*, 2 (2008), 279.

ministers abandoned both church and ministry in the mid nineteenth-century.[17]

The Groningen theologians took a similar position in terms of the prevailing culture of optimism: Christ would lead by example as humanity strode on towards moral perfection. However, their intense nationalism meant that the concept of the Dutch *volkskerk* (an ecclesiastical model whereby an elite-controlled church becomes intimately linked to national identity of the populace)[18] remained a key element in their model of Dutch culture. Thus, Christ would lead through the church.

As such, the Groningers staged this competition hoping not only to prove that *their* Łaski was more worthwhile than *Scholten*'s Calvin, but also to enforce that the Dutch *volkskerk* was a better option than the Leiden school's theories on church and State.

It is at this point that one finds a young Leiden student, Abraham Kuyper, entering the debate on the two most important live issues in Dutch theology: Calvin studies and ecclesiology. Kuyper's role in this competition, and the subsequent impact of intensive Calvin study on his own theology was described in Chapter 3 and will not be repeated at this point.

It will suffice to say that in engaging so thoroughly with Calvin's doctrine of the church, Kuyper came to espouse the classical Reformed distinction between the church as visible and invisible. Bavinck also upheld this categorization. Both theologians further defined the visible church as organism and institution.

IV. Reformed Ecclesial Visibility and Invisibility

Like the nineteenth-century Netherlands, Reformation-era Europe was the scene of much ecclesiastical upheaval. The Roman Catholic Church's emphasis on itself as the institutional mediatrix of salvation was dramatically challenged by Luther's claiming to have found peace with God through justification by faith alone, rather than through the institutional Roman Catholic Church. Roman Catholicism's institutional self-emphasis thus came under much scrutiny.

The Anabaptist movement, for all its chaos and fervent rejection of Catholicism, also developed a distinctly institution-based ecclesiology: by

---

[17] In this context, one finds the likes of Conrad Busken Huet, Allard Pierson and C.P. Tiele making high-profile exits from the church.

[18] Karel Blei, 'Volkskerk', *Christelijke Encyclopedie*, ed. George Harinck, 3 volumes, Vol. 3 (Kampen: Kok, 2006), 1819.

virtue of its emphasis on believer's baptism, its ecclesiology implied that all (re)baptized members were true Christians. In Münster, Anabaptists proclaimed themselves the first true believers in 1,400 years.[19] Those who, after adult baptism, vowed to abstain from alcohol, politics, war, friendship and clothing were, it was held, real Christians.

The Reformed, however, regarded such a one-sided, institutional ecclesiology as problematic and exegetically unsustainable. Their question was that if one can judge the true believers on the basis of participation in the visible institutional church, how does one deal with New Testament figures such as Judas, Ananias and Sapphria or Simon the Magician? All were undoubtedly active participants in the church on earth. Indeed, the latter three received Trinitarian baptism in the Apostolic church. However, the general consensus among the Reformed was that, ultimately, none was a true believer.

Luther's challenge was developed by Melancthon, Zwingli and finally Calvin. One finds the latter, in 1543, expressing a theology of the church as visible and invisible.[20] This is to say that the church is simultaneously visible in the world, thus being composed of believers and unbelievers, and invisible, made up only of true believers. Calvin regarded the latter element as 'invisible' for three reasons. First, it is the church catholic, spanning time and space, and thus cannot be fully seen in any single time or place. Second, it contains the full number of the elect, which is unrevealed before the end of time. Third, one cannot definitively distinguish on earth those who are 'elect'.[21] According to the Reformed, this visible–invisible distinction accounts for the temporary presence of Judas *et al.* in the visible church, while preserving the purity of the invisible church.

V. Neo-Calvinist Ecclesiology

Calvin's ecclesiology entered the British Reformed tradition via the Westminster divines. In Chapter 25 of the Westminster Confession of Faith, Calvin's basic position is restated. The invisible church is the church catholic, the elect of God. Conversely, the visible church is made up of those who profess Christian faith and their children. It is 'the kingdom of Jesus Christ, the house and family of God, out of which there is no

---

[19] Menno Simmons, *The Complete Writings of Menno Simmons*, tr. L. Verduin, ed. Harold Bender (Scottdale, PA: Herland Press, 1956), 158–9, 179–89, 212–15.
[20] Calvin, *Institutes*, IV.xvi.19.
[21] Calvin, *Institutes*, IV.i.1–9.

ordinary possibility of salvation'.[22] This basic position, however, is not expanded in the Confession.

In the Netherlands, however, Calvin's ecclesiology was received somewhat differently. This is unsurprising given that the minimal ecclesiological content of the Dutch confessional standard, the Heidelberg Catechism, makes no clear connection to the categories of visibility and invisibility.

54. Q. What do you believe concerning the holy catholic Christian church?

A. I believe that the Son of God, out of the whole human race, from the beginning of the world to its end, gathers, defends, and preserves for Himself, by His Spirit and Word, in the unity of the true faith, a church chosen to everlasting life. And I believe that I am and forever shall remain a living member of it.

55. Q. What do you understand by the communion of saints?

A. First, that believers, all and everyone, as members of Christ have communion with Him and share in all His treasures and gifts. Second, that everyone is duty-bound to use his gifts readily and cheerfully for the benefit and well-being of the other members.[23]

That the visible–invisible distinction made little obvious impact in Dutch ecclesiology is perhaps related to the general lack of study on Calvin until the nineteenth-century. It is also somewhat unsurprising that with the renewed study of Calvin by Scholten, Kuyper and Bavinck (albeit with a considerably different appropriation of Calvin's theology in the Leiden and neo-Calvinist schools of thought), these categories become prominent in Dutch ecclesiological debate.

In addition to this, the *ecclesiastical* nature of the neo-Calvinist movement (in its union of Bavinck's *Afscheiding* and Kuyper's *Doleantie* groups[24] in 1892) necessitated a considerable *ecclesiological* emphasis. In their appropriation of Calvin, Kuyper and Bavinck sought a clear definition of the visible church. Their pursuit of such a definition led to a specific ecclesiological claim: the visible church is an organism and an institution.

Calvin's accent comes across in Bavinck's ecclesiology. Listing the various biblical references to the church's members (sheep, living stones, children,

---

[22] Westminster Confession of Faith, XXV.2.
[23] Heidelberg Catechism, Questions and Answers, 54–5.
[24] For the background information on the *Afscheiding* and *Doleantie* groups, see p. 24.

brothers and sisters and so on), he highlights that among these are false members: chaff (Matt. 3:12), weeds among wheat (Matt. 13:25), bad fish among the catch (Matt. 13:47), wedding crashers (Matt. 22:11), the unchosen called (Matt. 22:14), unfruitful branches (John 15:2) and so forth. He proceeds to state that '[a]ll this makes it incontrovertible that in its essence the church is a gathering of true believers. Those who do not have an authentic faith may externally belong to the church; they do not make up its essential character. Though they are in the church, they are not the church'.[25]

Bavinck regarded the visible–invisible distinction as an ecclesiological necessity. 'The distinction between the visible and invisible church can only be applied to the church militant and then means that the church invisible with respect to its spiritual dimension and its true members. . . . The church is an object of faith. The internal faith of the heart, regeneration, true conversion, hidden communion with Christ (and so forth) are spiritual goods that cannot be observed by the natural eye and nevertheless give the church its true character (*forma*). No human being has received from God the infallible standard by which one can judge someone else's spiritual life.'[26]

Sharing fully in the Reformed conviction that there will always be 'chaff amongst the wheat', Bavinck quickly outlines why the organic motif is so ecclesiologically appropriate. 'The word "church", used with reference to the militant church, the gathering of believers on earth, therefore, always and among all Christians, both Catholic and Protestant, has a metaphorical sense. It is so called, not in terms of the unbelievers who exist in it, but in terms of the believers, who constitute the essential component of it and determine its nature. *The whole is called after the part.* A church is and remains the gathered company of true Christ-believers.'[27]

The classically Reformed distinction between the church as invisible and visible accommodates the reality that the visible church will be mixed.[28] As such, it already sets its own trajectory on the paradigm of unity-in-diversity. As will be explained in the following section, although *the whole is called after the part*, the church's catholic, invisible unity requires that its oneness precede its multiplicity.

Although Bavinck made great strides to incorporate the organism–institution definition of the visible church into neo-Calvinist theology, the

---

[25] *RD*, 4.298.
[26] *RD*, 4.303. Emphasis added.
[27] *RD*, 4.303. Cf. *CW*, 51.
[28] Bavinck nuances this point to say that '[u]nbelievers, accordingly, are not the essence of the church; they are not the church. The invisible and the visible church, therefore, are definitely not terms collectively describing the unbelievers and believers who exist in the church'. *RD*, 4.306.

concept was birthed by his colleague, Kuyper. In trying to account for the tension between the whole church and the individual believer, Kuyper first applied the organic motif as an ecclesiological solution.[29] It is interesting to note that when Scholten's solution to this problem is probed, the motif does not feature.[30]

If, as Spykman argues, the organic–institutional distinction was present in the theology of the Reformers (albeit in nature, rather than in name), it was discovered by the inheritors of Heidelberg rather than of Westminster.[31]

VI. The Visible Church as Organism

The ascription of a living element within the visible church is important to Bavinck's ecclesiology. The church, created by the living Holy Spirit, is a new community of faith and worship. Its spiritual essence is characterized by a necessary vitality. Bavinck draws on the heavily organic illustrations used in Scripture to refer to the church: it is a body, a vine, a field and so on.

Trying to simultaneously maintain Reformed doctrines of election and ecclesiology, Bavinck views Scripture's organic pictures of the church as referring to the visible, rather than invisible, *ecclesia*. The significance of this point should not be glossed over: the organic motif is employed here to convey the idea that through the Holy Spirit's creative power, there exists on earth a church teeming with spiritual life. Hendrikus Berkhof's account of Bavinck's ecclesiology suggests that the organic visible church idea is mentioned by Bavinck only 'in the passing'.[32] However, this seems to understate the significance of the motif within Bavinck's theology of church. Furthermore, Berkhof's highly minimalist portrayal of the

---

[29] 'A comparison of the ecclesiologies of the Groningers and Scholten as well as Chantepie de la Saussaye, shows that Kuyper designed a church model that was new to the Netherlands. Not only is the word "organism" completely lacking in the work of others, but also, none of them had thought so systematically about the role of the members of the congregation as such, let alone that any of them would have discussed the activities of the members before those of the church government.' Vree and Zwaan, *Abraham Kuyper's Commentatio (1860), The Young Kuyper about Calvin, a Lasco, and the Church, I: Introduction, Annotations, Bibliography and Indices*, 57.

[30] Scholten, *Dogmatices christianae*, 247.

[31] Gordon J. Spykman, *Reformational Theology: A New Paradigm for Doing Dogmatics* (Grand Rapids: Eerdmans, 1992), 431. Spykman's argument is based on the sequence of ideas in Calvin's *Institutes*, whereby Book Three discusses the everyday Christian life as the life of the Church, whereas Book Four explains the church in terms of government and so forth.

[32] Hendrikus Berkhof, *Christian Faith: An Introduction to the Study of the Faith* (Grand Rapids: Eerdmans, 1986), 399. 'Bavinck (GD IV, par. 53), however, refers in passing to the concept of "the church as organism" enunciated by Kuyper (over against "the church as institution").'

'church as organism' within Bavinck's thought seems odd when one considers the regularity with which Bavinck applies the organic motif to the church.[33]

The motif is applied to the church primarily to account for the visible church's marked unity-in-diversity.[34] The overwhelming focus of this, however, is the application of the second principle of organic thinking laid out in *Christelijke Wereldbeschouwing*: within the organism, unity precedes diversity.[35] 'In the first place, therefore, the ingathering of the elect must not be conceived individualistically and atomistically. . . . The church is an organism, not an aggregate; the whole, in its case, precedes the parts.'[36]

This grounding of diversity upon pre-existing unity is, according to Bavinck, the basis for the *ecclesia*'s catholicity.

'This oneness of all the churches does not just come into being a posterior by the establishment of a creed, a church order and a synodical system. Neither is the church an association of individual persons who first became believers apart from the church and subsequently united themselves. But it is an organism in which the whole exists prior to the parts; its unity precedes the plurality of local churches and rests in Christ. . . . The assertion that the universal *ecclesia* precedes the local churches is correct in the sense that while it is not historically prior it is logically so.'[37]

The same thought is applied to the *catholicity* of the church over time and space. The 'church militant' is, he writes, but a small portion of the invisible church. '[It] must be noted that the universal church is antecedent to the particular or local church. The church of Christ is an organism in which the whole is prior to the parts.'[38]

The same question of priority lies at the core of his section on 'The Church as Organism and Institution'.[39] Evidently, this is more than an *obiter dictum* for Bavinck. It does seem that in summarizing Bavinck's ecclesiology, Berkhof fails to give the concept of 'church as organism' adequate recognition.

---

[33] *RD*, 3.524, 4.280–1, 4.285, 4.301, 4.303–5, 4.330–32, 4.340, 4.375, 4.448.
[34] This point was marked upon Kuyper's ecclesiology by a trip to Brighton in 1875, where he found himself serving communion to French and Prussian officers who had previously been at war. See James Bratt, 'Raging Tumults of the Soul: The Private Life of Abraham Kuyper', 11. Cf. *CW*, 50.
[35] *CW*, 51; 'leert zij, dat het geheel aan de delen, de eenheid aan de veelheid voorafgaat.'
[36] *RD*, 3.524.
[37] *RD*, 4.280–81.
[38] *RD*, 4.301.
[39] *RD*, 4.329–32.

VII. The Visible Church as Institution

'Christ is the efficient as well as the exemplary and the final cause of the church. By the Holy Spirit he himself continues to live in it as prophet, priest and king and pours out into it all the gifts of his grace. He imparts these gifts exclusively by means of the offices and sacraments. The institution, accordingly, has priority over the organism. The church is the *mother* of believers before it is a *congregation* of believers.'[40]

In drawing on Scripture's richly pictorial ecclesiology, Bavinck is quick to note that the organisms in question possess a distinctly ordered existence. A body requires a head, every kingdom needs a monarch, a vineyard has a gardener and a flock must have a shepherd. Similarly, the visible church in addition to its status as an organism is also an institution. Bavinck defines this on two levels: first, it is institutional in terms of its elder and deacon-led government; and second, it is so in its possession of the means of grace.

Thus Bavinck's contention is that this institutional element is absolutely necessary. 'The church is not conceivable without a government. Granted, Christ could have exercised his office without any service from humans. If it had so pleased him, he could have dispensed his spiritual and heavenly blessings without the help of institutions and persons. But this was not his pleasure; it was his pleasure, without in any way transferring his sovereignty to people, to nevertheless use their services in the exercise of his sovereignty and to preach the gospel through them to all creatures. And also in that sense the church was never without a government. It was always organised and institutionally arranged in some fashion.'[41]

Again, his discussion of historical theology in relation to the institutional church is nuanced regarding the pre- and post-Reformation church. Unsurprisingly, Bavinck disagrees with the idea of continued apostleship.[42] The apostles were, he believes, instituted at a particular epoch to meet a specific need. The church's ongoing government, Bavinck maintains, is found in the ordination of elders and deacons.

What is fascinating about Bavinck's conception of the institutional church, particularly from the vantage point of modern Scottish Presbyterianism (with its highly developed and complex system of legal identities and institutional polity, and its often wholesale collapse into bureaucracy) is just how stripped down he renders the institutional church. In short, the visible

---

[40] *RD*, 4.285.
[41] *RD*, 4.329.
[42] *RD*, 4.337–58.

church's institutional essence is first that its leadership be composed of
ordained elders and deacons; and second, that it possesses and exercises
the means of grace. Christ has instituted that an elder-led church proclaims
the word, exercises diaconal ministries of mercy, baptizes its members and
declares his death in the Eucharist.

Bavinck's clear definition of that which Christ instituted gave him a
healthy perspective on the aspects of visible church life not instituted by
Christ. This clarity enabled Bavinck the churchman to manage ecclesial
change. As a young minister in rural, culturally conservative Franeker,
Bavinck initiated several (contextually) bold changes to the workings of
local congregational life. As a mature man, Bavinck, by then an elder
statesman of the Dutch church, was at the core of a major move for
denominational unity.[43]

VIII. The Visible Church as Organism and Institution

It should be acknowledged that Bavinck makes a great effort to keep the
pairings of visible–invisible and organism–institution separate.[44] By one,
he does not mean the other. Rather, the organism–institution is the
definition of the visible church. Those who regard the organic church as
the invisible church, he says, ignore that the as yet uncalled elect are not
currently members of the church militant. In this viewpoint, 'the church
becomes totally invisible, remains an idea, and has no corresponding
reality'.[45] Those who twin the visible church solely with the institutional
church, from Roman Catholicism to the Anabaptists, receive a parallel
critique: 'For external membership, calling and baptism are no proof of
genuine faith. Many are called who are not chosen. Many are baptized
who do not believe. Not all are Israel who are of Israel. So whereas the
former group fails to arrive at a visible church, the latter neglects the
invisible church.'[46]

---

[43] Indeed, this distinction lies at the heart of Bavinck's ecclesiastical strategizing: *RD*, 4.374–5.
Here, an explicit reference to the visible church as organism and institution is linked to a
high degree of organizational diversity within the church in differing social contexts.

[44] *RD*, 4.304. This point is stressed again in *RD*, 4.330: 'As stated earlier, this distinction is very
different from that between the invisible and visible church.'

[45] *RD*, 4.304. It has been argued elsewhere that due to the Westminster Confession's lack of
definition concerning the visible church, this criticism applies somewhat directly to much of
Westminster Calvinism in Scotland: James Eglinton, 'Some benefits of going organic: Herman Bavinck's theology of the visible church', *Theology in Scotland* (Vol. XVII, No. 1, Spring
2010), 23–36.

[46] *RD*, 4.304.

Worth stating in passing is that Bavinck posits a strict concatenation between the visible church's organic and institutional facets. Neither takes precedence: the presence of one always necessitates the other.[47] One cannot have a living church without the institutional factors established by Christ, and vice versa. Once again, then, the application of an organic idea finds itself dependent on such a concatenation: it must be both visible and invisible, and in its visibility it must be both organism and institution. 'From this it follows that the distinction between the church as institution and the church as organism is very different from that between the visible and the invisible church and may not be equated with it.'[48]

IX. Kuyper's Outworking of the Church as Organism

The concept of the visible church as organism was, as has been noted, also a significant feature in Kuyper's ecclesiology. It was a considerable focus of the first address given by Kuyper to his Amsterdam congregation in 1870 ('Rooted and Grounded').[49]

The organic–institution distinction, for Kuyper, represented the form and essence of the visible church. In breaking free of the Groningers' *volkskerk* model, which he regarded as tying the church too closely to the State, Kuyper instead proposed a 'free church' alternative. In terms of the visible church, this manifests itself in two directions. In relation to the State, Kuyper proposed that the visible church be institutionally independent; and in terms of the organic church, Kuyper envisioned the church as a highly relevant, but nonetheless voluntary society. By holding this view, he regarded himself as distinct from both the overly institutionalized spirituality of the Roman Catholic Church and the Leiden modernist attitude that the church had become obsolete (and that consequently, its sociological role should be taken by State services).[50]

---

[47] *RD*, 4.330. Cf. 4.340: 'The church, accordingly, was never without a government; and it did not provide its own but received it from God. Over and over the institution and the organism were called into being by God at the same time and in conjunction with each other.'

[48] *RD*, 4.305.

[49] Abraham Kuyper, 'Geworteld en Gegrond (1870)', *Predicatiën, in de jaren 1867 tot 1873, tijdens zijn Predikantschap in het Nederlandsch Hervormde Kerkgenootschap, gehouden in Beesd, te Utrecht en te Amsterdam* (Kampen: J.H. Kok, 1913), 328–9.

[50] Since the 1850s, the Thorbecke-inspired Dutch Government had been moving in this direction, particularly regarding social services towards the poor: Vree and Zwaan, *Abraham Kuyper's Commentatio (1860), The Young Kuyper about Calvin, a Lasco, and the Church, I: Introduction, Annotations, Bibliography and Indices*, 16. See also, Wood, 'Church, Sacrament and Society: Abraham Kuyper's Early Baptismal Theology, 1859–74', 279.

Perhaps because of their differing life circumstances, Kuyper spent more time than Bavinck in working out the consequences of the organic–institution distinction for the life of the church. These consequences can broadly be summarized in two parts: first, in the church-as-organism's role in wider society; and second, in the pluriformity of the church.

X. The Church as Organism in Society

Kuyper viewed the *volkskerk* model as directly opposed to the idea of the visible church as an institution and an organism.[51] He placed the two in antithesis[52] and moved to defend the organic–institution definition by paralleling and pairing it with the distinction between common and special grace. He does so by arguing for the existence of 'four terrains'.[53]

First, there is terrain abounding in common grace but which has not been touched by special grace. This terrain, he writes, is typical of non-Christian cultures which nonetheless display commendable sophistication. (Nineteenth-century China was Kuyper's chosen example.)

Second, there is the terrain of the institutional church, which comes about solely by special grace. Here, Kuyper has in mind 'those instituted churches' that make no effort to sanctify their host cultures.

Third, there is the terrain of common grace which is illuminated by special grace. This terrain is regarded as typical of much in late nineteenth-century Europe and North America, where the common grace-laden host cultures are benefited by Christianity, without the majority of those within the culture embracing special grace.

Fourth, there is the terrain of special grace which has been enriched by common grace. 'Finally you find the forth terrain wherever the church as organism manifests itself, i.e., where the personal confessors of Jesus in their own circle allow the life of common grace to be controlled by the principles of divine revelation.'[54] In this context, Kuyper explains that Christian art, schools and scholarship are 'Christian' in a very different

---

[51] Abraham Kuyper, 'Common Grace', *Abraham Kuyper: A Centennial Reader*, 194: 'This, then, is the system of the *national church*. Directly opposed to it is the system of the *church as organism*. . . . It maintains that the blessing of Christianity can only be truly effective in the wider circle [of human life] if the institutional church organises itself in accordance with the demand of Scripture, if Baptism as an ecclesiastical sacrament is administered only to believers and their offspring, and if church discipline is consistently exercised to purify the church.'

[52] Kuyper, 'Common Grace', 193.

[53] Kuyper, 'Common Grace', 199.

[54] Kuyper, 'Common Grace', 200.

sense to the Christian nation or state. The adjective applied to a nation, he believes, carries only a nominal meaning, whereas the organic church's role in society, whereby Christians understand and participate in common grace activities through the lens of special grace, is markedly different. For Kuyper, a Christian school is *Christian* in a way that a 'Christian' nation can never be.

Unlike Bavinck, who uses the organic motif primarily to emphasize that the church's unity precedes its diversity, Kuyper's outstanding emphasis is that the motif explains how and why church members conduct themselves outside of the church institute. Such a thought has a direct equivalent in Bavinck's writings. This equivalent, however, is expressed in Christ's own language, rather than the language of the organic: the New Testament image of the pearl and the leaven. In his penultimate Stone Lecture (1909), one finds Bavinck outlining the relationship of the church (by way of its individual members and in its congregational unity) to its host culture. Here, Bavinck states that the gospel is two things. It is first a 'pearl of great price' (cf. Matt. 13:46).

> But this is certain, – if the gospel is true, then it carries with it its own standard for the valuation of all culture. Jesus has shown this distinctly in the attitude which he adopted towards all earthly things and natural relations. He was no ascetic. . . . And he was as little an epicurean. . . . Neither shallow optimism nor weak pessimism finds in him an ally. . . . He accepted the social and political conditions as they were, made no endeavour to reform them, and confined himself exclusively to setting the value which they possessed for the kingdom of heaven. And in that connection he said, that nothing a man possesses in this world – food or drink, covering or clothing, marriage or family, vocation or position, riches or honour – can be compared with that *pearl of great price* which he alone can present.[55]

In this context, Bavinck, on the basis of common grace, praises the worth of human culture. However, on the basis of special grace, he admits that it is not that pearl of great price. To borrow Kuyper's language, the gospel gives Christians an institutional solidarity in a world characterized by common, rather than special, grace. However, the wider context of Bavinck's theology concerning common and saving grace means that he cannot lapse into pietism and withdraw the pearl from the world. To act consistently with his

---

[55] *PR*, 257. Emphasis added.

theology of common and saving grace,[56] he invokes another piece of New Testament imagery: the kingdom of heaven is like a 'leaven' (cf. Matt. 13:33). 'Christ did not portray for his disciples a beautiful future in this world, but prepared them for oppression and persecution. But, nevertheless, the kingdom of heaven, while a pearl of great price, *is also a leaven* which *permeates the whole of the meal.*'[57]

Thus, while the gospel (as the pearl of great price) provides an institutional haven for Christians in the world, it also (as the leaven) provides the impetus and rationale for their involvement therein. Although Bavinck relies on New Testament imagery, rather than the organic motif (*à la* Kuyper) to explain this dynamic tension, the picture is strikingly similar in both theologians.

In order to produce a Christian nation, the neo-Calvinist argument goes, one needs not a *volkskerk*, but rather a visible church which, as an institution is separate from the State (indeed, as the pearl of great price, it is worth more than nationalism) and which, as an organism, is the leaven that uses special grace to enrich the nation's pre-existing common grace. In his application of this principle, Bavinck attacks the thinking of both Groningen and Leiden schools, who both espoused the general spirit of passive optimism in nineteenth-century Europe. 'The kingdom of God, although analogous to a mustard seed and a leaven and a seed that sprouts and grows aside from any knowledge and involvement of human beings (Matt. 13:31, 33; Mark 4:27), nevertheless does not reach its completion by way of gradual development or an ethical process.'[58]

Bolt makes two helpful points on Bavinck's pearl and leaven ideal, both of which demonstrate that while Bavinck does not use the organic motif here, the principle operates out of the same paradigm. First, Bolt draws the reader's attention to the issue of concatenation: the church must hold the gospel as *both* a pearl *and* a leaven. Second, he highlights the issue of priority: '[F]urthermore, [the gospel] is a treasure or pearl first and foremost; the leavening role is *secondary.*'[59]

This point, it has been suggested, leads to a divergence between Kuyper and Bavinck. Presumably basing it upon Kuyper's wish to combat the

---

[56] Bavinck's idea is that common grace preserves the (corrupted) goodness of the creation until its restoration in special grace. See Bavinck, 'Common Grace', 51.

[57] *PR*, 268. Emphasis added. He also references the 'gospel as a leaven' idea in *RD*, 4.395–6, where the same idea is expressed.

[58] *RD*, 4.684.

[59] John Bolt, 'A Pearl and a Leaven', *John Calvin and Evangelical Theology: Legacy and Prospect* (Milton Keynes: Paternoster, 2009), ed. Sung Wook Chung, 263.

volkskerk emphasis on the church as a national institution (and, consequently, in his desire to emphasize the organic element), Heitink has argued that Kuyper played the organism against the institution.[60]

However, this presentation of Kuyper as a low-church theologian requires deeper investigation centred on the nature of his response to the Groningen school. Rather than respond to their *volkskerk* ideal *by* antithesis, Kuyper responded *with* an antithesis. This is to say, he did not react against their model by rejecting the institutional (or leaving it in a secondary place) and embracing the organic church. Instead, he drew an antithesis between his model of the visible church (as organism and institution) and the *volkskerk*.[61] Kuyper never set one aspect of the visible church against the other. Rather, he placed them in a mutually supportive, concatenous dynamic.[62]

'Kuyper recognised that both the organism and the institute were necessary aspects of the church, and that they had a reciprocal relationship: the organism naturally issuing in an external form or institution and the institution nourishing the organism.'[63]

There are perhaps various reasons that little has been previously written to demonstrate the coherence of Bavinck and Kuyper on the role of the church in relation to culture. Evidently, Kuyper has been portrayed in some quarters as a figure who opposes Bavinck on the priority of the organism–institution relationship. However, as has been seen, this is not a fair portrayal of Kuyper. Also it may be that because Kuyper wrote more on this application of the *church as organism* concept, more has been written on this as a Kuyperian, rather than Bavinckian, ideal.[64] Although their ecclesiologies use the same terminology in different ways (Kuyper's use of the 'pearl of great price' is very different to that of Bavinck),[65] one does well to remember the typically neo-Calvinistic distinction between essence and form. Between

---

[60] Gerben Heitink, *Practical Theology*, 72. 'Kuyper saw the church as an organism, that is, as the community of Christians who are present everywhere in society through the Christian organizations. This he viewed as essential: the church as an institution is of secondary importance and must serve the organism.'

[61] Kuyper, 'Common Grace', 193.

[62] Kuyper, 'Geworteld en Gegrond', 325–51.

[63] Wood, 'Church, Sacrament and Society: Abraham Kuyper's Early Baptismal Theology, 1859–74', 287–8.

[64] Herman Ridderbos, 'Het is taak van de "kerk als organisme" om een appel te doen op de samenleving', *De Kerk: Trefpunt van sociale en politieke akite?* ed. K. Runia (Kampen: Uitgevers-maatschappij J.H. Kok, 1987), 23–8; Jasper Vree, 'Organisme en instituut: De ontwikkeling van Kuypers spreken over kerk-zijn (1867–1901)', *Abraham Kuyper: vast en veranderlijk, De ontwikkeling van zijn denken* (Uitgeverij Meinema: Zoetermeer, 1998), eds. Cornelis Augustijn and Jasper Vree, 86–108.

[65] Abraham Kuyper, 'Calvinism: Source and Stronghold of Our Constitutional Liberties', *Abraham Kuyper: A Centennial Reader*, 303.

Bavinck and Kuyper, the form differs, but the essential agreement between Kuyper's emphasis on organism–institute and Bavinck's pearl–leaven concepts demonstrates that Bavinck should in no way be excluded from this discussion.

Although Bavinck prefers to express this aspect of ecclesiology with the language of the pearl and the leaven rather than the organic motif, the concepts behind the illustrations are cogent within the wider neo-Calvinist worldview. As such, this model of Christianity as culture-producing and culture-renewing depends on a balance of various neo-Calvinist principles, all of which originate in the unity and diversity of the Godhead.

XI. The Pluriformity of the Church

That the church should prize non-uniformity as its ideal is another application of the church as organism principle found in seed form in Bavinck's writings and in fuller form in Kuyper's work.[66] Particularly with regard to liturgical practice, this aspect of ecclesiology is an area of widespread current debate within Scottish Presbyterianism,[67] Roman Catholicism[68] and the Greek Orthodox Church.[69] In each of these examples, the debate focuses on whether one denomination or church should observe a strict uniformity of worship in every congregation and cultural setting.

Having explored both the origins and various applications of the Trinity *ad intra* leads to organism *ad extra* hypothesis, it should come as no surprise that Bavinck and Kuyper supported an ecclesiology which prized unity, rather than uniformity. As such, they are well placed to make an interesting contribution to the current debate. To return to Kuyper's speech 'Uniformity: The Curse of Modern Life', one notes that he regards uniformity as nothing less than a sinful parody of God's own glorious unity.

Those committed to dogmatics as the study of God and the conforming of all else to his perfect being, the neo-Calvinists claim, must strive towards

---

[66] Interestingly, Vroom's account of Kuyper's ecclesiastical pluriformity is that it grew out of the influence of Idealism on one hand, and his awareness of sin's effects on the other. Vroom, 'Understanding the Gospel Contextually', 43–4.

[67] James Eglinton and John S. Ross, 'Unity and Uniformity: Towards a Trinitarian Theology of Worship', *Scottish Bulletin of Evangelical Theology* (Autumn 2009), 131–54.

[68] Peter C. Phan, 'How much uniformity can we stand? How much unity do we want? Church and Worship in the Next Millennium', *Worship*, 72 no. 3 (May 1998), 194–210.

[69] In favour of liturgical uniformity; Bishop Demetri (Khoury), *The Need for Good Choirs and Good Music*, http://www.antiochian.org/1169507979, and *contra*, Anon. *Orthodox Liturgical Renewal and Visible Unity*, at http://www.wcc-coe.org/wcc/who/vilemov-07-e.html).

unity because uniformity is ungodly.[70] Its logical drive is to strip the cosmos and the church of their God-glorifying diversity, which must be reduced to the point of extinction. Within the church, a uniform paradigm sees diversity as inherently undesirable. Observing that although Islam has many sects (Sunni, Shi'ite and Sufi, Druze, Ahmadiyyah and so forth) and Judaism is divided culturally into Mizrahi, Ashkenazi and Sephardi communities and has many liberal and orthodox variants, it is nonetheless clear that in neither religion it is common to find diversity made a virtue. Rather, in both religions there exists a drive towards uniformity in which the differing sects expect conformity to their norms. For both, the core is the same: uniformity, at the expense of unity, is the ideal.

The Christian appropriation of uniformity maintains that Christ's body must be homogenized as Christianity takes on a greater similarity to its non-trinitarian monotheistic counterparts. The norms of the church's dominant cultural group are imposed on its minority subcultures with the goal that everyone look and sound the same.[71]

In applying a triniform pattern of unity-in-diversity to the church, Bavinck and Kuyper were convinced that a paradigm of unity-in-diversity (or pluriformity) was more triniform than that of rigid uniformity. 'The word [pluriformity] itself has always suggested a rich, blessed multiformity in contrast to all uniformity, which Kuyper called the curse of modern life, since uniformity left no room for genuine variation and meaningful differentiation. Pluriformity, then, makes room for variegation and distinction, both of which are so valuable to human life: because reality is not captive to uniformity, it is richer, not poorer!'[72]

However, the obvious objection to this is that within the Trinity, there is no disagreement in the diversity. While the three persons of the Godhead take distinct roles in the economy of salvation, for example, there is no discord. Their roles are wholly complementary. In addition, Paul's

---

[70] The distinctive positions of ecclesiastical uniformity (as typified by Roman Catholicism) and unity-in-diversity (as typified by neo-Calvinism) are apparent in Kuyper's debate with the Roman Catholic apologist, Th. F. Bendsdorp. See Martin E. Brinkman, 'Kuyper's Concept of the Pluriformity of the Church', *Kuyper Reconsidered: Aspects of His Life and Work* (Amsterdam: Vrij Universiteit Uitgeverij, 1999), 111–30; Martin E. Brinkman, 'Kuypers pluriformiteitsleer en de waarheidsvraag. Een konfrontatie met de kritiek van Th. F. Bensdorp', *Gereformeerd Theologisch Tijdschrift* 78 (1978), 115–27.

[71] Phan, a Vietnamese advocate for unity-in-diversity within the Roman Catholic Church, hints at the fascinating point that uniformity in a cross-cultural denomination is never a culture-neutral homogeneity. Rather, it works by the imposition of norms belonging to the denomination's dominant culture on its minority groups (in Phan's case, culturally inappropriate Roman norms being imposed on rural Asian villagers). Phan, 'How much uniformity can we stand? How much unity do we want? Church and Worship in the Next Millennium', 198.

[72] Gerrit Berkouwer, *The Church* (Grand Rapids: Eerdmans, 1976), 52.

application of the unity-in-diversity principle to the church as one body with many distinct members (Rom. 12:4–8) demonstrates the same principle of accord in diversity. Can one legitimately apply the unity-in-diversity paradigm to contexts where diversity is the product of disagreement? Can the fact of God's triunity go some way towards healing ecclesiastical rifts?

Bavinck believes this to be so.

> Undoubtedly the divisions of the church of Christ are caused by sin; in heaven there will no longer be any room for them. But this is far from being the whole story. In unity God loves the diversity. Among all creatures there was diversity even when as yet there was no sin. As a result of sin that diversity has been perverted and corrupted, but diversity as such is good and important also for the church. Difference in sex and age, in character and disposition, in mind and heart, in gifts and goods, in time and place is to the advantage also of the truth that is in Christ. He takes all these differences into his service and adorns the church with them. Indeed, *though the division of humanity into peoples and languages was occasioned by sin, it has something good in it, which is brought into the church and thus preserved for eternity.* From many races and languages and peoples and nations Christ gathers his church on earth.[73]

He is clear to distinguish this from the chaos of a multiform church where all disagreement is relativized.[74] In the background of Bavinck's argument, one hears Calvin's sentiments: 'Not all the heads of doctrine are in the same position.'[75] The Reformed tradition has historically understood that while all truths are important, they are not all of equal importance.[76] The position of Calvin, Bavinck and Kuyper is that the church must allow diversity proportionate to a doctrine's place in the hierarchy of truths. God's triunity, by a remote rather than a close, analogy provides a basis for principled pluriformity in the church; and as such, Bavinck uses a triniform ecclesiology as a model to unite those who disagree on non-fundamental matters. Berkouwer's analysis of Bavinck's ecclesiology observes that the above quotation is followed by the conviction that a key aspect of the

---

[73] *RD*, 4.318. Emphasis added.
[74] *RD*, 4.319.
[75] Calvin, *Institutes*, IV.i.12.
[76] For a thoughtful and helpful discussion of this hierarchy of truths within the Reformed tradition, see Donald Macleod, *Priorities for the Church* (Fearn: Christian Focus Publications, 2003), 100–16.

Reformation's return to Scripture was its departure from Roman Catholicism's insistence on ecclesiastical uniformity.

'Since the [sixteenth-century] Reformation the church has entered the period of pluriformity; and this fact forces us to look for its unity in the spiritual bond of faith rather than in the external form of its government.'[77]

Cornelis Veenhof has portrayed Bavinck as somewhat opposed to Kuyper in terms of attitudes towards ecclesiastical pluriformity.[78] However, when one considers the uncritical spirit with which Bavinck details the post-Reformation church's pluriformity, Berkouwer's counterargument (that Bavinck shared in Kuyper's large-heartedness and disliked disunity, rather than diversity) seems far more plausible.[79]

In redrawing its ecclesiology to the Trinity, the shared belief of Bavinck and Kuyper is that the church works for the redemption of its Edenic, pre-fall ideal diversity. Indeed, they regard this as the means by which it strides toward its *telos*; the sinless, heavenly unity-in-diversity wherein Christ's high priestly prayer for the church's oneness (John 17:21) will be positively and eternally answered.

---

[77] *RD*, 4.319.
[78] Cornelis Veenhof, *Volk van God: Enkele aspecten van Bavincks kerkbeschouwing* (Amsterdam: Buijten & Schipperheijn, 1969), 168.
[79] Berkouwer, *The Church*, 55.

Conclusion

This book, an attempt to explore Bavinck's pervasive organic motif via discussion of the divine paradigm of unity-in-diversity, began by charting the backdrop to Bavinck's theological development. Having done so, it justified a reinterpretation of the said motif by summarizing and developing the new general consensus in Bavinck scholarship: the 'two Bavincks' hypothesis has failed, and previous studies of Bavinck's theology led by its hermeneutics must be redrawn. It was noted that Jan Veenhof's *Revelatie en Inspiratie*, which reads Bavinck through the now discredited 'two Bavincks' lens, since the late 1960s, has influenced generations of Bavinck readers to regard the organic motif as the sole property of the 'modernist' Bavinck's followers. However, the collapse of the 'two Bavincks' model requires a new reading of the organic motif.

This new reading inverted Veenhof's methodology. Rather than beginning with Aristotle and working forward to Bavinck, it began with Bavinck's own definition of the motif and then worked backwards. This new methodology was chosen on the conviction that the best person to define Bavinck's use of a term will invariably be Bavinck himself, which he did in *Christelijke Wereldbeschouwing*. It was argued that although Bavinck uses terminology typical of his era, he did not use it in 'the universal sense of the time'. Rather, the organic motif was so useful for Bavinck because it reflected the paradigm of unity-in-diversity which so gloriously marks the Godhead and, by virtue of divine self-revelation, the entirety of nature and history. Accordingly, Bavinck loaded the term with trinitarian meaning. In so doing, he rooted himself in the Reformed, rather than German Idealist, tradition. Presupposing a reunited Herman Bavinck, it was proposed that the organic motif is, by virtue of its triniformity, the outstanding agent of unity within Bavinck's worldview. (This is, of course, a considerable departure from Veenhof's thesis that the motif is another symbol of disunity within Bavinck's theology).

As such, the hypothesis was developed that for Bavinck, a theology of Trinity *ad intra* leads to a cosmology of organism *ad extra*.

This hypothesis was worked out by first probing the doctrine of God in Bavinck's work. It was noted that the contours of his doctrine of God overwhelmingly emphasize the sense in which the Godhead is characterized by vast diversity (persons, names, attributes, economic roles and so forth) and profound unity of essence, volition and action. Bavinck's desire to "think God's thoughts after him and trace their lines of unity" formed the basis for this exploration. Furthermore, the structural theology of *Reformed Dogmatics*, which (after the *Prolegomena*) follows the Trinitarian pattern of the Apostles' Creed, fleshes out Bavinck's statement that God is the exclusive subject of dogmatics. Every loci of dogmatics is, for Bavinck, subsumed within the doctrine of the Trinity. Creation is understood in relation to the doctrine of God the Father, sin and salvation in relation to God the Son and ecclesiology and consummation through the doctrine of God the Holy Spirit.

Bavinck's desire to redeem the Augustinian concept of the *vestigia trinitatis* from the excesses of medieval natural theology lead him to diverge somewhat from the post-Reformed reticence to borrow from Augustine's theological lexicon in this area. However, his departure from this stream of the Reformed tradition is matched by his simultaneous rejection of the medieval emphasis on seeking triadic forms as the *vestigia*. Rather, Bavinck finds the Trinity revealed primarily in the non-numerically specific concept of unity-in-diversity. This accounts for his summary of the entire time–space continuum (which was created as the general revelation of the Trinity) as an 'organism' and as replete with the glory of the Trinity. In so doing, Bavinck has enriched the Reformed tradition by redrawing the reader to God's triunity and its consequences for all reality.

The proximity of the doctrine of God and the ways in which this God practices self-disclosure were then examined in chapters on general and special revelation. Particular attention was paid to the pattern with which Bavinck employs organic language in handling a theology of general revelation: while he explains its limited use until read through the lens of special revelation, it reveals very limited information on the Triune God. In the build-up to this point, the motif is used very sparingly. However, once Bavinck establishes that one ought to use special revelation to properly appropriate its general counterpart, the motif once again takes a prominent place in his thoughts.

The motif also proves highly significant in Bavinck's handling of God's special self-revelation in Scripture. Having noted the particularly crippling effects of the 'two Bavincks' hypothesis on readings of Bavinck on Scripture, this chapter demonstrated that the context within which he formulates the concept of organic inspiration largely accounts for the use of the motif here. In response to the pietistic handling of Scripture in his own ecclesiastical heritage, the low view of Scripture's divine authorship in his Leiden education and the low view of the human authorship in the Groningen school, Bavinck maintained a concatenation: the text is fully divine and fully human. To explain this, he invoked the formula of Chalcedonian Christology. In this idea, the organic motif was used to explain the unity of human and divine authorship. He also found the motif helpful in explaining the total cohesion of Scripture: in its differing languages, genres, human authors, stages in redemption history and so forth, it forms an 'organism'. A new reading of the reunited Bavinck makes sense of his doctrine of Scripture in a way that the 'two Bavincks' model cannot: it demonstrates that his desire is to hold diverse themes together.

Finally, the flow of this book focused on Bavinck's use of the motif in relation to the church, which, in its visible aspect, is called both an organism and institution. This creative development in the Reformed tradition, which Bavinck inherited from Abraham Kuyper, was shown to be a common feature in their vision for the church in relation to culture. Although Bavinck and Kuyper favour differing terminologies (where Bavinck prefers the image of 'a pearl and a leaven', Kuyper uses 'organism and institution'), it was shown that they shared a coherent vision for the role of the church in the modern world.

That Bavinck's theology has hitherto been read through a hermeneutic based on a highly particular interpretation of his personality, of course, lends a high degree of complexity to any study which departs from the previous norm. Notably, this book has rejected the notion that he was a simply an irreconcilably divided man producing similarly segregated theology. However, in creating a new reading of Bavinck, the sense in which one relates Bavinck *als dogmaticus* to Bavinck's *dogmatiek* must also change. The relationship between Bavinck's persona and his work is, needless to say, a highly complex one which no doubt merits a thorough study in its own right. The primary goal of this book has been to examine the use made by Bavinck of the organic motif. In order to do so, it has been necessary to make some initial foray into study of Bavinck as dogmatician. However, this foray is very much a secondary feature in this work. Although the organic motif appears to solve a great deal of the previously perceived tension in his work, and while the initial continuation of this study into areas concerning the 'reunification' of his persona seem promising, one is at this point quite happy to leave that investigation to a future work. This book has been on Bavinck's organic theology: one hopes that it will encourage study of the relationship between Bavinck's personal and intellectual histories in greater depth.

One shall attempt, however, to close this work by offering comment in the space between Bavinck the theologian and Bavinck's theology.

This book in no way attempts to say that Bavinck found his role as an orthodox participant in modern culture an easy one. Little could be further from the truth. (In that context, Harinck has recently argued that Bavinck's project to be an orthodox theological participant in the modern world was ultimately a failure).[1] However, it should nonetheless be maintained that the 'two Bavincks' hypothesis is overly simplistic, lacks scholarly foundation and has hindered, rather than helped, the development of Bavinck studies.

As has been apparent throughout this book, Bavinck's thought is full of tensions. God is three and one. God is and the cosmos becomes (and the *imago Dei* both is and becomes!). Revelation is general and special. The Christian is *simul justus et peccator.* Scripture's authorship is human and divine. The church is visible and invisible. In its visible aspect, it is both organism and institute. The gospel it possesses is a pearl and a leaven, which means it relates to its host culture in two directions at once (by recognizing the worth of common grace culture and its inferiority to special grace culture). As Berkouwer said, 'various undeniable themes' are 'manifest in Bavinck's work'.[2] Perhaps the great tragedy of the last half century of Bavinck scholarship is that these *onweersprekelijke* tensions have been consistently (mis)treated as *irreconcilable* rather than *undeniable.*

In summarizing this list of *onweersprekelijke motieven*, one observes that they share two factors. The first is that in Bavinck's thought, they can all be traced to the unity-in-diversity of the God whose being gives reality its contours: the Father, the Son and the Holy Spirit. The unity of the divine being, therefore, means that Bavinck has no expectation that these tensions are necessarily bad or undesirable. Rather, reality is non-uniform because it reflects its Creator. The second common factor is that throughout Bavinck's writings, it is in discussion of these 'undeniable themes in tension' that he chooses the organic motif, which provides him with the conceptual apparatus to convey something of the triune God's glory in the created realm.

---

[1] George Harinck, 'The Religious Character of Modernism and the Modern Character of Religion: A Case Study of Herman Bavinck's Engagement with Modern Culture', in *Scottish Bulletin of Evangelical Theology*, 29.1 (Spring 2011), 60–77.

[2] 'Het gevaar van een beschrijving en beoordeling van Bavincks levenswerk is, dat men hem annexeert voor eigen inzichten. Het is niet onmogelijk boven dat annexatie-gevaar uit te komen, doordat in het werk van Bavinck allerlei onweersprekelijke motieven zichtbaar worden.' Berkouwer, *Zoeken en Vinden*, 55.

The admission that tensions are not always inherently wrong, of course, is not to state that they are therefore automatically easy or problem-free. Indeed, holding together different things that nonetheless belong together is no easy task. The call of divine self-revelation to behold the living God is the case in point: it is a call to gaze upon the three-personned God who, in Paul's language, 'dwells in inaccessible light'. It is nothing less than to consider the one who is ineffably sublime. And yet, the unity-in-diversity on show in this example is archetypal blessed perfection.

To behold one's God is no easy feat. The divine undeniable tensions within the Godhead are perfectly balanced, non-contradictory and belong together: how difficult, then, to hold together lesser things in tension in a world so grossly ravaged by sin.

To orb a triniform worldview, therefore, is not easy. In trying to hold all things together, Bavinck consciously embarked upon that most difficult of tasks. Such is evident in a letter by Bavinck to his dear friend, Snouck Hurgronje.

> I do know the ideal I aim for is unattainable, but being human in the full sense of that word and then human in all things and a child of God – that seems to me to be the best of all. That is what I aim for.[3]

It is acknowledged, in closing, that this book has only begun to scratch the surface of the sense in which Bavinck saw the divine unity as rendering the rest of reality inherently coherent. However, one suspects that Bavinck, with characteristic humility, would say the same of his own writings. In probing the consequences of a reunited view of Bavinck's thought to this one particular area, that of the organic, one has also only made the first steps in a wider movement in Bavinck studies. If it is only appropriate to speak of a single Herman Bavinck, it is not simply the organic motif that must be reappropriated. Rather, the breakdown of the 'two Bavincks' model calls for nothing less than a paradigm shift in Bavinck studies.

Those who read a reunited Bavinck must be prepared to ask the hardest of questions in the quest to be orthodox Christians in the modern age.

> Naturally, it would be much easier to leave this age to its own ways, and to seek our strength in a quiet withdrawal. No such rest, however, is permitted to us here. Because every creature is good, and nothing is to be

---

[3] Cited in Harinck, '"Something that must remain, if the truth is to be sweet and precious to us": The Reformed Spirituality of Herman Bavinck,' 258.

refused, if it be received with thanksgiving, since all things are sancti-
fied by the Word of God and prayer, therefore the rejection of any creature were ingratitude to God, a misjudgement or under-evaluation of his
goodness and his gifts. Our warfare may be conducted against sin alone.
No matter how complicated the relationships may be, therefore, in which
the confessors of Christ are placed in this time, no matter how serious,
difficult and virtually insurmountable the social, political and especially
the scientific problems may be, it were faithlessness and weakness in us
proudly to withdraw from the struggle, perhaps even under the guise of
Christian motivation, and to reject the culture of the age as demonic.[4]

---

[4] Bavinck, *Our Reasonable Faith*, 10.

Bibliography

Primary Sources

Bavinck, Herman *De Ethiek van Ulrich Zwingli* (Kampen: G. Ph. Zalsman, 1880).

—. *De Katholiciteit van Christendom en Kerk* (Kampen: Zalsman, 1888).

—. 'Confessie en Dogmatiek,' *Theologische Studiën* 9 (1891): 258–75.

—. 'Godgeleerdheid en godsdienstwetenschap,' *De vrije kerk* 18 (1892): 197–225.

—. *De Algemeene Genade: Rede gehouden bij de overdracht van het Rectoraat aan de Theologische School te Kampen op 6 Dec. 1894* (Kampen: G. Ph. Zalsman, 1894).

—. *Education and Theology (Opleiding en theologie)* (Kampen: J.H. Kok, 1896).

—. *The Authority of the Church and the Freedom of Science (Het recht der kerken en de vrijheid der wetenschap)* (Kampen: G. Ph. Zalsman, 1899).

—. *Erudition and Scholarship (Geleerdheid en wetenschap)* (1899).

—. *The Office of 'Doctor' [in the Church] (Het doctorenambt)* (Kampen: G. Ph. Zalsman, 1899).

—. *The Theological School and the Free University* (Theologische School en Vrije Universiteit, 1899).

—. *Godsdienst en godgeleerdheid* (Wageningen: Vada, 1902).

—. *Christelijke Wereldbeschouwing* (Kampen: Kok, 1904).

—. *Principles of Education (Paedagogische Beginselen)* (Kampen: J.H. Kok, 1904).

—. *The Christian Family (Het Christelijke huisgezin)* (Kampen: J.H. Kok, 1908).

—. *Johannes Calvijn* (Kampen: Kok, 1909).

—. *Philosophy of Revelation* (London: Longmans, Green and Co., 1909).

—. 'The Reformed Churches of the Netherlands,' *Princeton Theological Review* 8 (1910): 433–60.

—. *Modernisme en orthodoxie: Rede gehouden bij de overdracht van het rectoraat aan de Vrije Universiteit op 20 oktober 1911* (Kampen: J.H. Kok, 1911).

—. *Education of the Teacher (De opleiding van den onderwijzer)* (Amsterdam: De Standaard, 1914).

—. *Education of Adolescents (De opvoeding der rijpere jeugd)* (Kampen: J.H. Kok, 1916).

—. *New Education (De nieuwe opvoeding)* (Kampen: J.H. Kok, 1917).

—. *The Imitation of Christ in Modern Life (De navolging van Christus in het moderne leven*, 1918).

—. *The Role of Woman in Modern Society (De vrouw in de hedendaagsche maatschappij)* (Kampen: J.H. Kok, 1918).

—. *Kennis en Leven* (Kampen: J.H. Kok, 1922).

—. *Our Reasonable Faith* (Grand Rapids: Baker Book House, 1956), tr. Zylstra, Henry.

—. *The Doctrine of God* (Edinburgh: Banner of Truth, 1977), tr. Hendriksen, William.

—. *The Certainty of Faith* (Grand Rapids: Paideia Press, 1980).

—. 'Common Grace,' *Calvin Theological Journal* 24 No. 1 (April 1989), tr. Van Leeuwen, Raymond: 35–65.

—. 'The Catholicity of Christianity and the Church,' *Calvin Theological Journal* 27 (1992), tr. Bolt, John: 220–51.

—. 'Herman Bavinck on Scripture and Science,' *Calvin Theological Journal* 27 No. 1 (April 1992), tr. Wolters, Al: 91–5.

—. *Reformed Dogmatics, Volume One: Prolegomena* (Grand Rapids: Baker Academic, 2003), ed. Bolt, John; tr. Vriend, John.

—. *Reformed Dogmatics, Volume Two: God and Creation* (Grand Rapids: Baker Academic, 2004), ed. Bolt, John; tr. Vriend, John.

—. *Reformed Dogmatics, Volume Three: Sin and Salvation in Christ* (Grand Rapids: Baker Academic, 2006), ed. Bolt, John; tr. Vriend, John.

—. 'Christianity and Natural Science, in *Essays on Religion, Science and Society* (Grand Rapids: Baker, 2008), ed. Bolt, John; trs. Boonstra, Harry and Sheeres, Gerrit: 81–104.

—. 'The Essence of Christianity,' in *Essays on Religion, Science and Society* (Grand Rapids: Baker, 2008), ed. Bolt, John; trs. Boonstra, Harry and Sheeres, Gerrit: 33–48.

—. *Gereformeerde Katholiciteit (1888–1918)* (Barnveld: Nederlands Dagblad, 2008), ed. van Bekkum, Koert.

—. *Reformed Dogmatics, Volume Four: Holy Spirit, Church and New Creation* (Grand Rapids: Baker Academic, 2008), ed. Bolt, John; tr. Vriend, John.

—. 'Theology and Religious Studies,' in *Essays on Religion, Science and Society* (Grand Rapids: Baker Publishing Group, 2008), ed. Bolt, John; trs. Boonstra, Harry and Sheeres, Gerrit: 49–60.

—. 'Theology and Religious Studies: Appendix B,' in *Essays on Religion, Science and Society* (Grand Rapids: Baker Publishing Group, 2008), ed. Bolt, John; trs. Boonstra, Harry and Sheeres, Gerrit: 281–8.

Bavinck Biographies

Bremmer, R.H. *Herman Bavinck en zijn Tijdgenoten* (Kampen: Kok, 1966).

Bristley, Eric, *Guide to the Writings of Herman Bavinck* (Grand Rapids: Reformation Heritage Books, 2008).

Gleason, Ron *Herman Bavinck: Pastor, Churchman, Statesman, Theologian* (Philippsburg: Presbyterian and Reformed Publications, 2010).

Hepp, Valentijn *Dr. Herman Bavinck* (Amsterdam: W. Ten Have 1921).

Landwehr, J. *Prof. Dr. Herman Bavinck* (Kampen: Kok, 1921).

Secondary Sources

Amyraut, Moyse *De mysterio trinitatis, deque vocibus ac Phrasibus quibus tam Scriptura quam apud Patres explicatur, Dissertatio, septem partibus absoluta* (Saumur: Isaac Desbordes, 1661).

Andrich, Gustav *Das antike Mysteriewesen in Seinim Einfluss auf das Christenthum* (Göttingen: Vanderhoeck und Ruprecht, 1894).

Aquinas, Thomas *Summa Contra Gentiles* IV (University of Notre Dame Press, 1991), tr. Vernon J. Bourke.

Augustijn, Cornelis 'Kerk en Godsdienst 1870–90,' *De Doleantie van 1886 en haar Geschiedenis* (Kampen: Kok, 1984), ed. Bakker, Wim: 58–62.

Augustine, *On the Trinity* (Cambridge: Cambridge University Press, 2002), ed. Gareth B. Matthews.

Bancroft, George *History of the United States of America* (New York: Appleton, 1890).

Barr, James *The Semantics of Biblical Language* (London: Oxford University Press, 1961).

Barth, Karl *Church Dogmatics*, Vol. I, Part 2 (Edinburgh: T & T Clark, 1956), trs. Bromily G.W. et al.

—. *Church Dogmatics*, Vol. I, Part 1 (Edinburgh: T & T Clark, 1975), trs. Bromily, G.W. et al.

Bascom, John *Aesthetics, or, the Science of Beauty* (Boston: Crosy and Nichols, 1862).

Bavinck, Johan Herman *An Introduction to the Reformed Science of Missions* (Grand Rapids: Baker, 1960), tr. David Hugh Freeman.

Beek, M. 'Abraham Kuenen,' *Vox Theologica* 7 (1935–36): 150.

Beiser, Frederick *Hegel* (New York: Routledge, 2005).

van den Belt, Henk *Autopistia: The Self-Convincing Authority of Scripture in Reformed Theology*, (Leiden: University Press, 2006).

Berkhof, Hendrikus *Christian Faith: An Introduction to the Study of the Faith* (Grand Rapids: Eerdmans, 1986).

—. *Two Hundred Years of Theology* (Grand Rapids: Eerdmans, 1989).

Berkouwer, Gerrit *General Revelation* (Grand Rapids: Eerdmans, 1955).

—. *Holy Scripture* (Grand Rapids: Eerdmans, 1975), tr. Rogers, Jack.

—. *The Church* (Grand Rapids: Eerdmans, 1976).

—. *Zoeken en Vinden: Herinneringm en Ervanngm* (Kampen: Kok, 1989).

Bertram, J.F. *Historia critica Johannis à Lasco* (Aurich: H. Tapper, 1733).

Blei, Karel 'Volkskerk,' *Christelijke Encyclopedie*, 3 volumes, Vol. 3 (Kampen: Kok, 2006), ed. Harinck, George: 1819.

Bloesch, Donald *Holy Scripture: Revelation, Inspiration and Interpretation* (Downers Grove: InterVarsity, 1994).

Bohatec, Josef 'De Organische Idee in de Gedachtenwereld van Calvijn,' *Antirevolutionaire Staatkunde: Orgaan van de Dr. Abraham Kuyperstichting ter bevordering van de studie der Antirevolutionaire Beginselen* 2ᵉ Jaargang (Kampen: Kok, 1926), 32–45, 153–64, 362–77.

—. *Calvin und das Recht* (Feudingen: Buchdruck und Verlags-Anstalt, 1934).

—. *Calvins Lehre von Staat und Kirche* (Breslau: Marcus, 1937).

—. *Budé und Calvin: Studien zur Gedankenwelt des französischen Frühhumanismus* (Graz: Böhlau, 1950).

Bolt, John *The Imitation of Christ Theme in the Cultural-Ethical Ideal of Herman Bavinck* (Ph.D. dissertation, University of St Michael's College, Toronto, 1982).

—. *Christian and Reformed Today* (Vineland, ON: Paideia Press, 1984).

—. 'The Trinity as a Unifying Theme in Reformed Thought: A Response to Dr George Vandervelde,' *Calvin Theological Journal* 22 No. 1 (April 1987): 91–104.

—. 'Trinitarian beauty and the Order of Common Grace,' *A Free Church, A Holy Nation: Abraham Kuyper's American Public Theology* (Grand Rapids: Eerdmans, 2001), 212–23.

—. 'Editor's Introduction' in *Reformed Dogmatics: Prolegomena*, ed. Bavinck, Herman: 11–19.

—. 'Grand Rapids Between Kampen and Amsterdam,' *Calvin Theological Journal* 38 No. 2 N. 2003: 263–80.

—. 'A Pearl and a Leaven,' *John Calvin and Evangelical Theology: Legacy and Prospect* (Milton Keynes: Paternoster, 2009), ed. Chung, Sung Wook: 242–66.

—. 'Bavinck Society Discussion # 1: The VanDrunen-Kloosterman Debate on "Natural Law" and "Two Kingdoms" in the Theology of Herman Bavinck' (published online via the Bavinck Institute: http://bavinck.calvinseminary.edu/wp-content/uploads/2010/06/Discussion_1_VanDrunen-Kloosterman_debate.pdf).

Bouma, Hendrik *Secession, Doleantie and Union: 1834–92* (Neerlandia, Alberta: Inheritance Publications, 1995), tr. Plantinga, Theodore.

Brakel, W. *Redelijke Godsdienst* I.iv.35 (D. Donner, 1881).

Bratt, James D. 'Raging Tumults of the Soul: The Private Life of Abraham Kuyper,' *Reformed Journal* No. 1 (November 1987): 9–13.

Brinkman, Martin E. 'Kuypers pluriformiteitsleer en de waarheidsvraag. Een konfrontatie met de kritiek van Th. F. Bensdorp,' *Gereformeerd Theologisch Tijdschrift* 78 (1978): 115–27

—. 'Kuyper's Concept of the Pluriformity of the Church,' *Kuyper Reconsidered: Aspects of his Life and Work* (Amsterdam: Vrij Universiteit Uitgeverij, 1999): 111–30.

Bristley, Eric *Guide to the Writings of Herman Bavinck* (Grand Rapids: Reformation Heritage Books, 2008).

Brouwer, A.M. *De modern richting* (Nijmegen, 1904).

de Bruijn, Jan and Harinck, George eds., *Leidse vriendschap* (Baarn: Ten Have, 1999).

Buel, Samuel *A Treatise on Dogmatic Theology*, Vol. 1 (New York: Thomas Whittaker, 1890).

Butin, Philip *Revelation, Redemption, and Response: Calvin's Trinitarian Understanding of the Divine-Human Relationship* (New York: Oxford University Press, 1995).

Calvin, John *Defensis Sanae et Orthodoxae Doctrinae de Servitute et Liberatione Humanii Arbitrii Adversus Calumnias Alberti Pighii Compensis, Johannis Calvini Opera Quae Supersunt Omnia*, Vol. VI, *Corpus Reformatorum*; Vol. XXXIV (Brunsvigae: C. A. Schwatschke et Filium, 1867).

—. *Contre la Secte Phantastique et Furieuse des Libertines qui se Nomment Spirituelz, Joan-nis Calvini Opera Quae Supersunt Omnia*, Vol. VII; *Corpus Reformatorum*, Vol. XXXV (Brunswick: CA. Schwetschke et Filium, 1868).

—. *Institutes of the Christian Religion* (SCM Press, 1960), trs. Battles, Ford Lewis and McNeill, John T.

—. *Commentary on Genesis* (Edinburgh: Banner of Truth Trust, 1965), tr. King, John.

Da Costa, Isaac 'Het Woord en de Schrift Van God,' *Opstellen van godgeleerden en geschiedkundigen inhoud* (Amsterdam, 1862).

Cremer, H. *Biblico-Theological Lexicon of New Testament Greek* (Edinburgh: T & T Clark, 1872) trs. Simon, D.W. and Urwick, William.

Dabney, Robert *Systematic Theology* (St. Louis: Presbyterian Publishing Company, 1871).

Dibelius, Otto *Das Jarhundert der Kirche* (Berlin: Furche-Verlag, 1926).

Bishop Demetri (Khoury), *The Need for Good Choirs and Good Music* (http://www.antiochian.org/1169507979).

Dooyeweerd, Herman 'Kuyper's Wetenschapsleer,' *Philosophia Reformata* 4 (1939): 193–232.

—. *Roots of Western Culture: Pagan, Secular, and Christian Options* (Toronto: Wedge Publishing Foundation, 1979).

Dosker, Henry Elias 'Herman Bavinck,' in *Essays on Religion, Science and Society* (Grand Rapids: Baker Academic, 2008), ed. Herman Bavinck: 13–24.

Dourley, John P. 'The Relationship between Knowledge of God and Knowledge of the Trinity in Bonaventure's *De mysterio trinitatis*,' *San Bonaventura Maestro* (Rome: Pontifica Facolta Teologica San Bonaventura, 1976), Vol. II, ed. Pompei, A.: 4–45.

Dowey, E.A. *The Knowledge of God in Calvin's Theology* (Grand Rapids: Eerdmans, 1994).

Dulles, Avery *Modes of Revelation* (New York: Orbis Books, 2002).

Dupré, Louis *The Enlightenment and the Intellectual Foundations of Modern Culture* (London: Yale University Press, 2004).

van Eck, Caroline *Organicism in Nineteenth-Century Architecture: An inquiry into Its Theoretical and Philosophical Background* (Amsterdam: Architectura and Natura Press, 1994).

Edwards, Jonathan 'An Essay on the Trinity,' *Treatise on Grace and Other Posthumously Published Writings* (Cambridge and London: James Clarke, 1971), ed. Helm, Paul.

van Eeden, Frederik *The Bride of Dreams* (Teddington: The Echo Library, 2009), tr. Mellie von Auw.

Eglinton, James 'Bavinck's Organic Motif: Questions Seeking Answers,' *Calvin Theological Journal* 45, No. 1 (April 2010): 51–71.

—.'Some Benefits of Going Organic: Herman Bavinck's Theology of the Visible Church', *Theology in Scotland* (Vol. XVII, No. 1, Spring 2010): 23–36.

—. 'How Many Herman Bavincks? *De Gemeene Genade* and the "Two Bavincks" Hypothesis,' *Kuyper Center Review, Vol. 2: Revelation and Common Grace* (Grand Rapids: Eerdmans, 2011), ed. Bowlin, John: 279–301.

—. 'To Be or to Become – That is the Question: Locating the Actualistic in Bavinck's Ontology,' *Kuyper Center Review, Vol. 2: Revelation and Common Grace* (Grand Rapids: Eerdmans, 2011), ed. Bowlin, John: 105–25.

Escher, D.G. *Disquisitio de Calvino, librorum N.T. historicorum interprete* (Utrecht: R. Nathan, 1840).

Fergusson, David 'John Baillie: Orthodox Liberal,' *Christ, Church and Society: Essays on David Baillie and John Baillie* (London: T & T Clark, 1993), ed. David Fergusson: 123–54.

Fernhout, Rein *Canonical Texts: Bearers of Absolute Authority* (Amsterdam: Editions Rodopi, 1994).

Gaffin, Richard *God's Word in Servant-Form* (Greenville: Reformed Academic Press, 2008).

Gérold, Charles Théodore *La Faculté de théologie et le Séminaire protestant de Strasbourg (1803–72). Une page de l'Histoire de l'Alsace* (Strasbourg: Librairie Istra, 1923).

Gleason, Ron 'The Importance of the "Unio Mystica" in Dr. Herman Bavinck's Theology' (http://www.hermanbavinck.com/OrganicThinking.doc).

—. 'Herman Bavinck's Doctrine of the Sacraments of the Church: The Sacraments as Means of Grace' (unpublished paper).

Gootjes, N.H. 'General Revelation in Its Relation to Special Revelation,' *Westminster Theological Journal* 51 (1989): 337–50.

Gousmett, Chris 'Bavinck and Kuyper on Creation and Miracle,' *Anakainosis* 7 No. 1–2 (September/December 1984): 1–19.

Grosart, Alexander B. ed., *The Complete Works of John Davies of Hereford* (Edinburgh, 1878).

Gunning, Johannes Hermanus *De wijsbegeerte van den godsdienst uit het beginsel van het heloof der gemeente* (Utrecht: Briejer, 1889), and *Het geloof der gemeente als theologische maatstaf des oordeels in de wijsbegeerte van den godsdienst*, parts I–II (Utrecht: Breijer, 1890).

Haeckel, Ernst *Riddle of the Universe* (Buffalo: Promotheus Books, 1992).

Harinck, George 'Herman Bavinck's indrukken van Amerika anno 1892,' *Documentieblad voor de Nederlandsche Kerkgeschiedenis na 1800*, 47 (December 1997).

—. ' "Something that must remain, if the truth is to be sweet and precious to us": The Reformed Spirituality of Herman Bavinck,' *Calvin Theological Journal* 38 (2003): 248–62.

—. 'Herman Bavinck and Geerhardus Vos,' *Calvin Theological Journal* 45 (2010): 18–31.

—. 'The Religious Character of Modernism and the Modern Character of Religion: A Case Study of Herman Bavinck's Engagement with Modern Culture,' *Scottish Bulletin of Evangelical Theology* 29 No. 1 (2011): 60–77.

Harris, Harriet A. 'A Diamond in the Dark: Kuyper's Doctrine of Scripture,' *Religion, Pluralism and Public Life: Abraham Kuyper's Legacy for the Twenty-First Century* (Grand Rapids: Eerdmans, 2000), ed. Lugo, Luis E.

Hatch, E. 'The Influence of Greek Ideas and Usages upon the Christian Church,' *The Hibbert Lectures, 1888*, 7th edn. (London: Williams and Norgate, 1898), tr. Fairbairn, A.M.

Hattiangadi, Jagdish 'Philosophy of Biology in the Nineteenth Century,' in *Routledge History of Philosophy Volume VII: The Nineteenth Century* (London: Routledge, 1994), ed. Ten, C.L.: 272–96.

Heerspink, J.B.F. *Dr P. Hofstede de Groot's level en werken* (Groningen: P. Noordhoff, 1898).

Hegel, G.W.F. 'The Spirit of Christianity and its Fate,' *Early Theological Writings* (Chicago: Chicago University Press, 1948), tr. T.M. Knox: 182–301.

—. *The Science of Logic* (Amherst: Prometheus, 1989).

—. ed. Houlgate, Stephen *The Hegel Reader* (Oxford: Blackwell Publishing, 1998).

Heideman, Eugene *Relation of Revelation and Reason* (Sheboygan Falls, WI: Van Gorcum & Comp. N.V. – Dr. H.J. Prakke & H.M.G. Prakke, 1959).

Heitink, Gerben *Practical Theology: History, Theory, Action Domains* (Kampen: Kok, 1993).

Hielema, Syd *Herman Bavinck's Eschatological Understanding of Redemption* (Th.D. dissertation, Wycliffe School of Theology, Toronto, 1998).

Hodge, Charles *Systematic Theology* (Edinburgh: Thomas Nelson and Sons, 1880).

Hofstede de Groot, Petrus *Beantwoording van J.H. Scholten, hoogleeraar te Leiden* (Groningen: A.L. Scholtens, 1859).

Huet, Conrad Busken *Vragen en antwoorden; brieven over den bijbel* (Haarlem, 1858).

Huet, D.T. *Wenken opzigtelijk de Moderne theologie* ('s-Gravenhage: J. M. van 't Haaff, 1858).

Huet, J.L. 'Iets over Calvyn,' *Nieuw christelijk maandschrift, voor den beschaafden stand* 5 (1831).

Jaarsma, Cornelius *The Educational Philosophy of Herman Bavinck* (Grand Rapids: Eerdmans, 1935).

van Jutphaas, Barthold Jacob Lintelo baron de Geer *De wet op het hooger onderwijs* (Utrecht: Bijleveld, 1877).

Käsemann, Ernst 'Vom Theologischen Recht historisch-kritisch Exegese,' *Zeitschrift für Theologie und Kirche* (1967): 259–81.

Van Keulen, Dirk *Bijbel en dogmatiek*, (Kampen: Kok, 2003).

Klinck, Dennis R. '*Vestigia Trinitatis* in Man and his Works in the English Renaissance,' *Journal of the History of Ideas*, Vol. 42, 1 (January–March 1981):13–27.

Klinefelter, Donald 'The Theology of John Baillie: A Biographical Introduction,' *Scottish Journal of Theology* 22 (1969): 419–36.

Kloosterman, Nelson D. 'A Response to "The Kingdom of God is Twofold": Natural Law and the Two Kingdoms in the Thought of Herman Bavinck by David VanDrunen,' *Calvin Theological Journal* 45, No. 1 (April 2010): 174–5.

Kuenen, Abraham *Verslagen en mededeelingen der Koninklijke Akademie van Wetenschappen, Afdeeling Letterkunde* (1883).

Kuyper, Abraham *Disquisitio historico-theologica, exhibens Johannis Calvini et Johannis à Lasco de Ecclesia Sententiarum inter se compositionem* (Den Haag en Amsterdam, 1862).

—. 'Geworteld en Gegrond (1870),' *Predicatiën, in de jaren 1867 tot 1873, tijdens zijn Predikantschap in het Nederlandsch Hervormde Kerkgenootschap, gehouden in Beesd, te Utrecht en te Amsterdam* (Kampen: J.H. Kok, 1913): 328–9.

—. *Onnauwkeurig?* (Amsterdam: J.A. Wormser, 1889).

—. *Lectures on Calvinism* (Grand Rapids: Eerdmans, 1931).

—. *The Work of the Holy Spirit* (Grand Rapids: Eerdmans, 1941), tr. De Vries, H.

—. 'Our Instinctive Life,' *Abraham Kuyper: A Centennial Reader* (Grand Rapids: Eerdmans, 1998), ed. Bratt, James D.: 255–78.

—. 'Calvinism: Source and Stronghold of our Constitutional Liberties,' *Abraham Kuyper: A Centennial Reader* (Grand Rapids: Eerdmans, 1998), ed. Bratt, James D.: 279–322.

—. 'Common Grace,' *Abraham Kuyper: A Centennial Reader* (Grand Rapids: Eerdmans, 1998), ed. Bratt, James D.: 165–204.

—. 'Uniformity: The Curse of Modern Life,' *Abraham Kuyper: A Centennial Reader* (Grand Rapids: Eerdmans, 1998), ed. Bratt, James D.: 19–44.

—. *Sacred Theology* (Lafayette: Sovereign Grace Publishers, 2001).

—. *Locus de Sacra Scriptura, creation, creaturis*, Vol. 2 (Grand Rapids: J.B. Hulst, n.d.)

Lane, Anthony *A Reader's Guide to Calvin's Institutes* (Grand Rapids: Baker, 2009).

Langley, McKendree R. *The Practice of Political Spirituality: Episodes from the Public Career of Abraham Kuyper, 1879–1918* (Jordan Station, ON: Paideia Press, 1984).

Lecerf, Auguste *Introduction à La Dogmatique Réformée* (Paris: Editions « Je Sers », 1931).

Leigh, Edward *A Treatise on Divinity* (London, 1646).

Leo XIII, *Aeterni Patris* (Inst. Surdo-mutorum, 1879).

Lossky, N.O. *The World as an Organic Whole* (Oxford: University Press, 1928), tr. Duddington, Natalie.

Lucas, Sean Michael 'Southern-Fried Kuyper? Robert Louis Dabney, Abraham Kuyper and the Limitations of Public Theology,' *Westminster Theological Journal* 66 (2004): 179–201.

McCormack, Bruce 'The Sum of the Gospel: The Doctrine of Election in the Theologies of Alexander Schweizer and Karl Barth,' *Toward the Future of Reformed Theology: Tasks, Topics, Traditions* (Grand Rapids: Eerdmans, 1999), eds. Willis-Watkins, David and Welker, Michael: 470–93.

—. 'Grace and Being: The Role of God's Gracious Election in Karl Barth's Theological Ontology,' *The Cambridge Companion to Karl Barth* (Cambridge: University Press, 2000), ed. Webster, John.

McGaughey, Don 'Thomas Aquinas and the Problem of Faith and Reason,' *Restoration Quarterly* 6 No. 2 (1962): 67–76.

McGowan, Andrew T.B. *The Divine Spiration of Scripture: Challenging Evangelical Perspectives* (Downers Grove: Inter-Varsity, 2007).

McKim, Donald and Rogers, Jack *The Authority and Interpretation of the Bible* (San Francisco: Harper and Row, 1979).

Macleod, Donald *Priorities for the Church* (Fearn: Christian Focus Publications, 2003).

—. 'Bavinck's Prolegomena: Fresh Light on Amsterdam, Old Princeton and Cornelius Van Til,' *Westminster Theological Journal* 68, No. 2 (2006): 261–82.

MacQuarrie, John *Jesus Christ in Modern Thought* (London: SCM, 1990).

Mannion, Gerard *Ecclesiology and Postmodernity: Questions for the Church in Our Time* (Minnesota: Collegeville, 2007).

Mattson, Brian G. *Restored to our Destiny* (Ph.D. dissertation, University of Aberdeen, 2008).

—. 'Van Til on Bavinck: An Assessment,' *Westminster Theological Journal* 70 (2008): 111–27.

Maurer, W. 'Das Prinzip des Organischen in der evangelischen Kirchengeschichtsschreibung des 19. Jahrhunderts,' *Kerygma und Dogma* (1962): 256–92.

Mead, George *Movements of Thought in the Nineteenth Century* (Chicago: University of Chicago Press, 1972).

von Meyenfeldt, F.H. 'Prof. Dr. Herman Bavinck: 1854–1954 "Christus en de Cultuur",' *Polemios* IX (October 15, 1954).

Miller, Benjamin *Calvin's Doctrine of the Church* (Leiden: E.J. Brill, 1970).

Mulder, M.J. 'Abraham Kuenen and His Successors,' *Leiden Oriental Connections 1850–1940* (Leiden: Brill, 1989), ed. Otterspeer, Willem.

—. 'Abraham Kuenen,' *Abraham Kuenen (1828–91)* (Leiden: Brill, 1993), eds. Dirksen, P.B. and van der Kooij, A.: 1–7.

Muller, Richard *Post-Reformation Reformed Dogmatics: The Rise and Development of Reformed Orthodoxy, ca. 1520 to ca. 1725, Vol. 4: The Triunity of God* (Grand Rapids: Baker Academic, 2003).

Nat, J. *De studie van de Oosterche talen in Nederland in de 18ᵉ en 19ᵉ eeuw* (Purmerend, 1929).

Oort, H. 'Kuenen als godgeleerde,' *De Gids* (1893).

Osterhaven, Maurice Eugene *The faith of the Church: a Reformed perspective on its historical development* (Grand Rapids: Eerdmans, 1982).

Packer, J.I. 'Foreword', xi, in *A Theological Guide to Calvin's Institutes* (Phillipsburg: Presbyterian and Reformed Publishing, 2008), eds. Hall, David and Lillback, Peter.

Parker, T.H.L. *Calvin's Doctrine of the Knowledge of God* (Edinburgh: Oliver & Boyd, 1969).

—. *Calvin: An Introduction to his Thought* (London: Continuum, 1995).

Partee, Charles *The Theology of John Calvin* (Louisville: Westminster John Knox, 2008).

Pierson, Allard *Brief aan mijn laatste gemeente* (Arnhem, 1865).

Potter, George R. and Simpson, Evelyn M. eds., *The Sermons of John Donne*, 10 Volumes (Berkley and Los Angeles, 1953–9).

Phan, Peter C. 'How much uniformity can we stand? How much unity do we want? Church and Worship in the Next Millennium,' *Worship* 72 No. 3 (May 1998): 194–210.

Praamsma, Louis *Abraham Kuyper als Kerkhistoricus* (Kampen: Kok, 1945).

—. 'Review of Revelatie en inspiratie: De Openbarings en Schriftbeschouwing van Herman Bavinck in vergelijking met die der ethische theologie,' *Westminster Theological Journal* 32 No. 1 N (1969): 100.

Puchinger, George *Abraham Kuyper: De Jonge Kuyper (1837–67)* (Franeker: Weaver, 1987).

Ridderbos, Herman 'Het is taak van de "kerk als organisme" om een appel te doen op de samenleving,' *De Kerk: Trefpunt van sociale en politieke akite?* (Kampen: Uitgeversmaatschappij J.H. Kok, 1987), ed. Runia, K.: 23–8.

Ritschl, Albrecht 'Über die beiden Principien des Protestantismus; Antwort auf eine 25 Jahre alte Frage,' *Gesammelte Aufsätze* (Freiburg: J.C.B Mohrl, 1893), 234–47.

Ross, John S. and Eglinton, James 'Unity and Uniformity: Towards a Trinitarian Theology of Worship,' *Scottish Bulletin of Evangelical Theology* (Autumn 2009): 131–54.

Rutgers, Frederik Lodewijk *Calvijns invloed* (Den Haag, 1901).

Schelling, F.W.J. *Werke*, II/3 (Stuttgart/Augsburg, J.G. Cotta'scher Verlag, 1856–61).

Scholten, Johannes *Disquisitio de Dei erga hominem amore* (Trajecti ad Rhenum, 1836).

—. *Oratio de vitando in Jesu Christi historia interpretanda docetismo, nobili, ad rem Christianam promovendam hodiernae theologiae munere* (in *Annales Academi, 1839–40*, Hagae-Comitis, 1842).

—. *De leer der Hervormde Kerk* (Leiden: P. Engels, 1848–50).

—. *Kritische inleiding tot de Schriften des Nieuwen Testaments* (Leiden, 1855).

—. *Dogmaticus Christianae*, 2nd edn. (Lyons: P. Engels, 1858).

—. *Vrijheid in verband met zelfbewustheid, zedelijkheid, en zonde* (Amsterdam, 1858).

—. *De vrije wil* (Leiden: P. Engels, 1859).

—. *Geschiedenis der godsdienst en wijsbegeerte* (Leiden: Akademische Boekhandel van P. Engels, 1863).

—. *Het level van Jezus door Ernest Renant. Toespraak bij de opening der akademische lessen* (Leiden, 1863).

—. *Herdenking mijner vijfentwintigjarige ambtsbediening* (Leiden, 1865).

—. *Afscheidsrede bij het neerleggen van het hoogleeraarsambt aan de Universiteit te Leiden* (Leiden, 1881).

Schreiner, Susan E. *The Theater of His Glory: Nature and the Natural Order in the Thought of John Calvin* (Durham, North Carolina: The Labyrinth Press: 1991).

Schweizer, Alexander *Die Glaubenslehre der evangelisch-reformierten Kirche, Dargestellt und aus den Quellen belegt*, 2 vols. (Zürich: Orell, Füssli und Com, 1844–7).

Silva, Moisés *Biblical Words and Their Meaning: An Introduction to Lexical Semantics* (Grand Rapids: Academie/Zondervan, 1983).

Simmons, Menno *The Complete Writings of Menno Simmons* (Scottdale, PA: Herland Press, 1956), ed. Bender, Harold; tr. Verduin, L.

Slis, P.L. *L. W. E. Rauwenhoff (1828–89): apologeet van het modernisme – Predikant, kerkhistoricus en godsdienstfilosoof* (Kampen: Kok, 2003).

Spykman, Gordon J. 'Sphere Sovereignty in Calvin and the Calvinist Tradition,' *Exploring the Heritage of John Calvin* (Grand Rapids: Baker, 1976), ed. Holwerda, David E.

—. *Reformational Theology: A New Paradigm for Doing Dogmatics* (Grand Rapids: Eerdmans, 1992).

Stromberg, Roland *European Intellectual History Since 1789* (New Jersey: Prentice-Hall, 1986).

O'Sullivan, Bernard and Linehan, Denis 'Regionalism in the Netherlands,' in *Regionalism in the European Union* (Bristol: Intellect Books, 1999), ed. Wagstaff, Peter: 99–114.

Tangelder, J.D. 'Dr. Herman Bavinck 1854–1921: Theologian of the Word,' *Christian Renewal* 19 (2001): 14–51.

Turretin, Francis *Institutio theologiae elencticae*, 3 vols (Geneva, 1679–85; new edition, Edinburgh, 1847).

Twesten, August *Vorlesungen über die Dogmatik der evangelisch-lutherischen Kirche* (Hamburg: Perthes, 1826).

Vander Stelt, John 'Kuyper's Semi-Mystical Conception,' in *Philosophia Reformata: Orgaan van de Vereniging voor Calvinistische Wijsbegeerte* 38[e] Jaargang 1973: 178–90.

Vandervelde, George 'A Trinitarian Framework and Reformed Distinctiveness: A Critical Assessment of *Christian and Reformed Today*,' *Calvin Theological Journal* 21 (1986): 95–109.

VanDrunen, David 'The Kingship of Christ Is Twofold: Natural Law and the Two Kingdoms in the Thought of Herman Bavinck,' *Calvin Theological Journal* 1 No. 45 (April 2010): 147–64.

Veenhof, Cornelis *Volk van God: Enkele aspecten van Bavincks kerkbeschouwing* (Amsterdam: Buijten & Schipperheijn, 1969).

Veenhof, Jan *Revelatie en Inspiratie: De Openbarings en Schriftbeschouwing van Herman Bavinck in vergelijking met die der ethische theologie* (Amsterdam: Buijten & Schipperheijn, 1968).

Verhey, Allen 'Introduction,' in 'Treatise Against the Libertines,' *Calvin Theological Journal* 15 No, 2 N (1980), trs. Robert G Wilkie and Allen Verhey; ed. John Calvin: 190–219.

Viret, Pierre *Exposition familière de l'oraison de nostre Seigneur Jésus Christ* (Geneva, 1548).

van der Vlugt, W. *Levensbericht van Abraham Kuenen* (Leiden, 1893).

Vree, Jasper *De Groninger godgeleerden. De oorsprongen en de eerste periode van hun optreden (1820–43)* (Kampen: J.H. Kok, 1984).

—. ' Hofstede de Groot en de armenverzorging door vrouwen. Een hoofdstuk uit de geschiedenis van de Groninger inwendige zending,' *Geloven in Groningen. Capita selecta uit de geloofs-geschiedenis van een stad* (Kampen: J.H. Kok, 1990), eds. G. Van Halsema Thzn et al.: 215–31.

—. 'Organisme en instituut: De ontwikkeling van Kuypers spreken over kerk-zijn (1867–1901),' *Abraham Kuyper: vast en veranderlijk, De ontwikkeling van zijn denken* (Uitgeverij Meinema: Zoetermeer, 1998), eds. Cornelis Augustijn and Jasper Vree: 86–108.

—. with Johan Zwaan, *Abraham Kuyper's Commentatio (1860): The Young Kuyper about Calvin, a Lasco and the Church, I. Introduction, Annotations, Bibliography and Indices* (Leiden: Brill, 2005).

De Vries, Simon 'The Hexateuchal Criticism of Abraham Kuenen,' in *Journal of Biblical Literature* 82 No. 1 (March 1963): 31–57.

Vroom, Henk 'Scripture Read and Interpreted: The Development of the Doctrine of Scripture and Hermeneutics in Gereformeerde Theology in the Netherlands,' *Calvin Theological Journal* 28 No. 2 (1993): 352–71.

—. *No Other Gods: Christian belief in dialogue with Buddhism, Hinduism and Islam* (Grand Rapids: Eerdmans, 1996).

—. 'Understanding the Gospel Contextually,' *Contextuality in Reformed Europe: The Mission of the Church in the Transformation of European Culture* (Amsterdam: Editions Rodopi, 2004), eds. Lienemann-Perrin, Christine, Vroom, Hendrik and Weinrich, Michael: 35–56.

Vos, Geerhardus 'The Idea of Biblical Theology,' *Redemptive History and Biblical Interpretation* (Philipsburg: Presbyterian & Reformed Publishing, 2001).

Wallace, Ronald *Calvin's Doctrine of the Christian Life* (Edinburgh & London: Oliver and Boyd, 1959); Lucien Richard, *The Spirituality of John Calvin* (Atlanta: John Knox, 1974).

Walton, Francis 'Athens, Elesius, and the Homeric Hymn to Demeter,' *Harvard Theological Review* 45 No. 2 (1952): 105–14.

Warfield, Benjamin Breckenridge *The Inspiration and Authority of the Bible* (Phillipsburg, NJ: P&R, 1948).

Wasson, R. Gordon, Ruck, Carl A.P. and Hofmann, Albert *The Road to Eleusis: Unveiling the Secret of the Mysteries* (New York: Harcourt Brace Jovanovic, 1978).

Wellhausen, Julius *Die christliche Religion: Mit Einschluss der israelitisch-judischen Religion,* I, IV, 1, 15, in *Die Kultur der Gegenwart,* 24 vols (Berlin and Leipzig: B.G. Teubner, 1905–23), ed. Hinnenberg, Paul.

Wells, David *No Place For Truth: Or Whatever Happened to Evangelical Theology* (Leicester: Inter-Varsity Press, 1993).

Wicksteed, Philip 'Abraham Kuenen,' *The Jewish Quarterly Review* 4 No. 4 (July 1982): 571–605.

Witsius, H. *Exercitationes* (Whitefish, Montana: Kessinger Pub Co, 2009).

Wobbermin, G. *Religionsgeschichtliche Studien zur Frage nach der Beeinflussung des Urchristenthum durch das antike Mysterienwesen* (Berlin: E. Ebering, 1896).

Wolters, Albert M. *Creation Regained: Biblical Basics for a Reformational Worldview* (Grand Rapids: Eerdmans, 2005).

Wood, John Halsey 'Church, Sacrament, and Society: Abraham Kuyper's Early Baptismal Theology, 1859–74,' *Journal of Reformed Theology* 2 (2008): 275–96.

Wright, David F. 'Calvin's "Accommodation" Revisited,' *Calvin as Exegete: papers and responses presented at the Ninth Colloquium on Calvin and Calvin Studies* (Grand Rapids: Calvin Studies Society, 1995): 171–90.

Wurth, Gerrit Brillenburg *J.H. Scholten als systematisch theoloog* ('s-Gravenhage: Van Haeringen, 1927).

Yarnell, Malcolm B. *The Formation of Christian Doctrine* (B & H Publishing Group: Nashville, 2007).

Zijnen, F.J. Sibmacher *Specimen historico-dogmaticum, quo Anselmi et Calvini placita de hominum per Christum a peccato redemtione inter se conferuntur* (Schoonhoven: S.E. van Nooten, 1852).

Zophy, Jonathan *A Short History of Renaissance and Reformation Europe: Dances Over Fire and Water* (New York: Prentice Hall, 2003).

Zylstra, Henry 'Preface,' in *Our Reasonable Faith* (Grand Rapids: Baker Book House, 1956), ed. Herman Bavinck; tr. Zylstra, Henry.

Zwaanstra, Henry 'Abraham Kuyper's Conception of the Church,' *Calvin Theological Journal* 9 (1974): 153–4.

Dutch History

Herderscheê, Jacobus *De Modern-godsdienstige richting in Nederland* (Amsterdam: Van Holkema & Warendorf, 1904).

Israel, Jonathan *The Dutch Republic: Its Rise, Greatness and Fall, 1477–1806* (Oxford: University Press, 1998).

Mackay, James Hutton *Religious Thought in Holland during the Nineteenth Century* (London: Hodder and Stoughton, 1911).

Pierson, Allard *Oudere Tijdgenooten* (Amsterdam, 1904).

Réville, Albert *Revue des deux Mondes* (Paris, 1859).

Roessingh, K.H. *De moderne theologie in Nederland; hare voorbereiding en eerste period* (Dissertation, Groningen, 1914).

de la Saussaye, Chantepie *La crise religieuse en Hollande – Souvenirs et impressions* (Leyde: De Breuk & Smits, 1860).

—. *Geestlijke Stroomingen* (Haarlem: Erven Bohn, 1907).

Sepp, Christiaan *Proeve eener Pragmatische Geschiedenis der Theologie in Nederland (1787–1858)* (Amsterdam: J.P. Sepp en Zoon, 1860).

Vanderlaan, Eldred *Protestant Modernism in Holland* (H. Milford: Oxford University Press, 1924).

Miscellaneous

Alberti, Leon Battista *On the Art of Building in Ten Books* (Cambridge: MIT Press, 1991), translation of *De re aedificatoria* (Florence, 1452), trs. Rykwert, Joseph, Leach, Neil and Tavernor, Robert.

Coleridge, Samuel *Coleridge's Criticism of Shakespeare: A Selection* (London: Athlone Press, 1989), ed. Foakes, R.A.

Gereformeerde Kerken in Nederland, Generale Syonde, *God met ons: over de aard van het Schriftgezag* (1979).

—. *God with Us: On the Nature of the Authority of Scripture* (Grand Rapids: Reformed Ecumenical Synod, 1982), trans. Secretariat of the Reformed Ecumenical Synod.

Hirt, Alois *Die Baukunst nach den Grundgesätzen der Alten* (n.p., 1809).

Picasso to Brassaï, *Conversations avec Picasso* (Paris: Gallimard, 1964).

Plato, *Timaeus* (Rockville: Serenity Publishers, 2008), tr. Benjamin Jowett.

Vatican Council I, session III, 'De fide.'

Waarheid in liefde, een godgeleerd tijdschrift, voor beschaafde christenen (1845 ff.: J. Zoon, 1837–72).

Subject Index

Index of Persons

Lightning Source UK Ltd.
Milton Keynes UK
UKOW04f1535141013

219045UK00001B/12/P